A Feminist Companion to Conceptual and Historical Issues in Psychology

Series: Feminist Companions to Psychology Series
Series Editors: Sarah Riley, Rose Capdevila & Hannah Frith

Other titles in the series:

A Feminist Companion to Social Psychology
by Madeleine Pownall and Wendy Stainton Rogers

A Feminist Companion to Research Methods in Psychology
By Hannah Frith and Rose Capdevila

A Feminist Companion to Conceptual and Historical Issues in Psychology

Katherine Hubbard and Peter Hegarty

Mc
Graw
Hill

Open University Press

Open University Press
McGraw Hill
Unit 4
Foundation Park
Roxborough Way
Maidenhead
SL6 3UD

Email: emea_uk_ireland@mheducation.com
World wide web: www.mheducation.co.uk

Executive Editor: Beatriz Lopez
Editorial Assistant: Hannah Jones
Content Product Manager: Graham Jones

British Library Cataloguing in Publication Data
A catalogue record of this book is available from the British Library

ISBN-13: 9780335252138
ISBN-10: 0335252133
eISBN: 9780335252145

Typeset by Transforma Pvt. Ltd., Chennai, India

Praise page

"*Katherine Hubbard and Peter Hegarty give students and researchers a much-needed accessible and lively feminist overview of the too-often neglected history of gender studies in psychology as well as pressing theoretical and conceptual issues. They skilfully lead students to consider fraught and complex questions pertaining, not only to gender studies, but to scientific practice itself, and provide them with the intellectual tools to address these issues in a socially-responsible, ethical, feminist way.*"
Stephanie A. Shields, Professor Emeritx, Psychology and Women's Gender, The Pennsylvania State University – University Park, US

"*Hubbard and Hegarty have provided a lively and accessible antidote to malestream history. With their engaging and sophisticated feminist companion, students will learn how gender and power are central to psychology while acquiring valuable tools to think critically about psychology's past, present, and future.*"
Alexandra Rutherford, Professor, Department of Psychology, York University, Toronto, Canada

"*In contrast to most psychology textbooks, this is a thoroughly engaging read. It introduces some of the enduring issues in psychology, but with a contemporary twist, including plenty of rich examples with real people, helping to bring the discipline of psychology to life, warts and all*".
Hel Spandler, Professor of Mental Health Studies, University of Central Lancashire, UK

"*This new Feminist Companion from Katherine Hubbard and Peter Hegarty provides students wanting to get to grips with some of the conceptual and historical issues in psychology (CHIP) with a highly accessible place to begin. The authors shine a historical lens on topics that are of interest to feminists such as gender and sexuality, as well as classic studies from the psychology curriculum, before bringing students up to date with an introduction to some of the contemporary voices in Feminist Psychology. Written in a personal style, it will serve as an introductory study companion to undergraduates everywhere.*"
Professor Katherine Johnson, RMIT University, Australia and author of Sexuality: A Psychosocial Manifesto

Contents

Series Preface

About the *Feminist Companion* Series

Series Editors: Sarah Riley, Rose Capdevila and Hannah Frith

As Series Editors we can each remember pivotal moments during our under-graduate psychology studies when we were exposed to feminist research and theorizing. These moments have shaped our own identities as feminists, our approach to teaching, learning and research in psychology, and our engage-ments with psychology as a discipline. There are some fantastic feminist psychology lecturers and mentors. For those of us who are fortunate to be taught by them, these are experiences that we never forget.

Hannah

For me, this came in the form of my second-year undergraduate module on research methods in psychology. On the first day of this module, in bounced my teacher (Celia Kitzinger) brimming with energy and enthusiasm, and burst-ing with exciting ideas about research. I was brought up short by a double whammy of learning about qualitative research for the first time and realizing (with some surprise) that research might involve talking with, learning from, and respectfully listening to people. Hearing the voices of women, talking about issues important to women's lives for the first time, lit a fire in me.

Rose

Reading feminist literature was an integral part of my undergraduate degree in politics. There were loads of stats and stories that could tell you the world wasn't fair, no convincing needed. However, the real revelation came when I attended a departmental talk shortly after starting my PhD in Psychology. Usually these talks revolved around experiments, controlling variables and producing sta-tistical analyses. However, the speaker that week (Christine Griffin) didn't do this. She talked about her research with young, working-class women; how they were constructed – both inside and outside of academia – as 'troubled' when they behaved in certain ways, and how this was used to manage them. The speaker described how, by using qualitative methods, researchers could explore the world in ways that valued experience and relationships, rather than converting them into variables to be measured and controlled. I had never thought of things in that way, and it opened up a whole new approach to mak-ing sense of world. Much reading followed.

Sarah

My story is slightly different. I had some great teachers and supervisors at undergraduate level, but none were explicitly feminist, other than a course on gender which was cancelled the year I could have done it while the lecturer was on sabbatical. In my research project though, I was supported to do feminist experimental research, but my greatest feminist education came from my friends Emma and Terry, who were studying Philosophy, Women's Studies and Russian Studies, and who taught me the art of thinking, arguing and drinking. There were also important books that gave me language for understanding my world; it felt like they explained what I already knew, but hadn't had the words to describe.

In our stories, we offer a range of experiences. Face-to-face with visionary feminist psychologists or peer taught – we had people with us on our feminist journey. But not everybody does. Although feminist research and theorizing has grown enormously over the many years since we were undergraduates (continuing a trend which began way before then), it remains marginalized in most undergraduate curricula and teachers can be unsure about how to integrate feminism into their classes. At the same time, feminist activism outside of academia is flourishing; Everyday Sexism, SlutWalks, #MeToo, Everyone's Invited, and the Million Women March are just a few examples. Curricula which fail to include feminist scholarship risk failing to engage students who want to see the psychology they study reflecting what is important in their lives.

The *Feminist Companions to Psychology* series was born out of a desire to address these gaps. It draws on the historic strengths of Open University Press of taking complex concepts and presenting them in a clear and accessible way, and aims to provide resources to support staff who are looking to incorporate the latest feminist thinking into their existing modules.

We wanted to develop short, snappy, pedagogically informed books which would sit alongside – as well as complement, complicate and contest – psychology textbooks and courses. We also wanted to support teachers and mentors in psychology by providing short, accessible books which speak to the British Psychological Society's curriculum areas (starting with the core areas of social, cognitive, developmental, biological, personality and individual differences and research methods). We wanted to engage undergraduate psychologists in academic work which might speak to their values, their activism, or help them make sense of their experiences. We also think psychology undergraduates are missing out! Feminist psychology is a diverse, multifaceted field of work creating cutting edge, energizing psychology that challenges all of us to think and act in new ways. It's important that we share it with the next generation of psychology students. This series is a celebration of the fun, fierce, fabulous and wonderful things that feminism has to offer to psychology.

About *A Feminist Companion to Conceptual and Historical Issues in Psychology*

Series Editors: Sarah Riley, Rose Capdevila and Hannah Frith

Acknowledgments

From Katherine

My life looked very different at the beginning of this project to how it looks now. Ironically for a book about history, I don't want to dwell on the past but instead want to take this moment to thank the absolute babes who have been with me during this journey.

This book owes a great deal to the wonderful series editors Rose Capdevila, Hannah Frith and Sarah Riley – this book series has made the world of Feminist Psychology a more accessible and even more exciting place to be thanks to you three. I especially owe Rose a great deal of thanks. Working with her on various projects and having her friendly guidance for quite a few years now has been invaluable and I'm exceptionally grateful for it. Of course this book wouldn't have been possible without the co-authorship of the one, the only, Peter Hegarty. I'm very lucky to have you in my life, Peter. I'm also so appreciative of the work of Alex Rutherford in helping us polish the book – her review was so encouraging and I'm so happy to have such a genuine icon of Feminist Psychology involved. The publishers, Hannah Jones at McGraw Hill, and everyone else there, have been a total pleasure to work with, thank you for all that you do. I'd also like to thank Lois Donnelly for being my feminist POWES companion and David Griffiths for being my brother-in-arms in almost all aspects of my life. The book would not be so lively and inviting without the brilliant illustrations by my fabulous wife Clare Butler. Thank you so much, Clare!

I'd also like to thank Jane Hubbard for being a wonderful sister and friend. I'm so lucky you arrived only a year after I turned up. Finally, I'd like to reiterate my immeasurable gratitude to Clare and David. Thank you both for everything (especially that one quite big thing). Much love, Kat.

From Peter

On *Psychology's Feminist Voices*, I refused to identify as a feminist. Writing acknowledgments for a feminist book seems more doable to this bloke. Many women nurtured my 'psychologist' and 'historian' sides across eight time zones, three countries and fifteen years, particularly Ruth Byrne, Michelle Fine, Joan Fujimura, Sheila Green, Mary Hegarty, Ruth Linden, Naomi Rogers, Felicia Pratto, Stephanie Shields and Abigail Stewart. Consequently, I learned more within CLAGS, the BPS Psychology of Sexualities and History and Philosophy Sections, and the SENS collective.

At Surrey, I supervised 100+ early career researchers. Too many to name, but Mona Al-Sheddi, Gavi Ansara, the late Sebastian Bartos, Tasha Bharj, Carmen Buechel, Lois Donnelly, Fabio Fasoli, Miranda Horvath, Tove Lundberg, Orla Parslow-Breen, Marta Prandelli, Patrice Rosconi, Annette Smith, Sapphira

Thorne, Francesca Trevisan, Nicola Tee and Jacy Young jump to mind. Katherine was, and is, a particular beacon of gorgeousness, even among these many teachers. I'm so glad she invited me into this project where her own transformative feminist insights and highly adhesive good humour, are abundant once again!

This is my first book for the Open University Press. Here Jean McAvoy encouraged me to embrace *openness*, the MSc Psychology (Conversion) module teams informed how I now write for students, and Open Psychology Research Centre colleagues tolerated this book's writing time.

At home, Andrew endured more book-related drama, Fergus was patient when 'the square' delayed walks, and GCC brought new embodied and partial openings into culture, history and psychology. I seem to be here now. Who knew?

Five reasons why you need A Feminist Companion to Conceptual and Historical Issues in Psychology

This series of Feminist Companions covers the breadth of Psychology, from Social Psychology to the Biological bits and bobs, and even the specific research methods adopted by psychologists are covered. This book in particular pays close attention to conceptual and historical issues in Psychology, or CHIP. Here, we attend to the feminist nitty gritty of the history of Psychology and the more abstract conceptual things underlying the discipline. All of the books in the series have moments where they refer to something or discuss something evident in one of the other books. So if you're especially interested in something we've covered, do check out the other titles in the series. Before we introduce ourselves and the book, we'll outline our top reasons for why you need a Feminist Companion for CHIP.

1. Psychology is political

It might be reassuring to think that Psychology is immune to political influence, but that is just not the case. Psychology is deeply imbued with politics. Beliefs about how the world is, and ought to be, matter at every level of Psychology. From *who psychologists are* and *what they measure and study*, to *how they do it* and *what they argue with the data*, are dependent upon political context. This books pays special attention to gender in debunking the myth that Psychology is apolitical. The political nature of Psychology has been somewhat hidden for the large part, which gives the impression that Psychology is always fair and objective. Feminism on the other hand has been considered political from the get-go. In drawing these together, and considering how both are political and intertwined, we believe it's possible to be more transparent about what Psychology does.

2. To gain important skills

There is no doubt that by exploring Psychology from a feminist angle a wealth of skills are gained, honed and developed. These skills are exactly those on which students are assessed at university and those that the British Psychological Society (BPS) and Quality Assurance Association for Higher Education (QAA) say students should get out of degrees in Psychology. By thinking in feminist ways, students learn to be *critical*. This isn't just about saying negative things, but questioning what is being said and why. Not only do we aim to teach critical thinking and reading throughout this book, but we also aim to promote independent and original thinking. Our goal is to not only make you question what you're being taught in constructive ways, but to really get you started on coming up with your own ideas.

3. To make the world a better place

Gender is a key social division through which the world is organized. This organization is largely patriarchal and therefore gender inequalities are rife. Feminists are those who are battling against this powerful tide and are, on the whole, trying to make the world a fairer place. We believe that taking a feminist stance on pretty much anything is going to improve it. That's because in our minds, feminism is about inclusivity, community and equity: everyone benefits in the end. By looking at CHIP from a feminist perspective, we're going someway to counter sexist and misogynistic takes in Psychology (that is, in its history and its present). CHIP is just one tiny slice of the patriarchal pie that together we can transform and make better for the future.

4. History matters in the present

History doesn't just remain in the past. It's echoed in the present all the time. Things in the past act as foundations or philosophies which underpin things now. There are long tendrils from the past which act as legacies evident in the present. In this book we are critical about the idea that 'things are always getting better' as if progress is inevitable (rather than because some people in the past worked really hard). By looking back at the history of Psychology it is possible to see the echoes, foundations, underpinnings and legacies which haunt Psychology today. We believe looking back can actually help make things better for the future. In particular, thinking historically often opens up and allows deeper and more critical deconstructions of things in the present, opening up future possibilities.

5. Feminists need feminist companions

In order to sustain feminism it's important that feminists do not feel alone or isolated. Feminists need other feminist companions to keep up the good fight. We need each other for support, to inspire us, to take the slack sometimes, and to care for one another. You know that lovely feeling when you don't have to explain everything from the very beginning to a really good friend because they just already know *you*, they *get* you? It's like that for feminist thinking. In speaking with other feminists we can just get on with it rather than going over old ground or covering the basics. This usually means we can learn from each other really well. That is not to say you have to be a feminist to get a lot of out this book. There's still lots to take away and people have all sorts of reasons for not identifying with feminism. You might not feel all that comfortable with the F-word because of some misconceptions or poor representations of feminism. In that case, then we believe this book (and the rest of the series) will show you what Feminist Psychology actually looks like; often ahead of the curve. Listening to what feminists have to say, and have said, can really show you where things are headed in Psychology now.

1 Introduction

Learning objectives

Study of this chapter will enable you to:

- Be introduced to us and the various different features of the book
- Gets to grips with the basic philosophical underpinnings of doing CHIP by paying attention to the constructed nature of history and by contextualizing gender and feminism alongside power
- Understand how 'Psychology' has different meanings and that its history even has a history
- See how the book maps onto the benchmarks set out for Psychology degrees and find other useful resources

Introduction

This book is a feminist companion to Conceptual and Historical Issues in Psychology, often called **CHIP**. Throughout these pages we're going to guide you through what can sometimes be the slightly confusing and more abstract aspects of Psychology with particular attention to feminism throughout. This book will act a bit like a hand-drawn treasure map. We will show you where some of the key areas of feminist CHIP are, give you some of the tools to help you, and introduce you to some fellow travellers.

The map is hand drawn because these are the bits that *we*, Katherine and Peter, think are the most prominent features of the field (like the mountains and shore lines of the map). So it's not to say there aren't other maps out there or other features and tools to use. Rather this book represents what we have found to be most useful, in our own navigations of this field. By sharing our map, we're aiming to be feminist companions on your voyage.

For this reason, the book doesn't outline what *the* history of Psychology is, but rather complements your learning about it and gives you a guide as to how to navigate it. We'll be highlighting the best tools to use to guide you through **CHIP** and lots of different areas of Psychology. At the end of the day though, this is all about your journey through and with CHIP; we are just *companions* here to help you on your own feminist adventure!

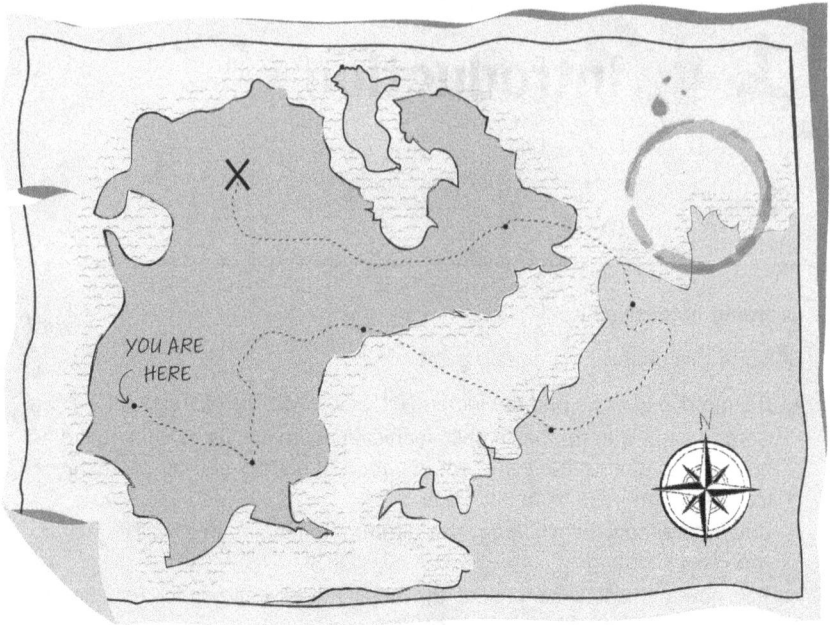

Psychology students across the UK encounter **CHIP** in really variable and inconsistent ways across universities. Surveys have shown that CHIP is not always well covered, and is less well covered in the UK than in the USA (Brock & Harvey, 2015). If you're doing an accredited degree, you'll be learning CHIP, but it can just be hidden away sometimes and not be as visible or explicit on your timetable. You may have a whole module called something like: History of Psychology, Conceptual and Historical Issues in Psychology, or CHIP/S. Or maybe you've never heard of these terms before and CHIP is integrated more into other modules. (Maybe so well *integrated* it wasn't flagged up at all.) When the British Psychological Society (BPS) and the Quality Assurance Agency for UK Higher Education (QAA, 2023) outlined what an accredited Psychology degree should contain, they specifically said students need to learn these topics (plus methods of research and enquiry):

- Biological Psychology
- Cognitive Psychology
- Developmental Psychology
- Individual Differences
- Social Psychology

They also considered it essential to learn conceptual and historical issues in Psychology too. And so this is where **CHIP** comes in. Different universities teach this bit in various ways and so our map here will help you through this area, which is essential for your degree, regardless of how you are taught it.

Introducing us

Katherine (she/her) and Peter (he/him) first met when Katherine was an undergraduate. Peter was a lecturer in her department and he gave a guest lecture on gender in her Social Psychology module. Peter's fate was sealed in that moment as Katherine decided that whatever kind of Psychology this lovely Irish chap was doing, she wanted in. A couple of years later, Peter was Katherine's dissertation supervisor. He talked her into a dissertation on sexual prejudice and *essentialist* beliefs about the history of sexuality categories, and together they published the data (Hubbard & Hegarty, 2014)!

Katherine left to go to do an MSc elsewhere, but Peter sneakily put the idea in her head that she should come back and do a PhD with him. That's exactly what she did. During Katherine's PhD, we published a special issue on the teaching of **CHIP** with Lovemore Ngyatanga in History and Philosophy of Psychology (Hegarty, Hubbard, & Nyatanga, 2015). Peter taught CHIP for over a decade at the University of Surrey and Katherine took over this duty for a year after her PhD. Peter has published two books focused on the history of Psychology: *Gentlemen's Disagreement: Alfred Kinsey, Lewis Terman and the sexual politics of smart men* (2013) and *Lesbian and Gay Psychology: From homophobia to LGBT* (2017). Katherine has published a queer feminist history of the Rorschach Ink Blot test *Queer Ink: A blotted history towards liberation* (2020). We are both invested in queer affirmative, trans-inclusive and anti-racist forms of feminism, history and Psychology.

Our queerness informs and enriches what we do and provides us with a particular lens through which to explore gender and sexuality. As queer feminists, we feel that transparency and liberatory practice are at the core of what we research and teach. Indeed, this book is another attempt to make transparent how we – and the field of Psychology – are indebted to feminist and queer scholars and activists who came before us. We mean this book to encourage, support and assist liberatory moments in the present, such as political and social efforts to advance the liberation of trans people, particularly in the hostile environment in the UK at present (Pearce, Erikainen & Vincent, 2020). You might notice that this feminist companion has lots of queer examples and themes – it's because it's who we are and it's what we do. We hope you enjoy the book all the more for it.

We are also both white, cisgender and able-bodied. We recognize the limits of our perspectives around other dimensions of human experience that become the basis for *privilege*. Even though we are both far out of formal education, we are constantly learning. In particular, we are supportive of efforts to decolonise Psychology, which are transforming how we think about Psychology's past and its concepts. Because there is a relationship between who draws your maps and how you will navigate this territory, we urge you to reflect on who you are talking with about Psychology. This active learning takes the form of paying close attention to those around us, not just scholars, but activists, writers and friends too.

The map key/legend

In order to fully utilize this book as map and the tools we outline, we first want to provide you with a key for what some of the things we'll be talking about mean. These are basically seven foundational aspects of our thinking about *CHIP* that we want to clarify early on before you get too deep into your adventure.

1. History is made up

That is of course not to say that things 'didn't really happen'. But rather that history is made up by the telling of stories about events from the past. History is subjective; stories depend heavily on what is *able* to be said and by *whom*. This subjectivity is related to power; what and who is considered important enough to write history about? Who is considered legitimate enough to write such history? What documents and materials are available to write history? What histories get told and retold? You may have heard the idiom that 'history is written by the victors' – it's the people with power who most often get to stake a claim on what gets written down and re-told about what apparently 'really happened'.

In other words, history is dependent upon interpretation. Fundamentally, histories are written from the perspectives and interests of the historian. Often in Psychology, the word 'subjective' comes with substantial negative baggage, such as accusations of bias, unrepresentativeness, or a skewed perspective that falls short of the heralded 'objectivity'. We however, don't mean subjective in a bad way. Instead, we mean it in an honest way – that all Psychology (and its history and concepts) are human creations that are subjective and depend on the context and positions of the researchers.

You see, who historians are impacts the kinds of history they do. We are led by particular questions we find interesting. Historians tend to most easily learn about and write histories of the topics they're most interested or invested in. Equally, we're also likely to engage in work that feels personal. Both Katherine and Peter, for example, have been especially interested in queer histories of Psychology and that's no coincidence. That does not mean we are 'biased' but rather that we have useful perspectives upon which to draw when telling such histories. Every single historian, psychologist and researcher is a person with beliefs, personal experiences, social identities and investments in what they are doing – we all have a perspective. Therefore, being more transparent about that is usually better practice rather than pretending otherwise (we talk more about this in Chapter 2 and in detail in Chapter 6).

History is not only *constructed* because it is centrally about story-telling, narrative and interpretation. It is also often based on analysis of primary sources, and historians are constrained by what is possible to know about the past too. We often only have accounts, documents and testimonies of people, things and events through *archives*. What is available in these depends so much on what was considered important enough to keep and make publicly available. This partial availability has implications for gender, as well as race, dis/ability, class, economics, geography, etc. too as the archive is also often a site where gender politics, colonialism and racism have all played a part in influencing what gets to be kept and whose records were considered worthy.

We would caution against thinking about *the* history of Psychology for these reasons – any history is *a* version, rather than *the* version. No account can claim to hold everything, historians make decisions about beginnings, middles and ends of stories and choices are made as to what is included.

There already seems to be an element of gender within the very word *history* itself. It's *his*-story after all (although some feminists have argued that instead they produce *her-stories* to counter this).

2. We are living in a patriarchal society

This will most likely not come as surprise to you to learn given you've picked up this feminist companion book, but we just want to explain what we mean here. *Patriarchy* is a complex and ideological system which permeates far, wide and deep, often rather insidiously. It impacts pretty much all aspects of life and promotes and reproduces the power of men and masculinity. It encompasses ideas, practices, assumptions and relationships of people as usually having distinct hierarchical gender roles typically based on a gender binary (women and men). It positions (cisgender) men and masculinity as having higher status and value than people who aren't men and femininity. That is of course, not to say that there is not substantial variation in the ways that individual people experience the world. There are of course many women who are exceptionally more *privileged* and have higher status than many men. But patriarchy is a global social structure which has historically ensured that power has remained in the hands of particular kinds of men. However, patriarchy is neither inevitable nor universal.

Because history has been constructed in a world in which men and masculinity have been favoured, patriarchy has affected what history looks like. Likewise, gender is also constructed – the things we think of as sex, gender, gender role, or masculine and feminine, have all changed over time and are all different in different historical and cultural contexts. Gender is both socially constructed and incredibly meaningful; it determines how we understand and talk about things in the world. We are therefore approaching both our ideas of history and gender from **social constructionist** perspectives. For example we are not convinced by the familiar gender binary – that is the assumptions that there are only women and men. Instead, we regard gender as a complex and wonderfully diverse thing. So it is no surprise to us that people identify with a variety of genders, including (but not exclusively): non-binary, agender, bigender, woman, man, genderqueer, etc. (There is more about this in Chapter 5.)

3. Context is vital

When doing history it is imperative to understand the **context** in which the thing you're telling a story about existed. This thing might be a person, a comment, an object, an event or a research study. Regardless of what's at the centre of your story, it's crucial to investigate and understand its **socio-historical** context. In particular for this book, we might be interested in what the gender implications were in this time and place, mindful that **patriarchy** intersects with other forms of power.

Context is not only important, it can be hard to recognize. It seeps into the background of stories, becoming invisible and implicit. But context is important to recognize because the context of the past is different from the context of the present. **Presentism** or **anachronism** happens when we apply understandings from the present context to the past inappropriately, often to dismiss the past as less 'advanced' than the present. The application of current or present understandings upon a historical period is anachronistic and can be considered poor history. The recognition of presentism was part of a shift towards the development of **CHIP** as a sub-field within Psychology in the 1960s (Stocking, 1965).

However, that is not to say we can't be highly critical of the values of the past. It is true that atrocious actions taken in the past were previously viewed as acceptable and that social norms have undoubtedly changed dramatically. And just because something was acceptable or a norm then, does not mean we can't still call it violent, problematic or unjust now. There are times when being presentist in history is useful. For example, some things done in the (surprisingly recent) past in Psychology were not then considered racist, ableist, transphobic, homophobic or sexist. But that does not mean that we don't understand them as such now and we can use terms like 'racist' to describe actions in the past. In fact, it is important to do so in order to investigate the actual effects that, for example, racist Psychology had on people and to consider how racist legacies continue to shape Psychology in the present.

When thinking about context it's important to reflect on the exact present context of this very book. We are bound by particular geopolitical and geocultural limits here, as we account critical histories of what has often been US and Eurocentric narratives about Psychology. What it means to **decolonize** the history of Psychology is discussed in Chapter 4 but we just wish to highlight this contextual note here.

4. It's all about power

From everything we've outlined so far about storytelling, construction, **patriarchy** and **context**, it is clear that a lot of what we might think about for history and gender is about power. (This is something we look at in more detail in Chapter 4.) What and who get valued and prioritized socially is about who has power. What gets said in history and by whom is about power. Power is not just possessed, it is also done. Indeed, writing history is one way of *doing* power. And of the possession and doing of power needs to be understood in (what is often a patriarchal) context.

When doing history it is not just important to think about the **context** of the past, but also the context of the present. What is the current **socio-historical context** in which you are speaking? How does your socio-historical context impact the kinds of questions you're asking? Reflecting on these questions helps you be critical, to reflect on what is – and is not – available to you as a historian. **Archives** are spaces where historians find their materials, but archives have their own histories too. Histories of medicalization, colonialism, pathologization, racism and sexism – histories related to power – have shaped what contemporary archives contain. Materials in archives are collected with an eye for what is considered important, and those materials are both written and read through the lenses of people's own perspectives, intentions, agendas, aims and beliefs. As historians and psychologists we hold substantial power – we get to be the ones who stake a claim on history looking a certain way.

5. Interdisciplinarity is really helpful

You'll notice throughout this book we mention people and ideas from outside of Psychology. That's because if we are looking at the historical and conceptual aspects of Psychology, it's usually necessarily, and incredibly useful, to look beyond Psychology itself. It's difficult to just use the tools that an individual discipline has to study it. Therefore it's handy to step outside of Psychology in order to be able to look at it. To do this we adopt an *interdisciplinary* perspective – one that borrows and uses ideas from other disciplines. Perhaps the most obvious is History. The fact that we're talking about the history of Psychology indicates we're already at the boundary of both History and Psychology. The fact we're thinking about feminism also suggests we're interested in gender studies, and we also take an interdisciplinary approach and also pay attention to Sociology, Philosophy, Politics and Biology among others.

Interdisciplinarity is really about working at the boundaries of disciplines. It's about the blurry line between where one discipline ends and another begins. It's sometimes difficult to say what discipline something *actually is* anyway, especially when we are thinking about feminism which is relevant across them all. *Multidisciplinarity* is a term used to describe borrowing from several disciples to do a piece of work. We find that working in *inter/ multidisciplinary* ways is often really productive and allows for more conversation across disciplinary lines. For example, there are historians who look at Psychology (and related fields), Psychologists who do history (sometime called psychologist-historians, this includes Peter), and people who do a combination of things without a clear title. Katherine falls into this category; she works in a Sociology department, but researches the history of Psychology and gender and sexuality studies.

6. There are different meanings of *Psychology*

Psychology actually refers to (at least) two different things and we think it's important to make the distinction. There is 'Psychology' the discipline, and 'psychology' the subject matter. 'Big P' Psychology is the discipline which studies 'small p' psychology (that is the psychology we each have in our minds). We are indebted to historian of Psychology Graham Richards (2010) for this distinction. Throughout the book, when discussing psychology as a studied subject, or somebody's psychology, we deliberately use the 'small p' version; psychology. But when discussing the discipline that studies psychology, we use 'big P': Psychology.

These distinctions are important for the clarification of the *reflexive* quality of p/Psychology; the ways in which psychology influences Psychology and vice versa. The P/psychology distinction is also useful when considering the relationship the public has with Psychology, through psychology. It is fascinating that every single person who makes up the discipline of Psychology has their own psychology! And when we study psychology, that impacts the discipline itself! To elaborate, what 'big P' Psychology says about someone (maybe their behaviour, their identity or something about an experience they have in their mental world) can affect how that person actually views themselves and therefore their 'small p' psychology. That shift in 'small p' psychology might then be measured or studied, or that person might decide they'd had enough and they'll do their own academic work in the field, and therefore changes the discipline 'big P' Psychology. We discuss this **reflexive** nature of Psychology more in Chapters 2 and 6.

7. There are different types of feminism

You may have heard of 'waves' of feminism spanning from over a century. These are often understood to have begun with the *first wave* starting at the early twentieth century with efforts to improve women's rights (the right to vote being a particularly prominent one at this time). *Second wave* feminism is usually thought to begin during the 1960s (characterized by a sexual revolution and ongoing fights for rights including women's rights as workers, reproductive rights and freedom from sexual violence). A *third wave* was named during the 1990s (inspired by riot grrl subcultures and it sought to broaden to discussions of feminism to more marginalized women). The *fourth wave* is thought to have emerged around 2010 (and tends to include technological revolutions around the internet as a format through which to enact feminism).

There are also different approaches and priorities in feminist thinking and action which somewhat correspond to these waves. In the *first wave* there were 'suffragists' (who campaigned using peaceful methods such as lobbying), and 'suffragettes' (who were more radical and direct in their approach). In the second wave, two approaches developed; *liberal* and *radical feminism*. Both focused on power as something that women and men possessed to an imbalanced or unequal degree. *Liberal feminist* theory often constructed power as a neutral or positive resource that can and should be shared equally. *Radical feminist* approaches viewed power differently. Instead of seeing power as neutral, radical feminists saw it as the expression of gendered dominance/submission (with men having dominance). Radical feminism had specific types, including Radical Separatist Feminism (which sought new politics involving only women), or Lesbian Radical Feminism (which understood feminism as the theory and lesbianism as the practice). *Socialist Feminism* (or *Marxist Feminism*) focused on the structural aspects of power, especially around labour, employment and work, taking gender and class as key axis of analysis and capitalist patriarchy as the central issue.

The *second wave* was also a period in which the 'sex wars' dominated a lot of feminist thought – there was a strong anti-pornography and pro-sex division in some areas of feminism. Crucially, second wave feminist thought and action made serious headway in many aspects of life in the UK, but it also tended to prioritize the experiences of white, middle-class, able-bodied, cisgender women.

In the 1990s the work of US-based Black feminists in particular moved feminism forwards in terms of being more inclusive and progressive. Some of these women include bell hooks, Patricia Hill Collins, Audre Lorde, Angela Davis and Kimberlé Crenshaw. The concept of *intersectionality* was developed by Crenshaw (1989, also see 1991) upon Black feminist thinking by Barbara Smith and this has substantially shifted feminist thinking in the twenty-first century. Crenshaw's work in this area is developed from Critical Race Theory and so centrally draws in race as well as gender as key factors which *intersect*, to give particular lived experiences. Intersectional feminist theory therefore examines power at multiple levels, unpacking the interacting axes of *privilege* and oppression that inform both social relations and individual identity. See Cole (2009) for a detailed overview of how to use intersectionality in psychological research.

Since the 2010s, thinking about gender, race, dysphoria and colonialism has advanced even further (e.g. Lugones, 2010; also see key work by Chandra Mohanty and Gayatri Spivak). *Decolonial feminism* moved beyond what *postcolonial feminism* attempted to highlight and de-centralizes Western colonial and white models of personhood. In addition, decolonial perspectives aim to dismantle these normative and limited constructions of applying what is known and knowable about the global *minority* to the global *majority*.

Throughout the history of feminism there have been tensions and it is not a linear simple story of a singular thing. Different types of feminism have often had different focuses and conceptualizations of power, or taken aim at different issues in society. A key area of division at present is around so called 'trans-issues' (Pearce, Erikainen & Vincent, 2020). This acts as a reminder that not everyone who calls themselves a feminist will have the same politics. We believe a ***trans***-inclusive feminism is the right way to go.

The history of Psychology has a history

Writings about the history of Psychology also, of course, have their own history. The first major influential history of Psychology was published by Edwin Boring in 1929. His book focused primarily on experimental Psychology which emerged in nineteenth-century Germany and was adopted in the United States and elsewhere as the 'proper' way to do Psychology. In 1951 Boring famously pondered why women had less eminence in Psychology (what he called the 'woman-problem', see Rutherford, 2015). In Britain, Hearnshaw's (1964) book on the 'short history' of British Psychology between the years 1840 and 1940 aimed to provide an outline of this period for both students and the general reader, during which, Hearnshaw argued, Psychology was becoming increasingly influential and in the 'public eye' (1964, p. v–vii). These histories valuably document the people, dates and places of events in these periods, telling us lots about the important institutions, and the powerful psychologists (who were very largely men) that occupied them. These histories were written by psychologists and *for* psychologists and are sometimes called ***internalist*** or celebratory accounts of 'great men' (Young, 1966). Only in the last few decades of the twenteith century, under the influence of second wave feminism, were the women who were involved in Psychology from its earliest days begun to be 're-placed' back into this history (but more on this in Chapter 2!)

Since the 1970s, feminist psychologists and historians have played a major role in shifting away from celebratory accounts of Psychology. Instead of merely accounting for the events in the history of Psychology, relevant scholars began to ask more conceptual questions towards more critical understandings of how the history of psychology is told and the importance of social *context*.

Shifts in the philosophy of science also opened up questions about how *socio-historical contexts* might influence the kinds of science that get done. To give a few examples here that were important for the field of the History of Psychology:

* Popper (1959) critiqued the notion that history had the same scientific nature that other disciplines are able to claim.
* Kuhn (1962) argued that science was not a slow accumulation of knowledge which developed in a linear fashion, but that change happened through *'paradigm shifts'*. A science can only be considered as such once a paradigm (that is a shared, often tacit, understanding of the discipline) has been reached. No singular approach in Psychology has been agreed upon, meaning a paradigm has not yet been reached in Psychology. So, according to Kuhnian thinking here, Psychology is not a mature science (more on this in Chapter 6).
* Stocking (1965) argued against the use of *presentism* in history; that is, the application of current present day understandings onto the past. Yet, understandings of the past are necessary to provide 'critical leverage' for problems in the present.

In the 1970s, the questioning of seemingly objective disciplines continued. Social psychologist Kenneth Gergen (1973) argued very directly that Social Psychology was in effect a 'historical inquiry'. Such thinking was instrumental in the introduction of using history to critique core aspects of disciplines. White (1973) in particular argued that historians had not accepted that the 'facts' they uncover are constructed by the types of questions they posed in the first place (which links closely to our keys above). Historians create the historical narrative and so history does not accurately reflect what actually happened and in creating narratives, particular *tropes* are drawn upon. He categorized historical writing into romances, tragedies, satires and ironies, with writers themselves being anarchist, conservative, radical or liberal. See for example, Herman's (1995) work on the ironic 'romance' of American Psychology.

Such *constructionist* and *relativist* thinking was initially considered somewhat radical. These critical approaches were reflective of, and engaged with, wider societal changes, such as the gay liberation, Black civil rights and anti-psychiatric movements, including the critique of psychological testing. Other social movements at the time also indicate a changing scene in both Psychology and society; wider effects of de-colonization began to be felt, the sexual revolution occurred and student protest movements developed.

Second wave feminism also began to influence the workings of Psychology, and the work of Naomi Weisstein (1968, reprinted and expanded in 1971) became better known. Weisstein argued that women were characterized by Psychology as emotionally unstable, weaker than men, nurturing and intuitive rather than intelligent. This, she argued, was because of the lack understanding of the social *contexts* in which women live. Social *context*, therefore, became not only something historians of Psychology began to study about the past, but was also shown to be influential on the practices of Psychology in the present, suggesting that what had been called objective' and universal was merely a partial male perspective.

By the 1990s, more constructivist accounts of Psychology emerged. In historicizing a number of themes in the history of Psychology, including the increase of the use and trust in statistics and group data, and the development of personality as a topic of study, Danziger (1994) helped reveal power relations in Psychology, and played a particularly key role in the development of constructivist approaches to the history of Psychology. Similarly, Hacking (1995) proposed that Psychology is characterized by 'looping effects' due to its *reflexive* nature whereby people categorized by Psychology respond back and can impact Psychology in a loop.

There was also an increase in the reclaiming of forgotten aspects of history, impacted by wider social changes. Cherry (1995) used this framework to consider the forgotten, or what she calls 'the stubborn particulars', in Psychology. The work of Morawski (1994) was particularly important here in her focus on gender and feminism in Psychology. Describing such work as 'liminal', Morawski aimed to highlight the importance of *reflexivity* in doing the history of Psychology (see also Morawski, 2005). The presence of women in Psychology in the past was central to this work (Morawski & Agronick, 1991). Feminist approaches in Psychology therefore expanded from a re-placing project to a *reflexive* one which included women's history as central. Throughout the twentieth century the relationship between Psychology and feminism has been complex. As Rutherford, Vaughn-Blount and Ball (2010) state, the two are bound with the concepts of gender, gendered roles and gender relations.

In the twenty-first century, historians of Psychology continued to broaden the theoretical scope in which they consider Psychology. Hacking (1999) argued that mental illness is a good example of the construction of 'human kinds' or negotiated classifications of people. He said these were historically situated, so things like hysteria, anorexia and schizophrenia were not 'real' *per se* but that they are situated and constructed in specific *contexts* (see Chapter 4 for more on constructions of diagnoses).

Many, though not all, historians of Psychology are psychologists themselves (see Vaughn-Blount Rutherford, Baker, & Johnson, 2009). Psychology is a particularly important discipline for historians to study because, as originally argued by Danziger (1994) 'the history of psychology, and the history of human subjectivity are not independent of one another' (p. 475). Zenderland (1997) argued that history of Psychology has become a potent weapon as a method to illustrate that science is not value-free; it has highlighted to psychologists and the public alike the importance of a critical perspective. Smith (2007) also argued that the history of Psychology was of particular importance, without which Psychology itself would be incomplete.

Vaughn-Blount et al. (2009) developed the argument that because the history of Psychology is so important, psychologists should be encouraged to become psychologist–historians. They argued that psychologist–historians' awareness of the internal processes and methods of Psychology gives them an advantage over historians who study Psychology. For example, your training in methods puts you in a better position to understand the history of IQ testing (e.g., Gould, 1981) than does a history student's training that does not include statistics courses. This is somewhat in contrast to the views of earlier historians of Psychology some decades before. For example, Young (1966) was very cautious about psychologists doing their own history. He thought that because many psychologists recorded history from writing textbooks they had the potential to work backwards from the present to the past increasing the chances of *presentism* (more on the unreliability of textbooks in Chapter 3).

Yet, Pettit and Davidson (2014) raised some concerns about the historian in Psychology adopting the professional norms of the historian. They particularly acknowledged Stocking's (1965) list of 'sins', which those who practise history in their own field may commit, including anachronism, misinterpretation, *context* neglect and oversimplification. In doing so, Pettit and Davidson (2014) argued that instead of recording the history of Psychology, perhaps historical methods could be better used to answer psychological questions.

As a discipline, Psychology is not located within a political vacuum. Instead it is very much embedded within powerful social (and usually gendered) structures. These structures not only influence Psychology, but also the stories which are told about its past thus leading to an emphasized *history*. More recent epistemological and philosophical considerations of feminism, gender and history of Psychology has furthered the arena of historical practice in Psychology. In recent years, historical efforts have begun to look at Feminist Psychology itself and consider its political motivations in and around the sub-field and how it ties to its own history (e.g. see Rutherford, 2020; Rutherford & Davidson, 2019; Rutherford, Vaughn-Blount, & Ball, 2010; Rutherford, Vaughn-Johnson, & Rodkey, 2015). In managing this complex consideration, Rutherford and Pettit (2015) discuss the relationship between feminism 'and/in/as' Psychology. They argue that the relationship between the two can be viewed as separate, as one within the other, or as feminism as a form of doing Psychology. They also discuss how there is a need for a growth in recent moves to include engage lesbian, gay, bisexual, trans (LGBT) and intersex histories by feminist historians of Psychology. Indeed, this is becoming more apparent as further efforts have also been made to begin to account for more varied gendered experiences beyond cis gender binaries (e.g. Barker & Scheele, 2019; Hegarty, 2018; Rigg, et al., 2019). Issues with the history of Psychology also go beyond gender. Efforts to *decolonize* the history of Psychology are very present at the moment as the stories told about dominant (or hegemonic) Psychology are so American and Eurocentric (Bhatia, Long, Pickren & Rutherford, 2024).

BPS and QAA Curriculum for CHIP

This book has been deliberately designed to directly correspond to the BPS and QAA benchmarks and framework for undergraduate Psychology degrees and postgraduate MSc conversion courses. In recent years the QAA benchmarks have expanded the relevance of *CHIP* to an even greater extent. For example, the QAA states, 'The purpose of a Psychology degree is to develop students' understanding of themselves, others and society through scientific investigation. The degree exposes students to the core domains of the discipline - from their historical roots to the present day.' The History of Psychology is therefore foundational and the QAA states that each area of teaching Psychology needs to address the 'historical and contemporary ethical issues associated with research and practice'. Upon graduating with an honours degree in Psychology or doing a conversion course, the QAA says that the first specific skill students should have 'understand the conceptual and historical underpinnings of psychology as a discipline'.

Under Subject Knowledge and Understanding, the *CHIP* section states:

Conceptual and historical issues are integral to all areas of psychology. Courses provide students with an understanding of epistemological and onto- logical issues to provide a foundation in the philosophy of science. Courses also address historical and contemporary positions within psychology, the dominance of privileged perspectives, and the impact of these. The value of interdisciplinary approaches is recognised throughout the course.

Accordingly, this book directly corresponds to the BPS and QAA requirements both for *CHIP* and across other areas (see Table 1 and Table 2).

Table 1: Mapping this Feminist Companion to the QAA Subject Statement

QAA Statement for Subject Knowledge	How this Companion corresponds
Understanding of epistemological and ontological issues to provide a foundation in the philosophy of science	Explains epistemology and provides accessible understanding of various feminist epistemological positions Identifies ontological issues when considering interdisciplinary approaches Explores how dominant epistemologies have been critiqued by feminists, and shifts in epistemology across time, including the current 'replication crisis'
Address historical and contemporary positions within Psychology	Clear outlines of various positions held within Psychology across time, spanning from traditional or past viewpoints to more contemporary concepts A range of feminist perspectives explored and explained in depth with attention to how they've developed and influenced the history of Psychology Positionality and reflexivity considered in depth
Address the dominance of privileged perspectives and the impact of these	Strong critical perspective throughout on issues related to the dominance of privileged positions Specific historical examples of this outlined with particular attention to gender, race and sexuality Specific guidance provided in how to attend to such issues in CHIP work
Recognition of the value of interdisciplinary approaches	Interdisciplinarity is at the core of this text and its value is expressed throughout Interdisciplinary approaches and their uses in CHIP is especially evident across the Tools feature

Table 2: Mapping onto other features of the QAA requirements

QAA Section	QAA Statement	How this Companion corresponds
Equality, Diversity and Inclusion (EDI)	Historically, the discipline has amplified the experiences of some, while marginalizing, misunderstanding and mischaracterizing others. It is essential that the discipline adopts a more socially just position which advances inclusivity for all, including those with protected characteristics that have often been excluded	The problematic history of marginalization in Psychology is evidenced throughout Many protected characteristics (including gender, sex, race, disability, class, sexuality and marriage status) are centralized An inclusivity ethos and approach is embedded throughout
	Many Psychology courses have historically been based on research and theory from homogenous white, educated, industrialized, rich and democratic countries and have not represented diverse voices and contributions to the discipline. Consequently, existing curricula may privilege a narrow range of voices and exclude or marginalize others	WEIRD (white, educated, industrialized, rich and democratic) samples and perspectives are discussed especially in relation to decolonial approaches Privilege is also a key area of consideration
	Course content emphasizes critical thinking, ethics, evidence-based decision making, and collaboration across interdisciplinary fields	Critical thinking is a crucial skill developed throughout, e.g. see textbook myths and Critical Reading tool Interdisciplinary fields are introduced and particular Tools from these are provided for student's use

	Contemporary Psychology courses encourage students to be critical of the dominant systems of thought that shape our language, perceptions and actions. They recognize that these systems are often intertwined with power and privilege, and that they can marginalize and oppress certain groups of people	The history of such power and privilege is outlined Power within Psychology is explored in depth Alternative approaches and feminist responses are outlined Ways of producing CHIP work which avoid such issues is explored
	For Psychology and related disciplines, discussions of mental health and wellbeing necessitate extending our thinking about equality and inclusion in a manner that embraces and values diversity and belonging. It also requires us to critically reflect on the language and terminology used within the discipline and make challenges where necessary. This commitment to EDI emphasizes not only the need to diversify curricula and improve representation, but to interrogate and challenge historical and dominant narratives about the 'psychological' world that continues to be reproduced	Shifts in language and the meanings of particular discourses is explored Extensive focus on depathologization of homosexuality as a key example Consideration of language when doing the history of Psychology is discussed Critiques of how CHIP curriculum has being predominantly about white cis men is highlighted and more diverse figures in the history of Psychology are provided
Design	Courses are designed to provide an understanding of both historical and contemporary psychological theories and research, and to prepare students for the application of psychological knowledge and skills to future issues. Historical and contemporary viewpoints will be integrated throughout the design of a course and represent culturally diverse perspectives	Issues in the present are identified as well as those in the past Guidance to avoid re-producing dominant and/or marginalizing work is provided Students are encouraged to apply their own thinking to psychological knowledge

Features of the book

Tools

In each chapter of this book we outline for you a metaphorical tool that can be used for and with **CHIP**. These are the tools we think are the most useful in helping us shift our thinking and be more critical about the history of Psychology and to think more conceptually. For us, these tools are like the compasses – finding aids that we might use while navigating the map of CHIP. There are of course lots of different tools, these are just the ones we think are most useful at this stage. But do add more to your own tool kits when you think other things are helpful too (more on this in Chapter 7).

Our ideas of tools has emerged from the writing of Sara Ahmed. In *Living a Feminist Life* (2017), Ahmed beautifully writes about the need for tools as a part of a feminist survival kit. These tools might be the things a feminist needs in order to be able to write, express or shout about feminism. We've taken these tools to be more conceptual in this book and aim to give you these tools to help you enact feminism in your scholarly life in Psychology. In this book the following chapters introduce these tools:

Chapter 2 – Feminist Science Studies
Chapter 3 – Critical Reading and Ethics
Chapter 4 – Queer Theory
Chapter 5 – Feminist Biology
Chapter 6 – Your Lived Experience

Ahmed also uses the term *Feminist killjoy* as a sort of reclamation of the idea that feminists suck the joy out of things. She uses this especially to argue that as killjoys, we 'recover a feminist history, turning it into a source of strength as well as an inspiration' (see her latest book *The Feminist Killjoy Handbook* 2023).

Boxes

Throughout the book we've used separated boxes to give you particularly pertinent examples. These work as case studies, or feature of key people etc. to demonstrate a particular point we're making. These have been designed to be entertaining and revealing. They might serve as a reminder that not everything that's relevant fits neatly into a single narrative.

Illustrations

We've been utterly inspired by the graphic books by Meg-John Barker and Jules Scheele (recommended below) and decided to include some illustrations throughout this book. We feel that these bring some of the people and issues we highlight 'to life' a little more and can make reading this type of companion book feel more familiar and enjoyable. We are indebted to Clare Butler (Katherine's wife) for these images.

Key questions/References/Index

At the end of each chapter we outline some key questions to think about or work on if you'd like to. We've included these to act as a teaching aid if helpful to lecturers and teaching assistants or for you to use. We also provide a short list of the key references we've cited in the chapter at the end of each one so you can see them easily. All references included in the book as a whole are cited at the end near the index. The index can be used to find key parts of the book which focus on a topic, person, subject, etc.

Glossary

As we are looking at conceptual issues as well as feminist ones, sometimes the terminology can be a bit confusing or opaque. We've explained terms in where appropriate throughout in the main text, but the glossary can be a handy extra feature to help you if you lose your footing on the journey. Whenever you see a word that is both *bold and italic*, you will find it in the Glossary.

Structure of the book

The book follows a rough chronological order. The chapters flows from thinking about how gender impacted the development of Psychology, to feminist analysis of such histories, to feminist action in and around Psychology towards social change, to deconstructing gender in the brain, and key issues in the present and future. The next Chapter (Chapter 2) covers early ideas in Psychology regarding gender and who was able to 'be' a psychologist to foreground how and why gender is an important analytic tool in the history of Psychology. Here we introduce the tool of Feminist Science Studies. In Chapter 3 we focus on classic experimental studies in Psychology, particularly the use of the Kitty Genovese's murder in social psychological studies of altruism, to equip you to debunk '*textbook myths*'. The tool in this chapter is Critical Reading and Ethics. In Chapter 4, we pay attention to how Psychology has been associated with *social change* and the political and powerful aspects of the discipline. This chapter historicises the depathologization of queer sexualities as introduces the tool of Queer Theory. In Chapter 5 we shift forward in time, and consider how *essentialist* biological *discourses* get used when thinking about gender. Using the tool Feminist Biology we show how feminism and biology are not incompatible. Chapter 6 considers live controversies in Psychology in the present about *open science*, and considers how present academic cultures impact the experiences of feminists in the field. Here, we propose your own *lived experience* as a key tool. In the final chapter we look forwards to feminist *CHIP* futures and frame you as a key feminist agent within that future! Here we will specifically outline how you can take what you've learned forward and do feminist work in your own research using the tools we've provided in this companion.

Other resources

This book works as a feminist companion, so it's not a replacement for a textbook or lots of readings that you might be doing to learn about *CHIP*. This book instead acts as an extra resource that gives you the feminist angle on CHIP that a lot of texts sadly lack.

However, there are some fantastic *CHIP* resources that we also recommend:

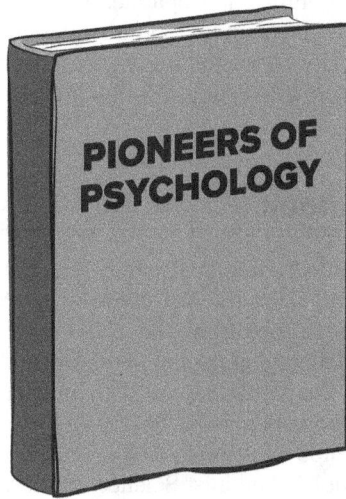

Pioneers of Psychology: A History (5th edition) by Fancher and Rutherford (2016). This is perhaps the most comprehensive history of Psychology book that thinks about gender throughout. Not surprising really, given it is co-written by Alexandra Rutherford, feminist badass historian of Psychology extraordinaire (we're pretty sure that's her official title).

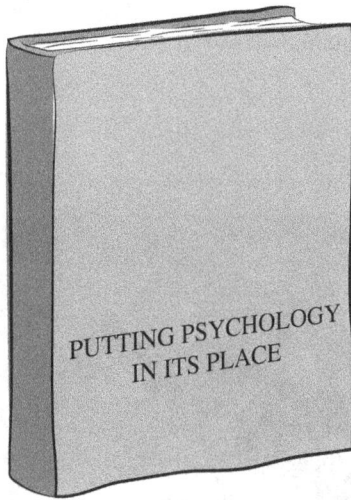

Putting Psychology in Its Place: Critical Historical Perspectives (4th edition) by Richards and Stenner (2022). This book gives a really strong critical lens to the history of Psychology. There is a chapter on gender, and we especially like how other areas are also considered critically, including: race, Psychology and war, mental distress, Psychology and the child, religion, and wider ethical issues.

Psychology's **Feminist** Voices

Outside of textbooks there are also some fantastic online resources. Psychology's Feminist Voices (PFV) https://feministvoices.com/ is brilliant and is run by the aforementioned feminist badass historian of Psychology extraordinaire Alexandra Rutherford (Katherine is also an international member of the team). Here you can read through profiles of feminists in Psychology past and present (including a profile on Peter!) and see all of the *oral history* interviews that the team have conducted (see Chapter 6 where we discuss PFV even more). Plus, there are great online exhibits, including one about Queering

Psychology that Katherine took part in, and one about the history of feminist Psychology in the UK that she was very involved with alongside Lois Donnelly and Rose Capdevila.

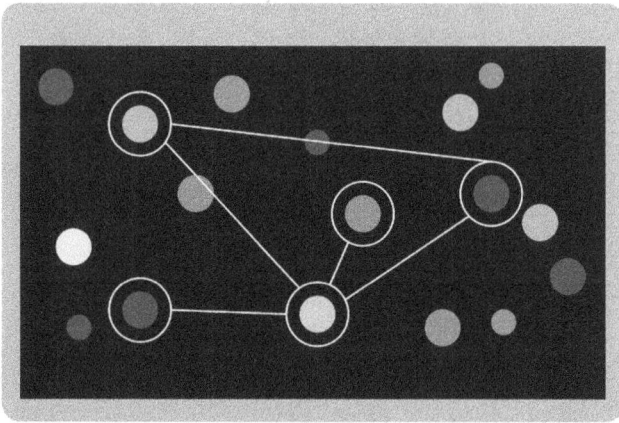

Another online resource that was developed by Rose Capdevila is the Open University Investigating Psychology *CHIPs* resource (Katherine was involved too!) You can find it by searching for 'Open University CHIPs'. It works to allow for a full interactive investigation into the history of Psychology, including people, contexts, perspectives, methods and narratives.

The online booklet 'Hidden Histories: Black in Psychology' is a great resource which not only outlines the contributions Black people have made to Psychology, but also provides loads of information for future career consideration too. Written by Parise Carmichael-Murphy and Adam Danquah and illustrated by India Joseph, it provides a wealth of key information. You can learn about Black Psychology, racial disparities and *social change* and *activism* plus loads of other things. Just search for the title and the main website links to the resource.

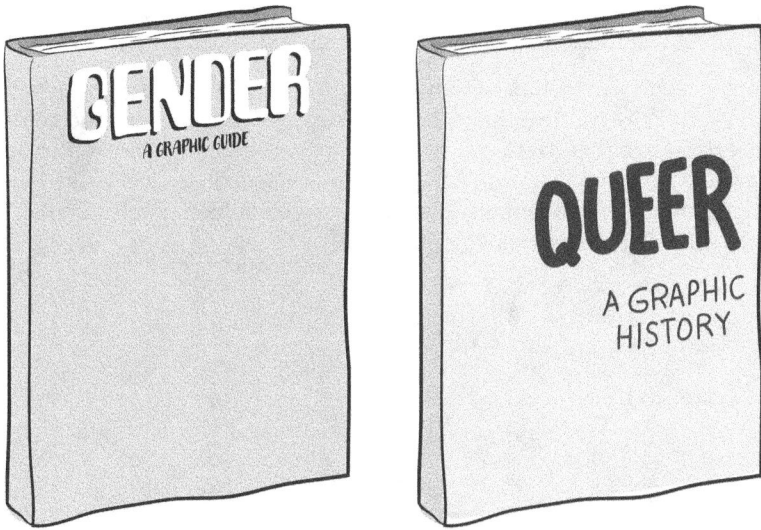

For more gender specific resources we really recommend two books by Meg-John Barker and Jules Scheele. *Gender: A Graphic Guide* (2019) and *Queer: A Graphic History* (2016) are superb. These are both really accessible and provide a wealth of information about gender and feminism as well as scholarly theory. Meet your gender studies heroes!

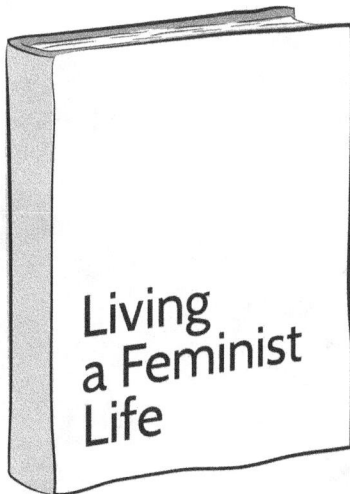

For feminist thinking especially, we recommend the aforementioned text *Living a Feminist Life* (2017) by Ahmed. If this feminist companion book had a companion, it'd be this. Ahmed also recently wrote *The Feminist Killjoy Handbook*. So if you feel like you need a bit of killjoy solidarity, we'd also recommend that.

Conclusion

Hopefully, you now feel all set and ready to begin your feminist adventure through *CHIP*. We've given you the map key/legend to understand the map, promises of tools that you'll get with full instructions in each chapter, and a background in what a history of the history of Psychology has looked like so far. In all, we want this feminist companion to embolden you to be your true feminist self when doing Psychology.

2 Who Has Made Up Psychology?

Learning objectives

Study of this chapter will enable you to:

- Question what you've been taught about the history of Psychology and importantly, *who* you've been taught about
- Understand how gender, race and class are key lenses through which to understand how women have been included and excluded in the history of Psychology
- Meet some of the women in Psychology's past
- Learn about the various epistemologies feminists have applied to deal with sexism in Psychology, including empirical, standpoint and poststructuralist feminisms
- Gain Feminist Science Studies as a critical tool for doing CHIP, allowing you to reconsider 'bias' and perspective and develop more confidence in your own epistemological standpoint

Introduction

If you were to walk up to someone in the street and ask them to name a famous psychologist, chances are they would first name a man. In fact, we'd be willing to bet there's a good chance that that man would be ... Sigmund Freud. If you asked them to name a famous psychologist called Freud, you'd be hard pressed to find someone who thought of Anna Freud ahead of Sigmund. Fair enough. Sigmund is pretty famous, his psychosexual stages of development and significant cocaine habit do make him spring to mind. But maybe there is also an ***androcentric*** pattern of thinking at work when we think about famous people in general and famous psychologists in particular? To get you into this chapter, we are going to ask if it's not just the general public who tend to be androcentric (that is, focused or centred on men). Perhaps the way we learn about Psychology's history at university also tends to make the story mostly about men.

In this chapter we're going to be writing against this androcentric trend. First, we will look at the history of women's inclusion and exclusion from Psychology. Was it just that there were no women psychologists until recent times? Or have they been there all along, we just haven't remembered them? Both explanations have some truth to them.

Second, we will look at what happened when feminists assembled and began to change both Psychology itself, and our understanding of its history. From the late 1960s onwards, feminists began to simultaneously reclaim lost knowledge about some of the unknown women from the past, and challenge *patriarchal* assumptions that had led those women's contributions to Psychology to be under-estimated. They established Feminist Psychology as a sub-field with new organizations, journals, questions and methods. Through these events, *second wave feminism* began to make lasting changes in the landscape of Psychology's culture; changing not only who got to be a psychologist (and who got studied) but also expanding the kinds of questions around gender were asked including new questions and theories about Psychology's relationship to science.

We will use these questions to introduce you to new friends in *Feminist Science Studies*. Feminist Science Studies is an interdisciplinary area of study that looks at Psychology critically from the outside – not as psychologists do, but as historians, sociologists and philosophers do (see Chapter 1). This interdisciplinarity (the words just get longer, don't they) was developed by feminists who were in dialogue with feminists in philosophy, history and other disciplines, giving us new tools for thinking about science – including psychology – as a kind of 'culture'.

The questions we will invite you to ask here can be applied broadly. By the end of the chapter, people might still immediately think of Sigmund Freud when you ask them to name a psychologist, but you'll be able to explain why.

Box 2.1: Two heritage 'Blue Plaques' at the Freud Museum

SIGMUND FREUD
1856~1939
Founder of
Psychoanalysis
lived here
1938~1939

ANNA FREUD
1895~1982
Pioneer of Child
Psychoanalysis
lived here
1938~1982

In the UK, these plaques on buildings commemorate people, places and events. Commemoration is always political – and gender is one thing that impacts who or what is considered important enough to be commemorated. Sigmund and Anna both moved in to 20 Maresfield Gardens, London, to escape Nazi persecution in Vienna, Austria in 1938. Sigmund died just over a year later, but Anna lived there until her death in 1982. In 1956 Sigmund's plaque was first installed, but Anna's plaque was not installed until 2002 when Sigmund's was updated. Anna established psychoanalytic Child Psychology and founded what is now known as the Anna Freud Centre. At her request the house was made into a museum which is well worth checking out if you're in London. You can even see Sigmund's actual couch (but you're not allowed to sit on it). Anna Freud is one of incredibly few very famous women psychologists in the early history of Psychology.

In an account of the 100 most eminent psychologists of the twentieth century, Haggbloom et al. (2002) used citations to psychologists' work and the opinions of living psychologists to estimate 'eminence'. Anna Freud was included in this list at number 99. There were only 5 other women included: Elizabeth Loftus (58th), Eleanor Maccoby (70th), Eleanor Gibson (joint 74th), Margaret Washburn (joint 88th) and Mary Ainsworth (97th). The authors acknowledged that their methods could have a pro-American bias, but said nothing about a possible *androcentric* bias.

The history of exclusion and inclusion in Psychology

Early psychologists were largely men, and they produced theories that women were inferior, weaker, more infantile and more emotional than men. They then baked these theories into medical and scientific concepts. Darwin's theory of evolution proposed that men were more variable in their abilities than women, explaining and justifying the limitation of women's scientific education (Milar, 2000). Women's 'emotional' traits were perceived as complementary to men's 'rational' traits and such differences were explained by sexual selection. This in effect justified the social hierarchy and women's apparently 'inferior' status within that hierarchy (Shields, 2007). In fact, it was thought an over-stimulation of education could cause women physical harm and detract from more 'natural' caring and nurturing abilities. Women were therefore excluded from higher education 'for their own good'.

In this *context*, where femininity and science were viewed as incompatible, the 'woman scientist' became a contradiction in terms (Bohan, 1990; Rossiter, 1982). Rather, 'proper' socially acceptable women were thought to be pious, pure, submissive and domesticized, *not* intellectual, ambitious and curious about science (Bohan, 1990). Henry Maudsley, the principal patron of the Maudsley hospital in London, a very influential institution for training psychologists, was explicit that women's nature was oriented around reproduction and men's around being clever:

'the affective life is more developed in proportion to the intellect in the female than in the male, and the influence of the reproductive organs upon mind more powerful'

(Maudsley, 1879 as cited in Shields, 2007)

This idea that wombs in particular were influential organs that disrupted women's abilities was common. While reminiscent of Sigmund Freud's theories of 'hysteria', Sigmund was actually the first person to apply the hysteria diagnosis to men and to argue hysteria was due to repression or childhood sexual abuse or childhood sexual fantasy or a mysterious influence of wombs. Nonetheless, the ideas that menstruation, menopause and uteruses caused emotional disturbance and instability remained.

Women entering Psychology in the late decades of the late nineteenth century (late 1800s) and early twentieth century (early 1900s) faced these theories that defined reason and science as best (and most safely) housed in male bodies only. They did not inhabit a psychologist-filled society like our own; only a few people were then beginning to call themselves psychologists. Unsurprisingly, most of them were men. For example, the first meeting of the British Psychological Society (BPS) in 1901 was attended by one woman (Sophie Bryant) and nine men. When the BPS had their very first reading of Sigmund Freud's work in 1913, all the women there were asked to leave the room! This was reported by Alice Woods who was very involved in the BPS at the time (Valentine, 2008a). These events illustrate how a) there *were* women in the history of Psychology from the start, b) they were *literally* excluded at the time, and c) their histories were forgotten and had to be later *reclaimed*.

In addition to sexist theories and being in the minority, early generations of women psychologists also faced *formal exclusion* from education. In Britain for example, the University of Cambridge didn't formally award women degrees until 1948.

Box 2.2: Christine Ladd-Franklin

One famous example of exclusion from early psychology involves Christine Ladd-Franklin (1947–1930), a pioneering psychological scientist who focused on colour perception.

Ladd-Franklin was admitted to the postgraduate programme in Johns Hopkins only by disguising her gender on her application form (cleverly using only her initials). She then became the first American woman to study logic and mathematics at the graduate level. Her theory of the evolution of colour perception described how the ability to distinguish black from white evolved first, and how the blue–yellow distinction evolved before the red–green distinction. It explains why more colour-blind humans struggle to distinguish red and green than blue and yellow (as do dogs)! In Ladd-Franklin's own time some of her ideas were stolen and attributed to other male psychologists, while other male psychologists whose theories she criticized ignored her altogether (Agler & Durmuş, 2013).

How and why was she excluded from Psychology's developing culture? Beyond the meetings of the American Psychological Association (APA) which did not exclude women, the largest meeting of psychologists in North America in the early twentieth century was a group called 'The Experimentalists'. It was organized by the Englishman Edward Titchener (1867–1927). The group met annually and informally at various universities on the East Coast of the USA where most psychologists in North American were then concentrated. Titchener excluded women, as a group, from The Experimentalists on the grounds that the argumentation in the group should be robust, and the room filled with smoke. This was an academic culture that the male scientists were supposed to all enjoy. Actually several men among The Experimentalists opposed the exclusion of women, while others thought that women could not engage in this boisterous culture.

Ladd-Franklin made an insistent demand to attend and to present her work. In 1912 in a letter to Titchener she even insisted that she herself always smoked in fashionable society and would be able to swear as well as the men. He refused her, and then the situation became critical in 1914 when the group were meeting at her own university. She made the case again. Titchener relented this time, but only after other (male) Experimentalists supported Ladd-Franklin explicitly. On that occasion, she then became the only woman who participated openly in this important scientific meeting for decades (Furumoto & Scarborough, 1986).

These historical stories of formal exclusion matter because they explain *how* psychology got assembled to be so **patriarchal**. As in any culture, there is a relationship between its social norms, who it includes and excludes, who has status, and how power is exercised.

Gender was not the only barrier to participation in early Psychology (see Guthrie, 2004). Psychology took shape in the decades immediately after the American Civil War which had ended slavery in the American South. Psychologist G. Stanley Hall, the first American to get a PhD in Psychology on American soil, and the man who supervised more than half of the PhDs granted in the USA in the nineteenth century in the country's first Psychology department, believed in the superiority of both men and white people. Nonetheless, Hall's research culture contradicted his own exclusionary logic. Francis Cecil Sumner, the first African American to earn a PhD in Psychology, was Hall's last PhD student

(Sawyer, 2000). Hall also used women extensively as research assistants, even though he also espoused the Darwinian theories described above (Diehl, 1986).

Early Psychology was characterized by beliefs about the primitiveness of non-white people as much as it was characterized by sexist beliefs about gender (Shields & Bhatia, 2009). In fact, these ideas *intersected*. In nineteenth century Europe, African women such as Sarah Baartmann, were *exhibited* by European male scientists who gazed at their bodies with fascination (Mitchell, 2020). Such thinking was highly associated with racist fascinations with the sexed attributes of women of colour, and the pathologization of lesbians (Somerville, 1994). In Psychology, white scientists argued using (pretty dodgy and culturally biased) IQ tests that white people (especially middle-class ones) were more evolved compared to people of colour, and that consequently the sexuality and reproduction of poorer women and women of colour should be controlled for *eugenic* reasons. Such *scientific racism* and sexism also linked to sexuality, so non-heterosexual people, women, poorer people and people of colour were viewed as 'primitive' compared to white middle-class heterosexual men (Somerville 1994; more on this in Chapter 4). Even in the 1990s, the best-selling science book *The Bell Curve* argued for the reality of class and race differences in IQ as the reason why the sexual revolution of the 1960s created freedoms that only white people with middle-class values could handle (Hegarty, 2013, Chapter 8).

Consequently Black psychologists were rarely able to influence theories of group difference in intelligence that raged across the discipline in the early twentieth century (a notable exception being the educationalist Horace Mann Bond). The first Black woman to receive a PhD in Psychology was Inez Beverly Prosser, whose dissertation at the University of Cincinnati concerned the impact of Black teachers on the personality development of their students (Benjamin et al., 2005).

She finished her thesis in 1933 and a year later sadly died in a car accident. In 1954 her research was very influential in the *Brown v. Board of Education Supreme Court* ruling which made state-sanctioned segregation (based on race) in public schools unconstitutional. (Note that *prior* to 1954, all education in the USA was racially segregated, including the teaching of Psychology, in extremely unfair ways.) The testimony of psychologists Mamie Phipps Clarke and Kenneth Clarke was also pivotal to this case. They developed their work at Howard University, a historically Black university whose psychology department was founded by Cecil Sumner.

Another important Black educational psychologist was Mollie Hunte. She was born in 1932 and began her work in schools in British Guiana (now Guyana). In 1961 she emigrated to the UK and gained an impressive education in Psychology over 12 years while working alongside her studies. She was pivotal in the Black Education Movement and greatly supported the African-Caribbean community in London (her collection is held at the London Metropolitan Archives).

'Re'-Placing Women in the History of Psychology

For decades the history of Psychology has been taught as the achievements of the great minds of (yep) mostly white men. In the United States, people particularly read a book titled *A History of Experimental Psychology* (1929) by E.G. Boring (we know, it doesn't sound super interesting). However, in the 1960s, historians began to look at science more critically, and to take scholarship in the history of science much more seriously. Following calls for Psychology to do more to challenge systematic sexism and racism in the late 1960s (for example, King, 1968), authors began to look back into the history of Psychology to rediscover people in it beyond the white men centred by authors such as Boring (1929). For example, Robert Guthrie's pathbreaking book *Even The Rat Was White* (2004, first edition published 1976) drew the history of Black psychologists in the USA together for the first time (great title, right?).

Spurred on by *second wave* feminism and wider social changes afoot (see Chapter 4), the 1980s and 1990s saw the beginnings of the 're'-placement of women in the history of psychology. Bohan (1990) rightly argues this is a 're'-placement because women have been there all along. The results of this (often feminist) scholarship were eye-opening. Despite its overarching sexist culture, women made major contributions even in late nineteenth-century Psychology (Bernstein & Russo, 1974; Furumoto & Scarborough, 1986; Milar, 2000; Rutherford, Vaughn-Blount & Ball, 2010). Selective US colleges such as Stanford University began to allow women to enrol in the late 1800s while gender-segregated women's colleges gave some American women access to degrees. Nonetheless, the options for women psychologists were limited. For example, even though Christine Ladd-Franklin was a lecturer at Columbia University, she was unpaid. She wrote in 1917 that she had no other option but to lecture for nothing (and was privileged to have the financial means to do so). She also wrote of the dilemma between work and family life that women psychologists faced. She also said that women:

> ought to be taught that she cannot serve two masters, that if she chooses the higher path of learning and wants to do herself and her sex justice, she must forgo matrimony
>
> (Milar 2000, p. 618).

Furumoto and Scarborough (1986) studied the lives of the first 22 women psychologists who joined the APA in the USA after it was formed in 1892, a group who achieved their doctorates around 1900. Every woman who became an assistant professor remained unmarried, and each experienced gender discrimination. Only 50 per cent were professors compared to 65 per cent of psychologists who were men (Milar, 2000). All of those professorial women were single and worked predominantly in women's colleges; many – like Ladd-Franklin – working for free or for very little pay.

Valentine similarly (2008b; 2010) researched the positions of 16 women in the early days of the BPS, including Beatrice Edgell, Alice Woods, Jessie Murray, Julia Turner and Susan Isaacs. Most were middle-upper-class women who worked in teaching roles, and two-thirds were unmarried. Valentine suggests that Psychology was more open to British women than some other disciplines at the time, such as physiology, because of the wish to 'swell the numbers' of the recently developed BPS. Men's dominance was not yet firm in British Psychology, but things like 'marriage bans' which allowed only single women to legally work did reinforce it. A marriage ban was applied to school teachers from the 1920s in Britain but did not impact the college- and university-level teaching these women were doing. However, as Valentine (2008b) points out, some institutions such as Liverpool University did try to enforce such a ban. It's worth noting however these bans only impacted middle-class women striving to enter male-dominated professions such as education. Working-class women regardless of their marriage status often worked in paid employment, for example in service or in manual roles.

Women psychologists opened spaces for each other in some specific areas of applied psychology in early twentieth-century Britain. For example, in 1913 physician Jessie Murray and teacher Julia Turner opened the Medico-Psychological Clinic in London. Psychoanalysis became more popular in Britain due to the social upheaval of the First World War, and reports of 'shell shock' from its trenches. Murray and Turner's leadership shaped women's greater engagement with Psychology. In 1924, 17 of 54 members (31 per cent) of the London Psycho-Analytical Society were women, compared to only 12–15 per cent of the International Psycho-Analytical Society (Hinshelwood, 1999). Murray and Turner were heavily involved with the suffragist movement and shared a close intimate relationship with one another. Their Clinic not only trained women psychotherapists, it also focused mainly on women clients (Valentine, 2009).

In the years between the First and Second World Wars, Psychology grew at an unprecedented rate. During the Second World War, psychologists were tasked with efforts aimed at assisting in the assessment and recuperation of soldiers. This military alliance also led to many men swelling the ranks of Clinical Psychology and lead to optimistic theories that psychological distress could in many cases be quickly addressed with the right environment. Indeed, while 12 per cent of soldiers were excluded on psychiatric grounds in the USA, self-help manuals for managing anxiety were circulated at an unprecedented scale, and many battle-weary soldiers were deemed psychologically able to re-enter combat after only a few days' rest (Herman, 1995). Following the war, men's employment was encouraged (and returning soldiers' college education was well-funded) while women were encouraged to give up the paid employment they had taken on during the war. Men's dominance in academic areas of Psychology, and Clinical Psychology in particular, therefore became even more ingrained.

Efforts to get back to more 'traditional' gender roles also ramped up after women had started to gain more independence during the war years. In an effort to get men back into workplaces that women had occupied during the war, there was a substantial effort to get women 'back into the home'. For example, sociologists described middle-class male 'breadwinners' and female 'homemakers' as the norm for all, even though only more affluent families could afford to have one potential wage-earner. Psychology was also very complicit in normalizing these gender roles. For example, John Bowlby developed the 'maternal deprivation hypothesis' based from studies of children evacuated from British cities during the Second World War. His theories were interpreted as the argument that children needed their mothers at home if they were to develop secure attachments. Indeed, the post-Second World War era is the high point of *mother-blaming theories*. During this time, the blame for so many things that were then deemed to be psychological problems – autism, homosexuality, schizophrenia – were laid at the feet of mothers (and arguably, this hasn't changed all that much since).

Despite efforts to get women out of the work force and into full-time caring roles, women psychologists continued to have impact, particularly in Child and Developmental Psychology (Anna Freud and Mary Ainsworth being just two examples). This is perhaps not all that surprising because old stereotypes specified that these areas were considered more appropriate for women. Because of beliefs that women's abilities and skills lay in nurturing, nursing and the caring professions, women were more likely to be accepted into roles in related areas of Psychology (Furumoto & Scarborough, 1986; Rutherford et al. 2015; Scarborough & Furumoto, 1989). This was in contrast to areas of experimental Psychology, where women were less represented and their work was less often cited.

The wars had also increased the importance of tests to Psychology. The First World War had seen the IQ testing of one million soldiers (Carson, 2006), while personality tests were used in military assessments in the Second World War (Herman, 1995). Furumoto (2003) argues that these testing practices had a large impact on the overall development of Psychology. Interestingly, it was actually often women doing the work of psychological testing. Testing was viewed, despite its importance and impact upon Psychology, as lower status and requiring less scientific understanding. It was therefore deemed suitable for women and so provided them with opportunities in lower salaried jobs than their male counterparts (Bohan, 1990). Not only this but the people who were being tested were men, resulting in it being men's averages which were considered the basis of determining what was a normal or abnormal score – leading to deeper entrenched form of **androcentrism** in Psychology.

Unsurprisingly, testing boomed in areas such as Occupational, Educational and Developmental Psychology. There were higher concentrations of women working in lower status testing as it was deemed a form of Psychology better suited to women's abilities than 'pure' scientific work in university laboratories (Bohan, 1990; Furumoto, 2003). Under the control of mainly women psychologists, applied Psychology and testing practices greatly advanced the profession. In the USA, the second generation of women in Psychology were also a bit more diverse than the first both in terms of ethnicity and religion (Johnston & Johnson, 2008) though this often meant they faced racist as well as sexist barriers (Rutherford & Granek, 2010).

From our contemporary perspective, the global effort to 're-place' women in Psychology's history (Bohan, 1990), revealed much about the lives of contemporary Psychology's forbearers. Feminist psychologists writing after the Second World War such as Georgene Seward and Ruth Herschberger were rare, and had little influence (but are well worth reading for their insight into these times). The feminist endeavour to account for the actions of women in the past that began in the 1970s is ongoing. We not only need to re-place these women, but also to analyse the **contexts** in which their erasure occurred to critique erasure continuing in the present. Such endeavours need to be intersectional, and cannot simply work for women who are **privileged** by race, ethnicity, class, age, sexuality and/or ability.

This intersectional approach is important because race and class were **privileges** that allowed many of those early women their slim chances to sit at Psychology's table. Nor did feminist historians re-place all the early women psychologists equally; there is more detail on the lives of early Black women psychologists such as Inez Prosser in Guthrie's work than in some of the work by early feminist historians. The issue of representation is also not just a historical one but lives in the present. The 100 Black Women Professors NOW campaign calculated that of the 22,000 professors in the UK, only 66 are Black women. That's 0.3 per cent, less than 1 in 500. A recent study by Cramblet-Alvarez et al. (2020) found men psychologists to be named far more often than women psychologists in five recent popular history of Psychology textbooks. Sigmund Freud topped the poll with 1807 namechecks in these books, while Anna got only 66. Mamie Phipps Clark was the most frequently name-checked Black woman psychologist (16 name checks), but her achievements were frequently misattributed to her husband Kenneth Clark (who got 82 namechecks, see also Chapter 4)

Parise Carmichael-Murphy and Adam Danquah's online document 'Hidden Histories, Black in Psychology' (2022) joins the dots between the stories of Black people from the history of psychology, current racial disparities in Psychology, *activism* and inclusion and the future of Black Psychology. Psychology's Feminist Voices also has a 'Women of Color in Psychology' project and the 'I am Psyched!' virtual exhibit which describe the histories of women of colour in Psychology. It is key to recognize that when erasure happens historically, it's not usually based on one particular characteristic, but rather there are many dynamics at play, including *privilege* (see Chapter 6).

Feminists assemble!

Feminist psychologists' attention to the history of women in Psychology occurred at the same time as an emerging fight against sexism and misogyny. The watershed moment occurred in the late 1960s. In the USA, the Association for Women in Psychology (AWP) was founded in 1969, and the Society for the Psychology of Women (Division 35 of the APA) was established in 1973. These groups certainly intersected with calls for psychologists to stand up explicitly for racial justice, following a controversial speech of Dr Martin Luther King to the APA in 1967, less than a year before his assassination (King, 1968). For example, the APA's Board for Social and Ethical Responsibility in Psychology (BSERP) was set up in response to the demands of both groups that Psychology engage in social justice struggles more directly (Pickren & Tomes, 2002), and BSERP became the platform for the first pro-lesbian/gay voices in the APA (Hegarty, 2018). The Society for the Psychology of Women, a Division of the APA, began publishing the *Psychology of Women Quarterly* research journal in 1976, a year after another journal of research, *Sex Roles*, began publication. *The Journal of Black Psychology* began publishing in 1974 and *Journal of Homosexuality* in 1976.

The feminist Psychology movement internationalized. In 1976 an Interest Group on Women in Psychology formed within the Canadian Psychological Association (now the Section on Women and Psychology (SWAP); see Austin, Rutherford & Pyke, 2006 on its wider influence in Canada). The Women & Psychology Interest Group of the Australian Psychological Society formed in 1984. While there are feminists working in Psychology all over the world, there aren't societies or official groups everywhere. Rutherford et al. (2011) reviewed the state of feminist psychology internationally. At this point in time, in countries such as Turkey, Spain, China, Brazil, India, and Israel and many others, no such formal structures for Feminist Psychology existed.

In Britain the development of a feminist Psychology group took some time to be established. But this wasn't because there were fewer feminists who wanted to organize – it was because they weren't allowed. Initially the feminist group WIPs (for Women in Psychology) was established and this became the basis for arguing for an official BPS feminist Section. Eventually, in 1987 the Psychology of Women Section (POWS) was officially founded after a substantial battle to organize it by Sue Wilkinson, Jan Burns, Paula Nicholson, Janet Sayers, Jane Ussher, Marilyn Aitkenhead, Linda Greenbury, Mat Idema, Sandra Oliver, Sheila Rossan and Alison Thomas (Burman, 1990; Wilkinson, 1990).

Looking at Britain in more detail, the problem was that the BPS wanted to see Psychology as a science distinct from politics. The BPS viewed a group of feminists as political and therefore would not allow them to form, and when they did form, did not allow them to call themselves feminists officially. This explained why the group was called the Psychology of Women Section or POWS. The irony that the BPS wouldn't allow them to call themselves feminists based on the BPS' political agenda was not lost on the women who were setting up POWS (Capdevila, Hubbard & Donnelly, 2019). In 2017, this BPS Section added 'equalities' into its name, becoming the Psychology of Women and Equalities Section (POWES). Their journal became *Psychology of Women and Equalities Review*, known as POWER – a clearer claim on the section's political stance. Tensions between POWES and the BPS have remained, as has the need for groups like POWES. Those feminists involved in the group value it enormously and have described it as an inclusive, nurturing, feminist community (Donnelly, Hubbard & Capdevila, 2022).

The challenges in setting up POWES illustrates tensions within Psychology about the legitimacy of explicitly political goals that comes with the recognition that psychology cannot be politically neutral by disengaging from social justice struggles (King, 1968). This history replayed itself a decade later with the setting up of the section for Lesbian and Gay Psychology within the BPS, now the section for the Psychology of Sexualities (Wilkinson, 1999). Terms like 'psychology of women' became popular, though they have always been contested (Burman, 2011; Capdevila & Lazard, 2015; Parlee, 1975). For some 'psychology of women' was a euphemism for feminist *activism* (Wilkinson & Burns, 1990; Wilkinson, 1999) so it sometimes acted as a trojan horse taking feminist scholarship into mainstream Psychology (Donnelly, Hubbard & Capdevila, 2022). But for others, it was too apolitical and implied a mere study of women rather than an engaged critique of the constrictive political world in which women live. In 1991 the journal *Feminism & Psychology* was set up which finally labelled feminist work in Psychology as explicitly feminist. Yet the term 'psychology of women' remained the most common for some years.

Box 2.3: Naomi Weisstein

An absolute classic text in this area from around this time is 'Psychology constructs the female' by Naomi Weisstein (1968/1971).

Weisstein (1939–2015) was, to use the technical term, an absolute feminist badass. She argued that Psychology had adopted the sexist norms of society unquestioningly with the result that Psychology knew nothing about women. Problems included: a) the tendency in Psychiatry and Clinical Psychology to develop theory without empirical evidence; b) a lack of recognition of the power of gender roles; and c) reliance on animal studies to explain gender differences. Weisstein made a pitch for a more social Psychology that recognized the importance of social **contexts** and expectations in producing gender differences. Without this, she argued, Psychology's knowledge was scientifically and politically empty. These days it seems sensible to think of 'gender' as separate from sex, but it was largely the generation of women psychologists in the 1970s, spurred on by Weisstein and by each other, that broke that assumption that gender differences were expressions of biological sex differences rather than the enforcement of gender roles, norms and stereo-types (see Unger, 1979, and Chapter 5). In order to understand women, or indeed anyone that isn't a cisgender man, Psychology needed to recognize the social **contexts** in which they live and the social expectations to which they are subject. Without this, Weisstein said Psychology was worthless to liberation efforts as its answers were just reflections of psychologists' prejudices.

Not only did Weisstein write this early and influential critique of Psychology, she was active in setting up the Chicago Women's Liberation Union, published in women's liberation periodicals, used comedy and cartoons to relay political messages, and was in the Chicago Women's Liberation Rock Band. You can hear a radio interview with her in 1972 and even listen to some of her rock music on the Psychology Feminist Voices site.

Feminist epistemologies: Three approaches to sexism in Psychology

Once the problems of sexism and misogyny in Psychology were pointed out, lots of different approaches for how to deal with the issue emerged. For some feminists, they could get behind the 'psychology of women' and just do the same sorts of Psychology as before but instead of just doing it on men, they could be broader in their sampling. For others that wasn't sufficient, instead they argued that women's experiences should be more firmly centred and not seen as an 'add-on' to 'malestream' Psychology. And for some, neither of these approaches would suffice and instead Psychology needed to be dis-mantled in order to be re-build it with a more inclusive ethos from the get-go. These led to various different approaches of how to actually do feminism in Psychology. Basically, what's the best feminist response to sexist scientific cultures: Beat them at their own game? Call them out explicitly? Or abandon them completely?

This dilemma was framed by philosopher Sandra Harding (1986; see also 1994). Concerned with **epistemology** – that branch of philosophy about the bases of knowledge – she described three broad approaches to science in feminist thought: **empirical feminism** (doing good science to drive out bad sci-ence), **standpoint feminism** (starting your theory from the feminist premise of women's subordination) and **poststructuralist feminism** (deconstructing the possibility of science). Stephanie Riger (1992) applied Harding's thinking to the Psychology of women at the time. Let's flesh out these three frameworks, or as they are known, **feminist epistemologies**.

Empirical feminism (or feminist empiricism)

Empirical feminism is the perspective that it is possible to use traditional *positivist epistemologies* and methods in Psychology to do feminist research. This positivist epistemology (the idea that a real world exists that can be objectively observed with the right methods) essentially uses the classic tools in Psychology, like experiments, quantitative statistical studies, etc., for feminist ends. It sort of assumes that the methods in Psychology are fine, but it's the way they are being used that is the problem. So from this perspective, the point is often to drive out misrepresentations of women among other issues with 'good science' that shows that they are wrong. For example, feminist empiricists since the 1970s continually emphasized the similarities of people with different genders, thus debunking ideas about gender differences that are taken to prove theories about women's inferiority or other sexist ideas (e.g., Maccoby & Jacklin, 1974; Hyde, 2005, see Chapter 5).

This empirical feminist approach requires acting as if the the core *epistemology* in Psychology is truly value-free. In a review of gender research in Psychology over 50 years, Eagly et al. (2012) showed that most research continues to follow a positivist-empiricist approach to examine gender differences and similarities. Quantitative studies of gender roles, gender stereotypes and sexist attitudes all fall under this umbrella (see Riger, 1992; Eagly et al., 2012). Feminist *empiricism* is the mainstream, safest way of researching 'the psychology of women'. However, lots of feminist psychologists said that this wasn't enough. It is the tools themselves *and* the ideas they are based on (their epistemologies) that are problematic. Critics of this approach said that it's not possible to be truly objective because all research methods are influenced by the social and political *context* in which they are happening.

Standpoint feminism (or feminist standpoint theory)

Is the approach which argues that people's position in the social world should be at the centre of the science. By understanding exactly how people are located and by paying close attention to *context* we get to answers which more accurately account what is actually going on for people. So it's not about trying to be objective, it's about embracing the *subjectivity* in methods and recognizing people's own *lived experience* as valuable expertise. This perspective, or standpoint, has *epistemic advantage* – this means it's actually a good thing to have experience of the thing you are studying (see Chapter 6). The subordinated knowledges of oppressed people (meaning the things people who are from marginalized perspectives think), are not simply good because they are more diverse – they are actually considered more likely to bring unique critical insights *because* they have been marginalized out in the past (see Intemann, 2010 for a discussion). This perspective solves one of the issues levelled at empirical feminism that androcentrism meant men's experiences were seen as the 'norm' and therefore women's were *othered*. Harding (1986) described feminist standpoint theories as borrowing from Marxist analysis of dominance and subordination. These socialist feminist theories assumed that *patriarchal* subjugation (oppression or control) not only oppresses women, but also suppresses women's knowledges and worldviews, which is exactly what *standpoint feminism* aims to emphasise.

However, standpoint theory was criticized for creating a rather generalized view of women and not paying enough attention to the differences among women (see Riger, 1992). Sociologist Patricia Hill Collins (1990) expanded this framework to explicitly consider standpoints in Black feminist thought created at the intersection of sexism and racism. Having particular, especially intersecting, marginalized positions can provide insight into problems around inequalities that aren't as visible for those from *privileged* positions, for example those marginalized by one dimension. However, as Hill Collins (1990) pointed out, being marginalized doesn't always give you an advantaged view of reality. Rather, a critical standpoint requires an *analysis* of both your location of subordination, and of the dominant system and of the relationships between them (see also Intemann, 2010). We will touch more on this in the first Tool on feminist science studies below.

Poststructuralist feminism (or postmodern feminism)

Poststructuralist Feminism was central to the wider poststructuralist and *postmodern* movements which argued that modern Western power and knowledge are entangled to such an extent that all 'truths' are constructed. That is, what modern Western society now holds to be normal and/or natural is dependent on sociohistorical *context*. It is not that there are things that are true, and some things that are not true, but rather our idea of truth is dependant. Poststructuralists made the natural sciences their particular target, taking Weisstein's criticism of Biological Psychology to new levels, basically arguing that any claim, scientific or not, is imbued with power and thus is political. So too is any category upon which you might base a claim for liberation. This impacts all claims about gender as we live in a *patriarchal* society. For poststructuralists, identities are therefore discursive and constructed; there is not universal or singular way to be a gendered person.

Consider Judith Butler's (1990; 1993a) influential work. Butler argued that it's not that gender is socially constructed and sex is based in a biological reality, but rather sex is equally as constructed as gender. Sex is discursive and it is through the repetition of the same *discourses* about sex that it becomes 'real'. Indeed, Butler went on to argue that sex could actually only be understood via gender, specifically how we talk about body parts in gendered ways. *Postmodernism* was voiced by discursive psychologists who similarly emphasized that language can *do* things. From a *CHIP* perspective, we would emphasise that scientific language does a lot more than other kinds of discourse because it is already constructed as a form of 'truth'.

Most feminist psychologists (us included) wrestle with this dilemma of which epistemology is best, and often engage in feminist research drawing from a couple, if not all, of these three perspectives. The idea that there are multiple positions but that one is better can set up a false dichotomy which is often not useful when tackling a problem. Let's take some of Peter's work as an example. He's used an empirical approach by using Psychology's methods of standard surveys and experiments to examine people's beliefs about sexual orientation (e.g., Hegarty, 2002; Hubbard & Hegarty, 2014), while also explicitly articulating his standpoint as a gay man in arguing that biological differences is a bad place from which to argue queer politics (Hegarty, 2017a) and used Butler's *postmodern* approach to point to norms re-iterated in biological articles about brain differences between gay and straight men (Hegarty, 1997).

The key thing to understand from this section is that despite Psychology's attempt to remove itself from politics, it hasn't been able to because politics is inescapably a part of everything Psychology has done. That includes the exclusion of women from its history, not allowing women to call themselves feminists officially, and the combination of racism and sexism many women of colour have experienced. Psychology is political because it cannot be removed from the social and political world in which it exists. (Indeed, how often do you hear psychologists say *both* that their work is apolitical *and* that they want it to be applied to change the world? Which is surely a claim grounded in political belief about what would make the world better). The same is true for the 'psychology of women', as Rutherford and Granek (2010) said:

> Given that the psychology of women, both as subject matter and professional discipline, was created almost entirely by women, often in response to personal experiences of sexism or an acute awareness of widespread sexist assumptions about women, it is impossible to disentangle the emergence and development of the psychology of women from the women who developed it and the gendered contexts in which they worked (p. 19)

Therefore feminist psychologists have to think about what their specific goals are when challenging the patriarchy. In translating the slogan 'the personal is political' into research, it is important to be aware of where you are coming from and where you want to go. This is especially important as as we are feminist psychologists doing Feminist Psychology, we often embody the thing we are actually studying (see Morawski and Agronick, 1991). Think not just about gender but other characteristics too. Black feminists in particular drew closer attention to the ways that race is important here. Patricia Hill Collins (1990) argued, among other things, that academia is based around the white male viewpoint, meaning that Black women experience multiple forms of exclusion. She also said that the *positivist epistemology*, which is heralded in Psychology, assumes the personal can be separated from the professional. The answer is not to remove the personal and the political from Psychology – but instead to recognize how the personal impacts the kinds of Psychology we produce. One way that we can do this is by paying close attention to what feminists have to say about science more broadly.

TOOL 1: Feminist Science Studies

Feminist Science Studies is a field which is *interdisciplinary*, drawing upon Philosophy, *historiography*, Anthropology, and Sociology to look at the practices of science and scientists. It's often thought of as a part of a broader field called *Science and Technology Studies*. Here, we outline what Feminist Science Studies has said and how you can use it as a tool to think about the history of Psychology.

A key component of feminist science studies is the emphasis on the idea that human sciences like Psychology need to have *reflexivity*, as we've previously mentioned. This means recognizing that the knowledge psychologists create about how people think can be applied, reflexively, to psychologists themselves. Psychology is not simply a natural science, but is a *human science*, because the positions of the people who produce it matter, and because when it is applied to people they can use their human agency to react against it in a number of individual and collective ways (Gergen, 1973; Hacking, 1995; Morawski, 1994).

Think of it this way – when a physicist says something about black holes ('It's a mysterious blob that sucks the life out of everything!') it doesn't affect the black hole at all. But imagine a psychologist saying the same thing about a group of people ('How dare you!'). People are impacted by the things psychologists say about them, and importantly, they can also respond, react and rally against it. Not only this, but psychologists are people too; we don't have black holes studying black holes. Unlike black holes, we embody the thing we are studying in Psychology, so that our knowledge is *reflexive* (see Morawski & Agronick, 1991). The foundational idea here is that science is *social*.

The fact that you are both the knower (someone who studies a thing) and the known (someone who identifies as the thing you're studying), makes this question about political influence complicated in Psychology. Acknowledging *reflexivity* is also a *risky business* in Psychology. Science is a powerful game of truth, and – ironically – the less political a science appears to be, the more politically impactful it can be (Shapin, 1996). For example, for much of the twentieth century, many queer researchers who were doing research on gay/lesbian subcultures had to be closeted, such as Alfred Kinsey, Thomas Painter and Jan Gay (see Minton, 2002). Researchers who came out about their own *lived experience* were often accused of being biased, which meant that to avoid this they often stayed in the closet. Relatedly (and returning to the black holes metaphor), Evelyn Hammonds said scientific research on the sexuality of Black women was like 'Black (w)holes' (1994). She argued that Black women's sexualities were known to exist but were only visible to the outside universe by its distorting effects on phenomena close by – scientific research didn't actually pay attention to Black women themselves. What *standpoint feminism* in particular argues here, is that being the thing and studying the thing give you a particular *epistemological advantage* – it can be a good thing, it's not bias. Your subjective understanding of your own life can helpfully inform your research. It's not actually always a good thing to be so separate from the thing you are studying.

Attempts to position oneself as objective and separate from the research is actually rather common in science. Donna Haraway (1988) — a key *feminist science studies* scholar – called this the '*god-trick*' (we meet her again in Chapter 5). The god-trick is when people try to make a scientific statement as if no human work was involved, as if they are sort of god-like and have no embodied perspective on the thing they are talking about. Think about pictures taken from space of Earth. In some ways these look like they were almost photographed by no one at all (she calls this the 'gaze from nowhere') – but we know that's not actually the case. There needs to be massive collective human intervention behind the image. There's a body somewhere, loads of technology, whole teams of people making it happen, we just can't see it when we stare at the image in wonder. That's the trick.

Haraway (1988) argued that everyone comes from a certain perspective; the lens through which they interpret information is impacted by their embodied experience. We cannot become disembodied people and thus 'see' the world without a certain perspective. She says this particularly around white men who are an unmarked category. White men are more often seen as being able to 'gaze from nowhere' because they are an unmarked category. Whereas others who are 'marked' in some way (e.g. women) are not seen in this way and instead can be accused of bias. It is therefore problematic in Psychology that women tend to get marked as 'having gender', people of colour get marked as 'having race', and queer people get marked as 'having sexuality' when of course straight white men still have all these things (Peter and his pals have a line of sneakily critical experiments on this stuff, Hegarty, 2017b; Hegarty & Bruckmuller, 2013; Hegarty & Pratto, 2001). We've mentioned this previously when Patricia Hill Collins (1990) similarly argued that academia is based around the white male viewpoint. There has therefore been a tendency to see white (straight) men as somehow being more 'neutral' about these issues and the marked people being more biased. Haraway named these **situated knowledges**. It is how we are *situated* that informs what knowledge we are able to have and able to interpret. However, we need to be careful and not take marginalized perspectives uncritically as they can still be impacted by the 'god-trick' and are not value-free positions (because no position is).

How might we *use* feminist science studies' tools to study the history of psychology?

1 **Give yourself permission to challenge** the basic assumptions behind what you're being told. Perhaps you have been told that there is one best way of understanding something. Generate alternatives and evaluate them. (Allow yourself to indulge seemingly ridiculous ideas). Is there really one way of understanding what's going on? Have you internalized beliefs that you are 'biased' for thinking otherwise?

2 **Ask 'What are the situated knowledges that we can see?'** Are they 'unmarked' or 'marked? Is there a 'gaze from nowhere'? Beware when psychologists call situated knowledges 'biased'. Ask others who use this word to define what 'unbiased' is. Get used to seeing your life experience as positioning rather than biasing.

3 **Read the original sources.** Textbooks are mass marketed for quick profits and they often misrepresent the past (more in the next chapter on this!) or at least present a partial view or a particular view only. Go back to see what the record shows originally (it's still an interpretation but you can analyse that). Get nosy. Snoop.

4 **Consider that what you have in a record is often a single perspective** (most often from those with more power?) and that it's the things they were willing to write down and keep. Where are the other, perhaps more marginalized, voices in the story? If they are missing, where did they go? Who lost them?

5 **Keep a record of the things that surprise you** (and what doesn't surprise you). What is it about *your* current worldview that means that something surprised and informed it? Often the things we find surprising and interesting and can't quite stop thinking about even though we don't know why, are the leads to follow.

6 **Use your imagination** – how else might this event have been interpreted? If you are not told enough about the research participants' experiences, wonder what they might have thought, done and felt (and why that didn't make it into the account of the research that you can access).

7 **Be creative.** There is more freedom, fun and flexibility in *CHIP* than you might have first imagined. What other narratives are possible to imagine? Ones which centres feminist perspectives? Ones that take an expansive and inclusive perspective on gender?

SUMMARY

We started this chapter by exploring the exclusionary and sexist history of Psychology, noting racist and colonial aspects of Psychology's past and how class and sexuality were involved as well. We next introduced how feminist psychologists began to question androcentric histories of Psychology, by 'replacing' women into this history and making the Feminist Psychology a sub-field of Psychology. Various epistemologies responded to patriarchal science: *empirical feminism, standpoint feminism*, and *postmodern feminism*. Jumping off from this we then introduced Tool 1: Feminist Science Studies. In this section we really challenged some of the core ideas that often underpin Psychology. So you may have found this difficult to grapple with at points. For one, we somewhat undermined objectivity and said everyone is biased (but that's not automatically a bad thing). Instead we gave you some new ways to think about science – one that has standpoints, advantages and embodied experiences. We urged you to reflect on your own **subjectivity** and where it came from, and not to think of it as a 'bias' but as a developing *standpoint* (more on how to do this in Tool 5: Your Lived Experience, Chapter 6).

In this chapter we have not meant to bamboozle you with a whole new way of thinking about Psychology, but we are hoping to have intrigued you about how there are different **interdisciplinary** feminist ways to think about Psychology. That's the thing about **CHIP** – it's historical and conceptual and we've aimed to show here how the history and philosophy are linked. That's why we've named the chapter 'Who makes up Psychology?', because it has two meanings – both of which we attend to in this chapter. One, who is it that literally is *in* Psychology and has been allowed to be a psychologist? This is our first section of the chapter about exclusionary practices. Two, who gets to construct or *make up* what Psychology is doing? This is our second section, where we deconstruct some of the frameworks and assumptions underpinning Psychology with a fresh perspective via feminist science studies. Our argument throughout has been that the two questions are braided together; there is a relationship between who makes Psychology up and what Psychology is made up to be.

QUESTIONS TO CONSIDER

1 Think about your education so far. What (if anything) were you explicitly taught about women in history and the various struggles they had? When women were mentioned, did they tend to be white women? Were they upper class women? Did you learn about women only as victims, or also learn about their strategies for empowerment?

2 What have you found *surprising* or not in this chapter? When did you feel 'that really opened my eyes'? And when did you feel 'I knew it all along'?

3 Thinking about knowledge is an important part of Feminist Science Studies. So based on who you are (e.g. gender, age, ethnicity, sexuality, etc.), what do you *know* based on your own personal experience? What is it about *your* own standpoint which means you know about something a lot already, precisely because it's who you are? And this is a bit trickier, but possibly more important: What are you *not* able to know because of your standpoint or perspective?

Key resources

Carmichael-Murphy, P. & Danquah, A. (2022). *Hidden histories. black in psychology.* https://documents.manchester.ac.uk/display.aspx?DocID=62182

Donnelly, L. C., Hubbard, K., & Capdevila, R. (2022). POWES is pronounced 'feminist': Negotiating academic and activist boundaries in the talk of UK feminist psychologists. *Feminism & Psychology*, https://doi.org/10.1177/0959353522110006

Furumoto, L., & Scarborough, E. (1986). *Placing women in the history of psychology. The first american women psychologists. American Psychologist, 41*(1), 35–42. https://doi.org/10.1037/10421-025

Haraway, D. (1988). *Situated knowledges: The science question in feminism and the privilege of partial perspective. Feminist Studies, 14*(3), 575–599.

Harding, S. G. (1986). *The science question in feminism.* London: Cornell University Press.

Harding, S. G. (1994). Is science multicultural?: Challenges, resources, opportunities, uncertainties. *Configurations, 2*(2), 301–330. https://muse.jhu.edu/article/8039

Hill Collins, P. (1990). *Black feminist thought: Knowledge, consciousness and the politics of empowerment.* Routledge: USA.

Johnston, E., & Johnson, A. (2008). Searching for the second generation of American women psychologists. *History of Psychology, 11*(1), 40–69. https://doi.org/10.1037/1093-4510.11.1.40

Milar, K. S. (2000). The first generation of women psychologists and the psychology of women. *American Psychologist, 55*(6), 616–619. https://doi.org/10.1037/0003-066X.55.6.616

Morawski, J. G. (1994). *Practicing feminisms, reconstructing psychology: Notes on a liminal science.* Ann Arbor, MI: University of Michigan Press.

Shields, S. A. (2007). Passionate men, emotional women: Psychology constructs gender difference in the late 19th century. *History of Psychology, 10*(2), 92–110. https://doi.org/10.1037/1093-4510.10.2.92

Scarborough, E., & Furumoto, L. (1989). *Untold lives: The first generation of American women psychologists.* New York: Columbia University Press.

Valentine, E. R. (2008). To care or to understand? Women members of the British psychological Society 1901-1918. *History and Philosophy of Psychology, 10*(1), 54–65.

Valentine, E.R. (2010). Women in early 20th-century experimental psychology. *The Psychologist, 23*(12), 972–974.

3 Textbook Myths and Narratives

Learning objectives

Study of this chapter will enable you to:

- Understand why textbooks often create myths when describing Psychology's past
- Look at the case of Kitty Genovese in a whole new light and take on a feminist understanding of this history
- Engage with key examples of textbook myths and evidence of sexual harassment in Psychology
- Gain Critical Reading and Ethics as a critical tool for doing CHIP, providing you with a stronger method of how to debunk further myths yourself

Introduction

Gentle reader, as you move into this next chapter, we remind you that this book is a *companion* to *CHIP*. Perhaps it is sitting upright accompanying your other textbooks, or keeping them company half-open in a pile on your desk. Or maybe it's an e-book co-habiting the same folder as other learning resources on your desktop. However you materialize your literature, this companion is about to become a critical friend to its fellows.

A critical friend is someone who believes in you and what you are doing, but knows you can do it better. A critical friend points out your shortcomings – not in enmity – but precisely because they are with you for the long haul. A critical friend is not a cynic. Rather they show that they believe in you so much, and in your ability to do better, that they carefully think about how your well-intentioned actions could be accidentally harmful. A critical friend reflects on the position that they are coming from, and acknowledges that their friendship might also need critique. That's how we are going to try to be critical to our textbook friends in this chapter.

Our topic is *textbook myths*. As textbooks tell you they are presenting 'facts' and 'science', the suggestion that they also contain mythic meaning sounds like a critique. The term 'myth' often signifies what truthful science and history are *not*. But in anthropology, the term also refers to the crucial origin stories that cultures use to explain their backgrounds (Williams, 2014). Thus myths can suggest a level of creative meaning that is beyond history and science.

The aim of this chapter's critical friendship is not to get you running from your textbooks. Rather it is to help you to be more critical of the versions of history and science that they offer you.

In this chapter, we are first going to explore the concept of textbook myths and then consider one myth in depth: the murder of Kitty Genovese. It's possible you've already heard about this case as it's often used in textbooks to frame social psychological research on bystander intervention. Feminist historian of Psychology Frances Cherry (1995) first saw the connections between the erasure of a story of violence against women in the Psychology textbook stories about Genovese, and the importance of sticking close to the 'stubborn particulars' of historical events. Psychologist Rachel Manning and her colleagues offered the most effective 'debunking' of the *textbook myth* (Manning et al., 2007). Social historian Marcia Gallo (2015) has done the most to restore the plurality of meanings made from the event in Social Psychology textbooks and other media, and her work allows us to frame what meanings are prioritized and de-prioritized by the abstraction of Genovese's murder into a puzzle to be solved by Social Psychology. Overall, we hope this discussion of the sense that has been made of Genovese's murder, repetitiously in Psychology textbooks and more diversely in other places, will allow you to see some general processes by which Psychology's history appears to have only one truth.

Textbooks and their myths

When you pick up your textbook you try to extract, summarize, highlight and memorize the key information it presents, as quickly and efficiently as possible. Stand back from those goals for a moment and consider your textbook from another standpoint. That textbook cost you money, and Psychology students make up a large market. Textbooks are not only books, they are also commodities. They are made up not just to be read by you but also to be sold to you. 'Like the telephone, automobile, and personal computer, textbooks can be viewed as meeting consumer demands and generating a new market, one open to innovation and competition' (Morawksi, 1992, p. 163). You may study textbooks to extract information, publishers study them as means of extracting profit from students like you.

Box 3.1: The myth of Little Albert

Perhaps the most famous **textbook myth** is the story of Watson and Rayner's (1920) fear conditioning of Little Albert. The basic story usually explains that Little Albert was a 9-month-old baby who was taught to fear white rats and other related furry things via classic conditioning because every time he saw the white rats Psychologists made a horrible loud noise near him. This study has been taken up to do different things. Behaviourist textbook authors (who tended to be nurture theorists) argued it showed the power of conditioning, and cognitive textbook authors (who tended to be nature theorists) that it demonstrated humans' natural propensities to form particular kinds of phobias. So what lesson the study told depended on who you asked. But the plot twisted again with claims that Little Albert's true identity had been found (Beck et al., 2009), and claims that Little Albert suffered from a neurological impairment (Fridlund et al., 2012). These recent controversies seriously questioned how reliable textbook narratives are about studies and how inapplicable such classic studies can be, yet the stories generated from them continue to be told (see Harris, 2011).

There are important feminist angles on this case that are not addressed adequately in the published literature on Little Albert's status as a **textbook myth.** For example, many students do not know that the 'Rayner' of 'Watson and Rayner' was a woman, Rosalie Rayner, whose romantic relationship with Watson (when a married man) scandalously lead them both to lose their academic positions. Romano-Lux's (2016) novel *Behave* puts Rosalie Rayner's life centre stage and provides a fictionalized account of women's early experiences of learning Psychology, their dependence on powerful men for access to laboratories, the difference between male experts' advice and women's practices of parenting their own children, and the tragedy of a smart woman reluctantly confined to raising her children in the home.

When **CHIP** experts have looked at textbooks critically, they have reached some broadly consistent arguments in the ways that textbooks construct both Psychology and the students' reading about it. First, textbooks present things in simplified form, and textbook authors bemoan the fact that they have to make tough choices about what to fit into a limited number of pages (see e.g., Matlin, 2010 on this dilemma in regard to Psychology of gender textbooks). Second, Psychology is usually presented as a *science*, and as a form of scientific understanding that is better than *common sense* (see Lamont, 2015). Drawing this kind of distinction between Psychology as a discipline and common sense about psychology is sometimes called 'boundary work' following the work of sociologist Thomas Gieryn (1983). Psychologist Mary Smyth (2001) argues that because Psychology has a precarious claim on being a science, its textbooks do their boundary work differently than biology textbooks do. In particular, psychologists presenting their knowledge as factual is... well... dodgy. '[P]sychological knowledge keeps its origins in the psychology textbook' (Smyth, 2001, p. 528), backing up each and every claim with a study to remember and a name and date to go with it. This might explain why you can end a session of textbook study with notes on a dizzying number of names and dates (and the procedures of studies), but very little direct new knowledge about human psychology *per se*.

Second, presenting Psychology as a science can have a strong influence on what is presented and how it is organized, and this fact has implications for how gender and feminism have been represented (or not) in textbooks. For example, feminist psychologist Jeanne Marecek (1993) described how Abnormal Psychology textbooks tend to adopt a natural science approach to psychological distress and to be organized by the psychiatric categories of the Diagnostic and Statistical Manual (DSM). The disease model organization of these textbooks abstracts people's distress, strips it out of **context** and presents the profile of psychiatric diseases as the key objects that students must learn about. The illness is prioritized to the cost of a de-prioritzation of people.

Third, textbooks are fascinating historical documents themselves, providing windows into the common sense of the past, and being described as 'documents frozen in time' (Unger, 2010, p. 153) or 'X-rays of the uncontroversial' of past times (Hornstein, 1992, p. 260). The history of textbooks designed to support courses with titles such as 'the psychology of women and gender' is relevant to the tensions and dilemmas between 'feminist psychology' and 'the psychology of women' considered in Chapters 1 and 2. To celebrate the 35th anniversary of the journal *Sex Roles*, four authors reflected on the history of their own and others' textbooks in this area since the 1970s (Basow, 2010). Their accounts showed a desire to write textbooks to convey academic legitimacy on the new field which lead them to boundary work that de-politicized it, particularly in the earliest years. For example, the first textbooks used in courses on the psychology of women were quite sexist, focused on sex differences, and were only later informed by social psychological perspectives on gender, but only included 'feminist' in their titles in the early 1990s (Unger, 2010). The American undergraduate market had a direct effect on how authors navigated these tensions, which as Matlin (2010) notes, involves presenting social justice issues to more conservative students without alienating them.

Finally, an ability to deconstruct your textbook is a very handy thing to be able to do. Recall that the history of Psychology also has a history, and the impact of patriarchy on that history can be glimpsed from textbooks. Both surveys of textbook contents and surveys of Psychology students' knowledge show that students (who are more often women than men) are vastly more aware of male psychologists, and white psychologists' achievements (see e.g. Cramblet Alvarez et al., 2020).

So in summary, as a critical friend to our textbook companions, this chapter approaches the Kitty Genovese myth with an understanding that textbooks get written not only to inform but also to entertain, to inspire a wide political spectrum of (mostly American) students to go further with Psychology and to extract money from students for corporations. We should expect textbooks to present a simplified and optimistic story about Psychology as (1) something more scientific than common sense, and (2) as a generally good thing in the world. As a result, our critique is going to focus on how textbooks can take historical events out of their social and political contexts and repurpose them as exemplifying how constructed psychological concepts and variables promise to help make sense of real world events and reduce the risk of emergencies. Finally, we are aware that gender, race, class and other intersecting axes of power and *privilege* might be obscured so that textbooks can reach general conclusions about individual psychology from particular events. With this understanding of critique in mind we now turn to the murder of Kitty Genovese.

38 Witnesses and bystander intervention

In this section of the chapter, we draw particularly on Gallo's (2015) account of the events surrounding the Genovese murder and its later historic consequences (see also Cook, 2014). On 13 March 1964, in Kew Gardens, a quiet suburb of the Borough of Queens in New York City, Winston Moseley assaulted and murdered Kitty Genovese. Both were in their late 20s. She was making her way home after finishing a shift at the bar where she worked. He had begun to live a secret double in life in which he went out and sexually assaulted and murdered women at night, holding down his job and providing for his wife and children during the day. Genovese was not his first victim.

When this murder was first reported in New York's newspapers it attracted little interest. But two later publications – an article by journalist Martin Gansberg (1964), and a short book by his boss *New York Times* editor Abraham Michael (A.M.) Rosenthal (1964) – both narrated this murder as the most extraordinary event with a powerful moral for changing times. Specifically, both publications rendered the murder exceptional by shifting attention away from the attack itself to the failure of Genovese's neighbours to intervene on her behalf. In Rosenthal's impactful telling of the event, 38 people witnessed it from their apartment windows while none of them did anything to help her.

Rosenthal's account of the non-intervention of the 38 witnesses constructed a *myth* of urban apathy, a lack of regard for fellow city dwellers for each other, and a breakdown of social mores that was more chilling than the murder itself. Rosenthal's account sent a sobering message. It was also a deeply conservative one. Empowered by the newfound support of the Equal Pay Act of 1963 and the beginnings of impactful feminist writings, such as Betty Friedan's (1963) *The Feminist Mystique,* and access to contraception, many women were beginning to enjoy the freedoms that the city had to offer. As Gallo (2015) notes, Genovese's murder occurred at a time when newspapers were increasingly obliged to interpret the news, not simply report it, and crime stories increasingly began to focus on victims. Rosenthal's account implied that young women, like Genovese, eager to enjoy the art, culture and social life of the city, were putting themselves in a new and poorly understood form of danger.

Kitty's murder was turned into more than one moral tale about the safety of women claiming new forms of independence in the modern world that was coming into being (with lots of victim-blaming to boot). Kew Gardens was a quiet, desirable and mostly white suburb. The fact that the attack happened in such a neighbourhood clearly added to the shock value of Rosenthal's story. In 1964, residents of New York City were beginning to see an escalation in the crime rates across their city, and that trend would continue for the coming three decades. Like every good myth, Rosenthal's tale got the New Yorkers of his time wondering who they were as a group, how they had gotten here, and where they were going.

In this context, Kitty Genovese became a kind of idealized innocent young female victim that now begged for explanation and for justice. Her murder occurred only one year after another famous murder in New York of two young 'career girls' in Manhattan which led the police to extract a false confession from a young Black man, an event that contributed to the development of all Americans' right to have their legal rights read to them upon arrest (called Miranda rights). The original reporting of the Genovese murder in the *Times* did not report that Winston Moseley was Black, but his picture appeared in several publications quickly thereafter. Race was erased in Moseley's crime career in other ways too. His earlier victim, Anna Mae Johnson, was also Black. She was very quickly forgotten and never depicted in popular media, while Kitty Genovese and pictures of her white face became iconic in Social Psychology textbooks and elsewhere. Moseley was convicted and given the death penalty for Genovese's murder, but never tried or convicted for killing Johnson.

Rosenthal's story of the 38 witnesses to Kitty Genovese's murder was amplified when it became a **textbook myth** in Psychology for about half a century. This account inspired social psychologists John Darley and Bibb Latané's research on bystander interventions. Darley, Latané and their colleagues conducted multiple studies to evidence that the presence of others inhibits helping in emergency situations, and referred back to the 38 witnesses as a real-world demonstration of the importance of their insight. Some of their studies were elaborate and theatrical deception experiments. In these studies confederates, playing the part of research assistants or other study participants, appeared to be in life-threatening situations. True participants were found to be less likely to take up the opportunity to intervene in apparent emergencies if they were in the presence of strangers than if they were left alone (e.g., Darley & Latané, 1968). More naturalistic experiments showed that people were less likely to help strangers who dropped coins or pens when in the presence of others in public elevators (Latané and Dabbs, 1975).

In one particularly gendered experiment (published under the title 'A lady in distress: Inhibiting effects of friends and strangers on bystander intervention'), participants were recruited to a Psychology laboratory for a study where they met a female experimenter who left them waiting while she went to an adjoining room. There she switched on a tape recorder which played a 10-second tape suggesting that she had fallen off a chair and was concerned that she had badly injured her ankle. 'Finally she muttered something about getting outside, knocked around the chair as pulled herself up, and thumped to the door, closing it behind her as she left' (p. 192). True participants were monitored for whether they intervened in this fake emergency, and for how quickly they did so. Participants were much more likely to intervene when they were alone in the waiting room (when 70 per cent intervened), than when waiting with another confederate who was acting passively (when only 7 per cent intervened). Two other conditions placed two true participants who either were friends or were strangers in the waiting room. Friends intervened to help the 'lady in distress' 70 per cent of the time, but strangers did so only 40 per cent of the time (Latané & Rodin, 1969).

As the researchers concluded, here, and in multiple other publications, the blame for inaction lay on the openness of emergency situations to multiple interpretations, and to the influence of factors such as 'the diffusion of responsibility' within it, where no bystander in the group feels 100 per cent responsible for the consequences of inaction. The researchers also considered the influence of 'pluralistic ignorance' through which each inactive bystander may use others' inaction as evidence that the situation truly is not serious enough to warrant anyone's intervention. The researchers thus accepted the essential truth of Rosenhan's account of the 38 witnesses, but offered a more understanding and situational interpretation of their behaviour via such social psychological concepts:

> Situational factors, specifically factors involving the immediate social environment, may be of greater importance in determining an individual's reaction to an emergency than such vague cultural or personality concepts as 'apathy' or 'alienation' due to urbanization.
>
> (Latané & Rodin, 1969, p. 190)

Debunking the myth

There were always other narratives available about what the residents of Kew Gardens did on the night of the murder, as the lawyers who prosecuted Mosely for Genovese's murder discovered earlier on. When bringing the case to trial, prosecution lawyer Charles Skoller could not draw on 38 eyewitness accounts to prove Moseley's guilt. Rather, he could only call on four individuals, none of whom had witnessed the whole of the attack. Part of Skoller's strategy was to keep the jurors focused on Moseley's guilt rather than the apparent culpability of the witnesses, which the *New York Times* reporting had already made a common topic of discussion. But it was also the case that most of the 38 witnesses had only heard the event, not seen it. One who did see it had actually shouted at Moseley, leading him to temporarily call off his attack; this neighbour effectively intervened in a way that generations of Psychology students have long been told that Genovese's neighbours never did. Rather than the chilling image of Kitty Genovese dying alone, long used to motivate interest in the Psychology of bystander intervention, one of Genovese's neighbours came out of her own apartment and held her in her arms as she lay dying. The neighbours saw less and did more than the textbook account would have you believe.

In 2007, Rachel Manning (2007) and her colleagues drew on such evidence from the trial documents to contest three key features of the '38 witnesses' narrative. Without disputing the value of Darley and Latané's work per se, Manning et al. (2007) focused on 'the functions of the story as a parable' with 'an iconic place in social psychology.' But, here we must remind our textbook friends that even when provided with a corrective, they do not always change the narratives within their pages. Griggs (2015) examined popular introductory textbooks published after Manning et al.'s (2007) article. Manning et al. (2007) had begun to be cited in introductory textbooks but not so much in Social Psychology textbooks, and the narrative of the apathetic 38 witnesses persisted in both. The persistence of the 38 witnesses story, particularly in Social Psychology textbooks, raises the question of why textbooks might persist in reproducing a simple story about this event when it had been so openly and convincingly challenged.

If you pick up a contemporary textbook today, you may find that this story about the 38 witnesses is reproduced therein, to introduce Darley and Latané 's work, bystander intervention and the Psychology of helping and altruism. Or you might find reference to the 38 witnesses as a story that has been challenged or debunked. For example, Myers and DeWall's (2018) best-selling introductory textbook introduces research on bystander intervention via the 38 witnesses narrative of the Genovese murder, crediting Darley and Latané for showing the importance of situational factors over the common sense interpretation in terms of apathy and indifference. Towards the end of the section, students are asked to self-assess their knowledge that presumes the simple truth of the 38 witnesses story with the following 'Retrieval practice' question:

> Why didn't anybody help Kitty Genovese? What social psychological principle did this incident illustrate?"
>
> (Myers & DeWall, 2018, p. 519)

This looks like a really innocent and common type of textbook question, doesn't it? But consider how this banal feature of this textbook *constructs* the facts of history as simple truths beyond matters of interpretation and perspective. This question is not just presenting information, it is engaging its readers to check their learning and constructing the 'right way' to think about history. The question illustrates how textbooks tend to present the past as a set of stable facts with undisputed meanings and no value-laden moral lessons, even when they are functioning as parables or myths in the textbooks at the same time. Indeed, it is teaching students to believe that the key thing to be learned is in this section is that the 'right answer' is that nobody helped Kitty Genovese. That is not only not true, it is also miles away from the sense that feminists made of this event (as we shall shortly see).

We are not saying that the evidence of these well-known ways that Psychology textbooks do their boundary work and sell Psychology to you mean that Darley and Latané's experiments are themselves meaningless. Manning et al. (2007) also avoided making that kind of direct and damning criticism. They did accuse both the original 38 witnesses story and the Darley and Latané explanation of bystander apathy of distorting emphasis in Social Psychology. Specifically, Manning et al. described the textbook story as falling within a larger body of social psychological theory that tends to problematize collectives as a cause of mindless irrational behaviour, taking an overly positive view of the individual and an overly negative view of the influence of 'the crowd'. They described this partial perspective as a particularly American take on Social Psychology, evidenced also by Philip Zimbardo's work, and they contrasted it with European social identity traditions of research that emphasize the importance of group identities in determining social actions, thoughts and feelings (see Hornsey, 2008, on the history of this social identity tradition). Of course, this distinction between two traditions of social psychological thought, emphasized by Manning et al. (2007) gets us back directly to the business of feminist collective thought, action and feeling and social change.

Box 3.2: Misogyny and serial killers

The death of Kitty Genovese was a horrific tragedy, eclipsed by an apparently bigger story – the 38 'witnesses' who 'did nothing'. This is a frustratingly common thread that runs throughout a lot of reporting on stories about women who are killed. Misogyny runs rife in violence against women and this remains the case in extreme examples such as those of serial killing. Take a moment to name five serial killers. Can you do it? Can you also name five victims of serial killers? Maybe that's harder. Remember the gendered nature of serial killing – men are more often the serial killers and women the victims. The tendency of reports about such murders is often to focus on the killer as a fascinating figure and to forget the victim.

One person who has taken great umbrage with this is Hallie Rubenhold. She was so fed up with the focus on Jack the Ripper, that she wrote *The Five* (2019). This books tells the stories and lives of five women who were killed by Jack the Ripper (there may have been more). It highlights the experiences of these poor Victorian women and the misogyny they faced, including the misconception that they were sex workers. Indeed, very troublingly, when women who sell sex are killed there is historical evidence of this dramatically affecting how the police and the public respond. For example, in the 1970s Peter Sutcliffe killed 13 women, 7 of whom were engaged in sex work. He became known as the Yorkshire Ripper precisely because of this apparent link to Jack the Ripper. The misogyny in the case, in part because of the assumptions that Sutcliffe was targeting *sex workers* rather than *women* (horrid, right?), led to numerous incidences of police misconduct, including overlooking vital eye-witness testimony from women who escaped his attack. Because those women did not seem to the police to be sex workers, their evidence was not taken to be relevant to the case (see Wattis, 2017).

Despite feminist efforts to tell the stories of women who are victims, there remains a strong focus and interest in the killer primarily. These people (more often men) are treated by media as if they are extraordinary people. But Lisa Downing (2013) argues, despite efforts to conceptualize killers as separate and special kinds of beings, they are really ordinary people reflecting society. So society's ideas of gender and violence are key. To find out more about misogyny and serial killers we recommend the podcast Hallie Rubenhold runs called Bad Women, plus 'Serial Killers and Misogyny' (ep 51) with Kate Lister on Betwixt the Sheets.

Feminist analysis of Kitty Genovese

Nothing about the standard textbook treatment of Kitty Genovese's murder would necessarily get you thinking about the impact of patriarchy. Feminist historian of Psychology Frances Cherry (1995) became curious about what she called the '*stubborn particulars*' (that is the persistent **contextual** details) of the Genovese case, which had been obscured by Psychology textbooks, as a result of her involvement in the feminist movement. Although Moseley's crime against Genovese is often remembered as a murder, feminists have also emphasized that it was also a rape – a crime of sexual violence against a woman. Indeed, in feminist author Susan Brownmiller's (1975) pivotal early feminist analysis of sexual violence, *Against Our Will: Men, Women and Rape*, Moseley was described as a paradigm of the dangerous male serial rapist–murderer. Cherry (1995) considered Brownmiller's account but went beyond it in examining later events in Moseley's criminal career.

Sometime after the guilty verdict, Moseley's death penalty for Genovese's murder was commuted (meaning it was changed to life imprisonment), and he briefly escaped from prison in 1968, and hid out in an empty house where he held a Black woman called Zella Moore hostage. Moseley sexually assaulted her and threatened to kill her children. When the white couple who resided in the house returned, Moseley tied up the husband of the couple, sexually assaulted the wife, and escaped in a stolen car. All three victims survived his attack, and Moseley was later apprehended and re-sentenced for these crimes. He spent the rest of his life in prison. But Zella Moore was also initially charged with aiding an escaped felon! Brownmiller does not mention it, but Cherry notes that the irony of her treatment as a Black woman was so different from the ideal victim status accorded to Genovese (and the white couple). Indeed this intersectional injustice was articulated very clearly at the time by Barbara Sims, Zella Moore's African-American lawyer who was moved by this injustice to defend Moore against this charge in court.

In 2004, a further *'stubborn particular'* of Kitty Genovese's life was made public. Mary Ann Ziolonko, who was Genovese's lesbian lover at the time of her murder, broke her silence. Zioloko and Genovese had met the year before and shared the apartment in Kew Gardens that Genovese was attempting to reach the night she was murdered. Later that night, Ziolonko was awakened by the police who subjected her to an invasive interrogation that included questions about the two women's sex lives. Zioloko gave evidence at Moseley's trial, identifying some of Genovese's personal possessions which she had about her on the night she was murdered. But at the trial, the Genovese's family funeral, and in the media coverage, the lesbian relationship between Ziolonko and Genovese was kept firmly in the closet. When Ziolonko broke her silence, she did so with *lived experience* of how homophobia had silenced so many stories about lesbians; she herself had twice been beaten up for being gay.

Gallo (2014) places the Genovese murder within its social and historical *context* and made the erasure of her lesbianism central to the story of how the myth took form. As Gallo notes, Rosenthal remained a conservative editor-in-chief of the *New York Times* for decades after his book exploiting the Genovese murder. The closeting of Genovese was essential to his story, not because the *New York Times* was reticent to discuss homosexuality in general, but because the paper was already describing the city's lesbian/gay scenes in mythic terms as portends of a city under threat of decay from modernizing trends. In sum, a lesbian Kitty Genovese would not have fit with the ideal white victim model, nor anchor the moralizing myth of urban apathy that the *New York Times* used the 38 witnesses and lesbian/gay subcultures to represent.

Rosenthal's position of power as editor of the *New York Times* also had consequences for the continued representation of lesbian and gay New Yorkers' stories for decades. Gallo describes how Rosenthal created a workplace where LGBT reporters often remained closeted. He was still editor of the newspaper when it was so unbelievably slow to recognize or report on the effects of the HIV/AIDS pandemic on gay communities in the 1980s (see Shilts, 1987 for a critique of the *New York Times'* and other American newspapers' homophobic neglect of HIV/AIDS in the early 1980s).

In more general terms, Gallo (2014) describes the changing geography of class- and race-*privilege* across New York's five boroughs in a way that goes beyond the mythical account of urban apathy in Rosenthal's telling. In so doing she draws on Marxist geographer David Harvey's compelling alternative image of New York as an urban landscape that became characterized by 'islands of privilege' located 'in the midst of large areas of decay' (Harvey, p. 119). Her social history shows that the Genovese murder inspired diverse forms of collective action organized by people who shared gender, race, and/or geography. '[S]ilences in the story promoted by the *Times* inspired feminists to make explicit the prevalence of sexual assaults against women' (Gallo, 2015, p. 118). In particular, feminists challenged the assumption, which held sway at the time of Genovese's attack, that it was acceptable to *not* intervene when a man is attacking a woman in public if the event seems like a 'lover's quarrel'. Such collective actions by ordinary Americans resonate with Manning et al.'s (2007) concern that the 'parable' presents Social Psychology students with a too-individualist view of collectives and neglect the importance of social groups as agents of *social change* (see Chapter 4). By so doing, Gallo's work restores the sense and importance of the *'stubborn particulars'* of this narrative that are stripped out so that it could serve as a historical introduction to the psychological topic of bystander intervention in your textbook.

Box 3.3: Sexual harassment and Psychology

Sexual harassment has a long, and surprising (to some), history in Psychology. One of the most well-known recent histories in this area was conducted by Jacy Young, feminist historian of Psychology superstar, when working with Peter, on their article (2019) 'Reasonable Men: Sexual harassment and norms of conduct in social psychology' which caused some waves within Psychology. The article charts multifaceted histories combining: a) the use of sexual harassment as a tool, variable or manipulation *within* Social Psychology experiments; b) the later conceptualization of sexual harassment as a psychological object (and the work by feminist psychologists to move such work forwards); and c) the sexual harassment experienced by women within social psychology by Henri Tajfel, the founder of the social identity tradition.

Young and Hegarty's (2019) article draws upon Frances Cherry's description of her first faculty position in the mid-1970s:

> the days before sexual harassment policies when I would arrive at work to find sexually explicit notes under my door from a colleague in a position to judge my work and the feelings of helplessness, disillusionment and self-blame that would ensue
> (Cherry, 1995, p. 54, also see Young and Hegarty, 2019, pp.460)

Young and Hegarty (2019) chart the development of feminist empiricist research in the 20 years between Cherry's experience and her writing about it that allowed us to talk about **sexual harassment** as a genuine concern (including in the law).

This paper caused a re-thinking of the conceptualization and presentation of eminent psychologist Henry Tajfel and led to deeper discussions of the histories and ongoing issues of **sexual harassment** in Psychology. In response to the paper, the European Association of Social Psychology announced that they would rename their most prestigious lifetime achievement award (previously known as the 'Tajfel Medal') citing the revelation that he 'showed reprehensible and unacceptable behaviors towards female members of his lab' (EASP, 2019). The organization also created new structures for its members to report instances of sexual harassment. Histories therefore do not just remain in the past; they impact and shed light on the present. Young and Hegarty (2019) also demonstrated how the sexual harassment of women participants by male researchers was positioned as the traditional way to do experiments in some handbooks for decades. However, no social psychological organization has yet responded to the article to re-consider the history of using that experiment in those handbooks.

TOOL 2: Critical Reading and Ethics

Critical reading is essential when doing history. You may have heard about it as a key academic skill – it helps you evaluate, analyse and gain a more critical perspective. It boils down to not necessarily believing what you read at face value. Critical reading is all about getting an in depth comprehension and understanding – the specific nitty gritty aspects of texts. You might apply a particular lens, perspective, idea or question to what you're reading. You're probably doing this all the time already when you evaluate key studies – you might think, 'Hmmm, well that's not a representative sample so the conclusions are rather stretched and not applicable to everyone,' or, 'Well this is all well and good but the study has very little ecological validity.' To make those sorts of conclusions you're being critical of what you're being told. Being critical of course doesn't always mean negative. You might also think, 'Wow this study is really using an intersectional approach,' or, 'I really like how reflexive the author is in this.' These are still critical points to raise but they are positive ones! Close *critical reading* pays lots of attention to language and *discourse*. So it's not just about what is being said, but how it's being said and what is not being said. What evidence is being used to back up what claims?

Such techniques have not only disproved myths in the history of Psychology but have even revealed fraudulent data by some of the most eminent psychologists. Perhaps the most famous example of this is Cyril Burt and the highly suspicious twin data that he used to argue for hereditary IQ. Tucker (1994) outlined the history of how Leon Kamin exposed Burt (and many of his supporters) by paying very close attention to the specifics of Burt's data. By investigating Burt's publications, Kamin found that Burt hadn't actually really clarified how he measured IQ. In fact, it appeared he had sometimes just decided it via 'observation'. Among other problems was the strange statistical finding that despite Burt claiming he had a growing sample, from 15 to 53 pairs of twins in his studies, the correlations reported were coincidently exactly the same. Tucker (1994, p. 339) described Kamin's inspection of primary sources as 'open-heart surgery on the IQ literature, cutting away error, exaggeration, and myth, and certainly raising fresh questions' about what was believed to be the most compelling evidence in Psychology that IQ was hereditary. In Chapter 3, we return to the topic of IQ testing and racism and in Chapter 6 we consider dubious research practices and fraud in the context of Psychology's current *replication crisis*.

By drawing on the skills of more than one discipline, Kamin was acting as a psychologist–historian (Vaughn-Blount et al., 2009). Close reading (even of the statistics) can reveal a great deal about Psychology's present and past, but it also tells us a great deal about Psychology and *ethics*. Research psychologists have several ethical duties. You're probably encountered some thinking about ethical issues in psychological studies and experiments. We have to think about consent, deception, honesty, confidentiality, etc. Crucially, our understanding of what is considered to be ethical has changed quite a lot since Psychology was formulated as a discipline. Look back at Box 3.1. The Little Albert study would not get ethical approval nowadays, though at the time there were no ethical approval processes and its methods were considered acceptable. We must also remain cognisant that what we think of as ethical now, may *not* look ethical in the future. Reflecting on LGBQTI Psychology, Katherine and fabulous colleague David Griffiths (2019) stated:

> Throughout this history, people, institutions, and those in positions of authority often understood their practices to be the most moral, the most kind, the most humane. Yet this has not always proved to be the case, especially in hindsight.
>
> (Hubbard & Griffiths, 2019, p. 251)

Working ethically for the long term is therefore much more complex than it first appears. It's well worth thinking in the present, what side of history you'll be on in the future.

It's not just psychologists who need to think about ethics, but historians do too. As explained in Chapter 1, historians have enormous power of interpretation, and their professional claims about the past carry a certain weight. After all, it is possible for history, just like Psychology, to be abused and used for manipulative or deceptive ends (we discuss this further in Chapter 7). Doing history is embroiled in ethics: which materials you use, how you present people in the past, avoiding **anachronism**, truth-telling and the social implications of what you're arguing.

How might we use **critical reading** and ethics as a tool to study the history of psychology?

1 **Get comfy**. Both physically and mentally. Critical reading can take some time, so make sure you've got the space to get really familiar with your materials. Such work is usually best done with regular breaks and with time to write notes on your thinking and ideas. (You want to ensure when you're working on your materials you're in a suitable place where you can really concentrate. We recommend snacks.)

2 **Develop close reading skills**. What precisely is being claimed and what dynamics are at play? In what context was the work produced and from what perspective? (Top tip: don't just take it for granted, do some fact checking and go to other sources.)

3 **Speak to someone you trust** who can advise you on your reading. (Is it a logical argument you're developing, what are the key points, what issues, concerns, evaluations are arising? Are they able to follow your train of thought and see how the evidence supports it?)

4 **Think not only about the judgements being made in the materials, but also the judgements you're making**. History is written from a perspective, what's yours? (Perhaps the most obvious one being a feminist, but are there others too. What are you contributing to the dialogue and conversation?) Aspects of your perspective that affect your reading may not be the aspects that are foremost in your conscious mind.

5 **Interrogate how ethical your history is.** Are your materials suitable/trustworthy for what you're claiming? What is at stake? What are the implications of your work? Are you using them to speak truth to power? Whose side are you on? (Remember what Ginetta Sagan said: 'Silence in the face of injustice is complicity with the oppressor.')

6 **Remember history is about real people**. Are you giving all due respect to those you're speaking about? Consider the ethics of speaking about people who are dead and cannot respond, and the issues of confidentiality and anonymity for others if they are alive or recently dead. (That's not to say you can't be critical – there are lots of people in this chapter who were strikingly critical and feminist but still doing excellent history.)

SUMMARY

The genre of Psychology textbooks can repeat simplified stories. In stripping out social and historical context, they often present acontextual stories about psychological variables that, in the case of Kitty Genovese, and elsewhere, cleanse events of their embeddedness in complex social historical contexts, including feminist and other forms of collective action. Your aim is to try to weave different – more feminist – stories from the research events that are presented to you in textbooks.

In contrast, experiments and textbooks are written from a point of view of the research psychologist, not those of the other characters in the drama. In Psychology, as in medicine, we can have disappointingly few first-person narratives of research encounters 'from below', from patients' or research participants' vantage points (Porter, 1985). As the case of Kitty Genovese shows, psychologists often write *partial* accounts of history that strip out the stubborn particulars so that the events are used to illustrate the psychological concepts (and to convince readers that those concepts have real-world relevance).

We are putting into your feminist toolkit the permission to let your imagination run wild about what various actors might have experienced in the research events that are tidied up into simple stories in your textbook (and in journal articles). To push your imagination in this direction beyond familiar human subjectivities, look at Michael Pettit's (2012) research on how queerly rats in early sex research might have felt. (Maybe you are already wondering what the rat in the Little Albert experiment was feeling.) Perhaps write your own narratives from the different perspective of adults, children, animals and even *things* that have played important roles in key psychological research, but which have also been written about as if they were merely passive, and the psychologist–researcher was the only active hero in the story. How does the received dominant story look *partial* – clearly written from one self-interested perspective – when you can call to mind alternative narratives?

Hopefully, this tool will make you less of an apathetic bystander to your textbook's socialization of you into Psychology's dominant narrative about its scientific basis and humanism. As Cherry, Manning and Gallo's work on Genovese have all shown, looking for who else has made sense of events, with what purpose, and to what effect, helps to bring into relief the dominant myths within Psychology textbooks so that you can see them for what they are. *CHIP* research therefore helps you to see that what you have learned about Psychology in your textbook is *a* narrative and not *the* only right one, and that feminist alternatives are possible. Indeed, they have been there all along.

QUESTIONS TO CONSIDER

1 What have you learned about the Kitty Genovese case that has surprised you? Did you learn something that you wish was in your classic Psychology textbook?

2 Can you think of any other textbook myths? Are there any other classic studies in Psychology that you now want to investigate for potential myths?

3 This chapter has thought a lot about misogyny and violence against women. Are there any other psychological areas/topics that you think misogyny plays a role in the way stories get told about it?

4 If you were to write an ethical code of conduct for doing the history of Psychology, what would you include? What do you think are the big ethical issues in doing history?

Key resources

Beck, H. P., Levinson, S., & Irons, G. (2009). Finding Little Albert: A journey to John B. Watson's infant laboratory. *American Psychologist, 64*(7), 605–614. DOI: 10.1037/a0017234

Cherry, F. (1995). *Stubborn particulars of social psychology: Essays on the research process.* London: Routledge.

Cook, K. (2014). *Kitty Genovese: The murder, the bystanders, the crime that changed America.* New York: Norton.

Darley, J. M., & Latané, B. (1968). Bystander intervention in emergencies: Diffusion of responsibility. *Journal of Personality and Social Psychology, 8*(4p1), 377–383.

Fridlund, A. J., Beck, H. P., Goldie, W. D., & Irons, G. (2012). Little Albert: A neurologically impaired child. *History of Psychology, 15*(4), 302–327. DOI: 10.1037/a0026720

Gallo, M. M. (2014). The parable of Kitty Genovese, The New York Times, and the erasure of lesbianism. *Journal of the History of Sexuality, 23*(2), 273–294. https://doi.org/10.7560/JHS23206

Gallo, M. (2015). *"No one helped": Kitty Genovese, New York City, and the myth of urban apathy.* Ithaca, NY: Cornell University Press.

Griggs, R. A. (2015). The Kitty Genovese story in introductory psychology textbooks: Fifty years later. *Teaching of Psychology, 42*(2), 149–152. https://doi.org/10.1177/00986283155731

Harris, B. (2011). Letting go of Little Albert: Disciplinary memory, history, and the uses of myth. *Journal of the History of the Behavioral Sciences, 47*(1), 1–17. https://doi.org/10.1002/jhbs.20470

Latané, B., & Rodin, J. (1969). A lady in distress: Inhibiting effects of friends and strangers on bystander intervention. *Journal of Experimental Social Psychology, 5*(2), 189–202. https://doi.org/10.1016/0022-1031(69)90046-8

Manning, R., Levine, M., & Collins, A. (2007). The Kitty Genovese murder and the social psychology of helping: The parable of the 38 witnesses. *American Psychologist, 62*(6), 555–562. https://doi.org/10.1037/0003-066X.62.6.555

Morawski, J. G. (1992). There is more to our history of giving: The place of introductory textbooks in American psychology. *American Psychologist, 47*(2), 161–169. https://doi.org/10.1037/0003-066X.47.2.161

4 Feminist and Queer Social Change

Learning objectives

Study of this chapter will enable you to:

- Consider feminism and gender studies alongside sexuality to a greater extent
- Pay close attention to the concept of power especially in relation to when and how psychologists have been involved in efforts for social change – including from a decolonial feminist perspective
- Understand how pathologization, aversion therapy and activism have all been integrated in queer histories of Psychology
- Gain Queer Theory as a critical tool for doing CHIP, allowing you to recognize heteronormative assumptions and how politics is inescapable in Psychology

Introduction

The chances are that you've decided to study Psychology because you'd like to *do good*. Maybe you'd like to understand people; make changes to the world. Perhaps you've witnessed or experienced some form of mental distress and want to try to alleviate that for other people. Or maybe you've recognized social injustices and you want to try to make the world a fairer place. These are common reasons for studying Psychology. However, Psychology isn't just one thing that always does the same action. And the actions that it does do, aren't always good (even when that is the goal). By looking closely at Psychology's history it's possible to see where Psychology really has done good things, where it's done some not so good things, and where it's done some downright atrocious and appalling things.

In this chapter, we're going to be paying closer attention to the concept of *social change* and how psychologists have been involved in it (for both the better and for the worst). Social change is not only about what individuals do, but also about how, as groups and within certain roles, we might embody and enact certain kinds of power. Extending out further there are structural powers at play too. In exploring Psychology and social change in this chapter, we're going to be thinking about feminist action as well as sexuality – so linking gender and sexuality together more.

In the first section, we will be asking the question: is Psychology a force for good? Here, we consider Psychology's role within racist policies and ideologies, including what some people did that was terrible and what others did that was good. Then, we pay close attention to what feminists have said about power and recognize the power of Psychology. Second, we look at the relationship between *activism* and Psychology, and consider the example of *depathologization* as one area where activism made a real difference to Psychology's actions. Throughout, there are some key examples to illustrate the points we're making including learning about aversion therapy and how feminist psychologists were involved in the fight for equal marriage.

By the end of this chapter you'll probably have been on a bit of a journey. Going from 'I chose Psychology, it's a good discipline' via 'How awful, I can't believe psychologists did that!' to 'Okay, so it's often around power and what you use that power to do'. You'll meet a few excellent activists and psychologists, and eventually learn how to use *queer theory* to do your own queer affirmative forms of Psychology in the future.

Psychology: A force for good?

It is really common to talk about Psychology as a 'thing' – a unified discipline which does things. There is after all, the British Psychological Society, an organized group that's been going for over one hundred years which manages, organizes and is comprised of psychologists. There are particular benchmarks and criteria that university degrees have to fulfil in order to say they are teaching Psychology. For example, 'Graduate Basis for Chartered Membership' (GBC) is a standard set by the British Psychological Society (BPS). You have to get certain qualifications before you can be a psychologist. There are rules, regulations and guidance. Psychology is organized. This is all true and because of all of this, Psychology has a certain level of power and being a psychologist is powerful as they make real life interventions into people's lives.

While Psychology is a powerful thing, it does not exist outside of the people who are doing Psychology. It is made up of people, who are the ones actually taking actions. It is psychologists, as individuals and groups, who make up the discipline. As we learned in Chapter 2, science is *social* and made up of people (including, their beliefs, opinions, their own attitudes, positions, etc.). That is why we argued it is important to be *reflexive* and why Feminist Science Studies (the Tool in Chapter 2) emphasizes the power involved in doing science and speaking in its name.

But with great power comes great responsibility. Psychologists have used the power that they have to do some good things, but there's also lots of examples where psychologists have done some very bad things. So Psychology itself as a discipline isn't necessarily intrinsically or automatically good or bad. We also wish to highlight that often these histories are more complex than fights between good heroes and bad villains. Psychology is a science which is made up of people and so it depends on what those people decide to do with it (as well as the unintended consequences of what they do). It's all in the application.

For example, let's for a moment think about how Psychology has been involved with racism and *eugenics*. For a long time, many psychologists were very convinced that white people were more intelligent than Black people. They grounded these ideas in what they thought were very scientific practices, such as reaction time experiments (Carson, 2006). We now know that race categories are constructed and are not natural. At the high point of European colonization of African peoples, Francis Galton (who was Charles Darwin's cousin, an explorer of South West Africa himself, and whose inherited wealth came from making the guns material to Britain's colonial conquests) argued that white people were most intelligent, and that the human race should be improved by only letting 'appropriate' people procreate (see Brookes, 2004). He called this philosophy eugenics and it became internationally popular and disturbingly it still has supporters even now. Eugenics often supported *scientific racism*, that is, theories that assume there are distinct human races that vary in their value and capabilities. Science was reflecting societal racism and further legitimizing it. These ideas were very much grounded in broader ideologies that were also dangerous and violent. These include *imperialism, colonialism,* and *white supremacy*.

Psychology specifically really promoted these ideas and key people, including Galton, said that intelligence was hereditary. Such ideas were highly influential and permeated popular culture (see Ladd-Taylor, 2001). *Eugenic* ideas were particularly taken up in the early part of the twentieth century in the USA, where several states introduced sterilization laws. In California – where over 20,000 forced sterilizations occurred during this period – women from immigrant families were those most often subject to eugenic sterilization. Sterilization programmes in the USA increasingly focused on Black women and persisted into the 1970s (see Kline, 2001; Roberts, 1997). The majority of such sterilizations took place in mental hospitals and so this is not only a racist history but one which intersects with class, dis/ability and mental health specifically.

IQ tests were often used to diagnose and justify surgical procedures to ensure some people couldn't have children. Such tests were highly culturally dependant and biased; they were after all written by older white cisgender men, so it's what they thought was important that was tested (you could apply Tool 2 from Chapter 3, Critical reading and ethics, to expose such bias). Nonetheless, debates and issues around intelligence and race raged on for most of the twentieth century and the same sorts of arguments were still being published at the end of this period. See Gould (1981) *The Mismeasure of Man* for more details, plus Winston (2004) *Defining Difference: Race and Racism in the History of Psychology*. Peter's book, *A Gentleman's Disagreement*, connected this well-worn territory to the new interest in the history of sexuality in twenty-first century history of Psychology.

This isn't to say that while a lot of this was going on, that some psychologists weren't using Psychology for good. Mamie Phipps Clark for example, alongside her husband Kenneth (introduced in Chapter 2), did a series of experiments which demonstrated the vast psychological impacts of racism and segregated schooling on children. In her postgraduate studies in the late 1930s at Howard University, Mamie, and Kenneth, famously conducted doll experiments and colouring experiments. These studies showed that Black children both pre-ferred white dolls as they were 'good' and tended to draw themselves with lighter skin than their actual skin tone. Their work demonstrated that children as young as five recognized that Black people had inferior status in the USA and that self-hatred was especially pronounced for children in segregated schools.

Their research would continue to be influential and less than a decade later their studies were used in the ***Brown v. Board of Education Supreme Court*** case in 1954. The court highlighted that it was several psychological studies that revealed the impact segregation had on Black children (i.e. that it made them feel inferior and it interfered with their learning) that led to their unanimous conclusion: to abolish segregated education. The work of Mamie Phipps Clark and Kenneth Clark was influential despite the backdrop of exten-sive racism (and sexism for Mamie) in Psychology. Mamie Phipps Clark was the first Black woman at Columbia University to be awarded a PhD (in 1943) and the second Black person ever after her husband Kenneth. Her supervisor there actually even supported segregation! The wider culture of Psychology at the time was incredibly exclusive, discriminatory and biased, yet they used Psychology to do good.

What we deem 'good' is also incredibly personal. For us, we are thinking of 'good' Psychology as that which is liberatory and oriented towards equity. We are pro Psychology that is anti-racist, anti-ableist, anti-sexist and anti-cisheteronormative – especially a Psychology which recognizes the historical and cultural **contexts**, and which has deeply considerate ethical practices. We think of 'bad' Psychology as that which intentionally or unintentionally acts to oppress, enact violence, discriminate and evoke power against, marginalized and vulnerable groups. While we think it's clear in the brief history outlined above that that the eugenicists are very much the 'baddies' and the Clarks were the 'goodies' (in attempting to motivate significantly social change around educational segregation), it's not always clear who the 'goodies' and the 'baddies' are. It's often far more complicated, especially because one can have perfectly good intentions but precipitate bad effects. While the outcomes from the Clarks' research was positive for civil rights in the USA, it has still gained some critique. For example, Eve Tuck (2009) has highlighted how the Clarkes' research is 'damage-centred' which she argues is, in the long term, a flawed approach to change as it continues to suggest marginalized people are ruined (e.g. by self-hate). History, people and Psychology are all more complex than our comic book heroes and villains. And so is the power that is linked to all those things.

Katherine and colleague Natasha Bharj recently tried to untangle questions about feminism, Psychology and power when they wrote 'Power/History/

Psychology: A Feminist Excavation' in *Psychology, Power and Gender* (in press). In the following text, we'll be taking you through some of the excavations Katherine and Natasha made.

One excavation was around conceptualizations of power. A key thing to recognize when thinking about power is that it's been rather difficult to define what we mean by 'power'. For example, Celia Kitzinger (who we also meet in Box 4.2) wrote that feminist psychologists have a reluctance to explicitly define power. Allen (2016) argued that power was most often conceptualized in two main ways: 1) power is thought of as a quantifiable entity held by *individuals* in different amounts; and 2) power is thought of as a force exerted by broader *structures* of society. Claims that 'science is not political' construct science as an activity that is not an exercise of power, and ironically this has allowed power to be wielded through natural science for centuries (Shapin, 1996). Michel Foucault particularly thought about that ironic exercise of power in relation to medicalization, prisons, sexuality and the construction of human sciences like Psychology to justify such exercises of power. (He crops up later again in Tool 3 when we think about *queer theory*). Feminist thinking that recognizes the political and the power in Psychology is therefore important.

Different forms of feminism (including feminism outside of Psychology) can also conceptualize power in different ways. As we explored in Chapters 1 and 2, feminism is multifaceted and has various approaches, and the same is true for how it understands power. For example, Allen (2016) highlights how liberal and radical feminist theory tended to conceptualize power as a thing between individuals. *Liberal feminist* theory constructs power as a neutral or positive resource that can and should be shared equally. In contrast, radical feminist approaches view power as the expression of dominance/submission which is often gendered (with men having dominance). Alternatively, *socialist feminism* focuses on the structural aspects of power and sees those as dominant (often through labour). Intersectional feminist theory however, examines power at multiple levels, unpacking the interacting axes of *privilege* and oppression that inform both social relations and individual identity (Allen, 2016). These ideas can be similarly mapped onto our descriptions of *empiricist, standpoint* and *postmodern* feminist epistemologies in Chapter 2.

Another excavation was around the issue that people differ on the extent to which they think power can be used for good. There is a tendency to create a bit of a binary here: power is bad in the wrong hands, but good in the right hands. This is an area of debate. Is it possible for power to a be a positive thing when it is in the hands of women and other marginalized groups (see Allen, 2016)? This question hangs on the difference between conceptualizing a dominating and controlling 'power-over' others versus a transformative and liberating 'power-to' marginalized people. We can't help but be reminded of the Spice Girls' 'Girl Power' slogan when thinking about this (and the critiques of the commodification of feminism for capital gain, i.e. feminism 'sells'). But there are lots of (more contemporary) examples as 'power-to' forms of power are often linked to the idea of empowerment. These basically encompass the idea that individuals can choose, or act in ways and that leads to, personal empowerment. These are often associated with more personal level changes we make in the world for and about ourselves and tend to avoid the negative connotation of the 'power-over' version (see Yoder & Kahn, 1992).

Conceptualizing a positive form of power is useful for feminist action, for example, as a means of justifying *liberal feminists* striving for 'equal' power, or to reimagine how power or agency might look in a radically different world. It is also this type of power which tends to be the most dominant understanding in Psychology. However, these perspectives rarely provide a clear explanation of how these forms of power can be used for good and how it's actually that different from 'power-over' forms of power. Another important issue is that 'power-to' versions tend to be about the individual self which tends to ignore wider structural constraints and obligations (Kitzinger, 1991; Kurtiş, Adams, & Estrada-Villalta, 2016).

Feminist psychologists have identified a number of these problems and have thought about power in Psychology in detail. For example, there was a special issue of *Psychology of Women Quarterly* in 1992 all about feminist psychological analyses of power. Particularly influential in this issue were Griscom's (1992) history of power in Psychology and Yoder and Kahn's (1992) editorial introduction explicitly outlining the 'power-over' versus 'power-to' framework as described above. More recently, feminism, and Feminist Psychology by implication, has been critiqued for focusing too much on individualist understandings of 'power-to' forms of power. The argument is that the emphasis on empowerment in turn implies women are responsible for their own lack of power and ought to adapt to current unequal and unfair structures (see Rutherford, 2018). Consequentially this can suggest that when women and others such as gender non-confirming people do not feel empowered, it is their own beliefs and sense of self-efficacy which is the cause (not the unequal power structures which exist in the first place). See Kitzinger and Frith (1999) for an analysis of this in relation to sexual refusal.

In the book chapter they wrote, Katherine and Natasha argued that in order to resolve this issue it was essential to recognize the wider contexts in which people are situated and therefore include the structural aspects more. Indeed, some feminist psychologists have been long making arguments against individualistic understandings of power, for example Kitzinger (1991) decried individualist notions of power as not only troublingly narrow but overtly harmful:

> The notion of the free, autonomous, self-fulfilled and authentic woman possessed of a personal power innocent of coercion - an ideal which informs most feminist psychological engagement with the concept of power - is simply an individualist myth which actively obscures the operation of power.
>
> (p.124)

bell hooks (2013, who by the way, always has her name in lower case) claimed that individualistic perspectives can actually disconnect gender from power.

Decolonial feminists also argue that individualistic understandings of empowerment are mostly based on colonial Western models of the person (Kurtiş et al, 2016). For example, the idea that somehow knowledge based on research about white men (conducted often by white men) applies to all other people, has been a common idea and one that has required substantial tackling. In particular much of the knowledge produced by Psychology tends to be based on WEIRD samples and from WEIRD perspectives (that is, from western, educated, industrialized, rich and democratic, people and contexts). Psychology as a science is therefore 'inextricably linked to the legacy of (gendered) colonialism, orientalism and Euro-centric assumptions' (Macleod, Bhatia & Liu, 2020, p. 299). Tuck and Yang (2014) provide a detailed discussion of how research might not be what decolonial approaches needs and the issues of whether research even deserves some forms of (indigenous) knowledge (also see aforementioned Tuck, 2009; Bharj & Adams, 2023).

It is therefore important to not only think about what sort of power we mean, but also to consider how we are conceptualizing power. For Feminist Psychology, it is imperative that feminist psychologists continue to be critical of how wider Psychology views power and the individual, as these are often based on ***androcentric***, and ***colonial*** ideas of personhood. Decolonial perspectives aim to dismantle these normative and limited constructions of applying what is known and knowable about the global *minority* to the global *majority*. In the introduction of the special issue 'Feminisms and Decolonising Psychology' for *Feminism & Psychology*, Macleod, Bhatia and Liu (2020) argued:

> Feminist decolonising psychology is complex because what is at stake is not only deconstructing psychological science but also, firstly, dominant Euro-US-centric versions of feminism that have, advertently or inadvertently, replicated colonialist and racist ideologies and, secondly, decolonial theory that sidelines gender
>
> (p. 287)

Crucially, decolonial perspectives often grapple with aspects of history. Perhaps the clearest example of this is how efforts to decolonize the curriculum have been made in order to rectify the white-washing of the past evident in history (see e.g., Cramblet Alvarez et al., 2020). In two special issues for the *Journal of Social Issues* (2022a, 2022b, also see 2021), Reddy, Ratele, Adams and Suffla as the 'Readsura Decolonial Editorial Collective' outline a whole range of key areas in relation to Decolonial Psychology including historical trauma and violence and present epistemological violence evident in and around Psychology. They argue that colonial violence is not a past issue like it's often presented as (i.e. colonialism as a thing that happened) but instead persists as 'coloniality' very much in the present.

In order to interrupt such coloniality in Psychology, Bhatia, Long, Pickren and Rutherford (2024) argue that is critical to centre the experiences and knowledges of those who have been erased or marginalized within its history. In undertaking a historical decolonial 'turn', the power dynamics between coloniality and knowledge can be further revealed. Subsequently, Psychology could have a new historical footing; one that is removed from the hierarchal and elitist histories associated with colonial understandings of knowledge.

So is Psychology a force for good? It can be – but it's vital to recognize the types of power and the structures of power underneath it. Or, to be more specific, psychologists can utilize the power of Psychology and be empowered by it. What is critical to recognize though, is that in writing about power and Psychology, power itself is implicated. Power has a history too. There is a 'history of the power Psychology has wielded' (Hegarty, 2007, p. 76) and clearly there are unequal extents to which people in Psychology can utilize its power to make claims about other people, depending on the power they hold.

As a discipline, Psychology can throw its weight around – it's very much a 'power-over' entity. And it can be way more complicated than that when we consider people's intentions, contexts and positions. As explored below, this power is also more likely to be enacted upon those with less power, who are more marginalized, pathologized and stigmatized. However, in work aimed to counter this, issues remain. Tuck (2009) calls for researchers to not re-ascribe, even unintentionally, discourses of marginalized people as broken when doing 'damage-centred' research that aims to hold those in power accountable for psychological damage.

Box 4.1: Aversion therapy

Not many Psychology students realize that a few decades ago it was possible to be diagnosed as 'homosexual'. This constituted a mental illness according to the *Diagnostic Statistical Manual* (DSM) which is the main manual used by the **psy-disciplines** to diagnose and categorize mental illnesses. Indeed, psychologists were fascinated by homosexuality and tried to not only understand what apparently 'causes' it (a dangerous game as explored in Chapter 5), but diagnose it, and 'treat' it. Interest in homosexuality in Psychology and Psychiatry gained a particularly homophobic and **pathologizing** tone from the middle of the twentieth century (Jennings, 2008). The medical, social and psychological sciences were engrained with thinking that LGBT people were 'sick', ill and pathological, and capable of being 'cured'. King and Bartlett (1999) reviewed British psychiatry and homosexuality paying particular attention to treatments offered for homosexuality. These included behavioural treatments first developed at the Maudsley Hospital, such as electro-shock treatments and aversion therapy.

Aversion therapy is the practice of attempting to alter someone's sexuality (in the direction from queer to heterosexual) or sometimes their gender identity (in the direction of **trans** to **cisgender**) utilizing conditioning-based techniques. These techniques were grounded in **behaviourism** and usually took the form of presenting an individual with queer sex-related material and either simultaneously giving them electric shocks, or giving them drugs to make them exceptionally unwell (causing sickness and diarrhoea in an enclosed space with no access to a toilet). Sometimes 'anticipatory' methods were used where waiting for a shock caused more distress and so was used to prolong the extreme discomfort for an individual. These 'therapies' or 'treatments' were provided in all sorts of places, across hospitals and universities in the UK (and the wider British commonwealth), as well as the USA, Australia and former Czechoslovakia (Davison, 2021).

Oral histories from both the professionals involved in such treatment (King, Smith & Bartlett, 2004) and the patients of such treatment (Smith, Bartlett & King, 2004) revealed the horrific impact treatments had on patients and a worrying trend that some professionals continued to support homophobic and abusive treatments (see also Dickinson, 2015). It goes without saying really, that these 'treatments' did not work as intended and at best caused people to be relatively unaffected, and at worst caused suicidality.

John Bancroft published an article in the British Journal of Psychiatry in 1969 which detailed the use of electric aversion therapy on 10 gay men in attempt to 'cure' them of their homosexuality. Only one 'case', was deemed completely 'successful', though seven were said to have a change in 'sexual attitude' after 'treatment' but only three men sustained this change short-term. Despite the subsequent anxiety in several men and depression detailed in all the descriptions of the participants, Bancroft was encouraged to continue his research to see if he could continually justify the use of what he called 'an inherently unpleasant method'. Bancroft later admitted he would no longer give aversion therapy citing a shift in social attitude as well as the ineffectiveness of treatment (King and Bartlett, 1999).

Aversion therapy and other 'treatments' for homosexuality were primarily targeted towards gay men. However, that is not to say other people didn't get exposed to such abuse – for example, lesbian women also underwent such 'treatment'. In 1967 MacCulloch and Feldman published 'Aversion Therapy in Management of 43 Homosexuals' in the British Medical Journal. This research included two lesbian women in the sample. One of these women, Pauline Collier, has recently spoken to Helen Spandler and Sarah Carr for their 2019 article outlining the evidence of queer women being treated and has even written about her experience in The Psychologist (2023). Likewise, Dickinson (2015), who conducted **oral histories** from people who underwent aversion therapies, interviewed two trans women. Understandings at the time about gender identity and sexuality were often mixed and this demonstrates the use of aversion therapy across gender as well as sexuality lines (see Hubbard & Griffiths, 2019, for a history of British LGBTQI psychology).

It has only been in recent years that these practices are being historicized and those related institutions are beginning to recognize how the power they held allowed this sort of psychological practice to occur (see Davison, in press).

It's not that doing this impacted people's careers negatively, quite the oppo-site. For example MacCulloch and Feldman's research was conducted at the Crumpsall Hospital, Manchester following donations of between £6,000 and £7,000 to set up a unit specifically for the purpose of 'curing' homosexuality. Feldman then went on to develop their career at Birmingham University where there has recently been a historical investigation and report of the university's involvement with aversion therapy (the report 'Conversion Therapy' and the University of Birmingham, c.1966–1983' is available online as is the panel event launching the report that Katherine took part in).

It is also worth noting that the vast majority of those who underwent such treatment did so voluntarily. Such is the power of fear, stigmatization and pathologization. In MacCulloch and Feldman's study, of the 45 people invited to take part, only 2 declined (see Dickinson, 2015). Pauline was one of the women in the study. In fact, they even employed her as a receptionist so that she would be able to be in the hospital regularly for treatment. And while aversion therapy is no longer practised by mainstream Psychology, forms of conversion therapy, which still aims to shift someone's sexuality and/or gen-der identity, are still about today. Bartlett, Smith and King (2009) found that 17 per cent of UK practitioners had attempted to change a client's gay or lesbian feelings (222 of 1328 psychologists, counsellors, psychiatrists and psychotherapists surveyed). More recently again, efforts to ban conversion therapy in the UK have faltered because of attempts to only develop a ban for lesbian, gay and bisexual people and not trans people. Fully inclusive bans exist elsewhere, including Brazil, Malta, Canada and Uruguay. So despite historical evidence that gender conversion has been rife and just as problem-atic and violent as that on LGB people, there remains a reluctance from the Government for a full ban, leaving trans people especially open to further abuse (see the Stonewall, 2020 report on conversion therapy for LGBT people).

Activism and Psychology

In this section we're going to look at one example of *social change* which happened in Psychology that was deeply related to *activism*. The relationship between Psychology and activism can be rather complicated. As aforemen-tioned, the power Psychology has can be used for good, but it's also been a force used against marginalized people. So there are issues of trust. Plus, there's a wider debate in feminism as to whether it is possible to use the tools from an oppressor to make change.

Audre Lorde, who beautifully described herself as 'black, lesbian, mother, warrior, poet', famously wrote 'For the master's tools will never dismantle the master's house' about this exact issue. We think her quote her is worth looking at within the wider paragraph:

Those of us who stand outside the circle of this society's definition of acceptable women; those of us who have been forged in the crucibles of difference – those of us who are poor, who are lesbians, who are Black, who are older – know that survival is not an academic skill. It is learning how to take our differences and make them strengths. For the master's tools will never dismantle the master's house. They may allow us temporarily to beat him at his own game, but they will never enable us to bring about genuine change. And this fact is only threatening to those women who still define the master's house as their only source of support.

(Andre Lorde, 1979/2018)

If we apply what Lorde here is saying to Psychology, we could argue that while using Psychology's tools might make some temporary or small changes happen, it will never make dramatic changes necessary to remove structural and institutional abuses of power. To relate this to our earlier understandings of power, it might be that individuals feel empowered by Psychology, or have 'power-to' do something, but Psychology will continue to have the 'power-over'. (The metaphor of tools is also integral to this book and we explain more about their meaning and use in Chapter 7.)

Nonetheless, that is not to say that activists inside and outside of Psychology have not still made changes that have real life impacts on lots of people. One central area of study for psychologists is mental illness, and Psychology's understanding of mental distress is based on contextual, and therefore changeable, ideologies. Foucault (1954) argued not only for this constructed nature but that Psychiatry was used as a social institutional force to control people (see Joranger, 2016). Others have critically developed arguments for the social constructed nature of madness itself (Samson, 1995). Hearing voices for example, has dramatically different meanings across different cultures (Luhrmann, Padmavati, Tharoor & Osei, 2015). The same is true for disability as activists argued for more *social* models rather than medical models of disability. These make clear that it is the way the world is set up, which impairs certain people from engaging in it rather than their bodies per se. Activists in this area have worked hard to stake a claim on the knowledges that they have and famously argued research should have 'nothing about us, without us' (Charlton, 1998) meaning disabled people should be engaged and consulted to a much greater extent. One key change that activist efforts from inside and outside of Psychology have focused on has been around diagnosis. Diagnoses have changed dramatically over time, depending on what the **psy-disciplines** think of as 'mental illness'. The *Diagnostic Statistical Manual* (DSM) published by the American Psychiatric Association which outlines such diagnosis has changed substantially over the decades (see Grob, 1991) removing, adding and changing what psychiatrists agree mental illness is and what it is not.

One key example relevant to this chapter's focus on sexuality is the removal of 'homosexuality' as a mental disorder from the DSM in 1973. This change happened somewhat later than you might expect (see Minton, 2002). In fact, aversion therapy was still commonly practised when the Sexual Offenses Act decriminalized sex between men in 1967 in England and Wales (well, that is *two* men, *aged* 21 or older, in *private* who *aren't* in the military). This change in law came a decade after the Wolfenden report which had recommended it. (In 1994 the age of consent for sex between men was lowered to 18 and in 2000 it was lowered to 16 to match the age of consent for sex between men and women.) The law and Psychology are therefore related and both have complex relationships to social norms. It's clear that while the law was decriminalizing, Psychology was still 'treating'. It wasn't until 1990 that homosexuality was removed from the International Classification of Diseases (ICD) (the exact date, 17 May, is now celebrated as the International Day Against Homophobia, Biphobia and Transphobia).

This messy and complex history is well narrated by Minton (2002) and includes of course people working within, as well as outside of, Psychology and Psychiatry. Minton especially identified the Rorschach research of psychologist Evelyn Hooker (1957) as pivotal in this story – Hooker used Psychology's masters tools, the Rorschach ink blot test and the statistical comparison of groups, to argue that there were no differences between gay men and straight men. This research provided pivotal to breaking up consensus that homosexuality was a mental illness in the decades after her work was published.

Gay Liberation activists (such as Frank Kameny and Barbara Gittings) started protesting at Psychology and Psychiatry conferences sessions about homosexuality from 1970. At one American Psychiatric Association meeting, they chanted: 'Stop talking about us and start talking *with* us' (emphasis original, Minton (2002) p. 256). In a session about aversion therapy, the heckling became so disruptive the chairperson halted the talk. Perhaps in the most succinct description of the issues at play between psychologists and activists is the following exchange described by Minton:

> 'I never said homosexuals were sick, what I said was that they have displaced sexual adjustment.' – Irving Bieber
>
> In response a protestor retorted, 'That's the same thing, motherfucker.'
>
> (p. 256)

By the end of this conference some psychiatrists started back room conversations about the possibility of deleting 'homosexuality' as a mental disorder from the DSM (see Minton, 2002). It was therefore the direct action of activists (who were not using the 'master's tools) which began the important changes underfoot. The following year a presence of gay activists was once again on the conference proceedings, but also included, for the first time, a panel which included a gay psychiatrist: 'Dr Henry Anonymous' (who later came out as Dr John Fryer). Fryer was disguised by large suit, wig, mask and a voice distorting microphone for the session and described the suffocating difficulty in being gay in Psychology (Minton, 2002).

Fryer wasn't the only queer person working in the ***psy-disciplines*** at the time but as Fryer's experience shows, such work was incredibly difficult. The gay British psychologist and sociologist Michael Schofield wrote under a pseudonym (Gordon Westwood) and initially embraced the pathologizing model of homosexuality despite being gay himself. Later he shifted perspective and viewed the struggles faced by queer people in Britain as being based on the social stigma they faced rather than because of a 'disordered' sexuality (Hubbard & Griffiths, 2019). Indeed, Hooker wasn't the only person using the Rorschach test to argue there was nothing wrong with queer people. June Hopkins did similar work but with a different perspective in Britain and later came out as a lesbian herself (Clarke & Hopkins, 2002; Hubbard, 2017a, 2017b, 2018, 2020). Some of her research was even published in the same issue of the *British Journal of Psychiatry* as Bancroft's aversion therapy study. Some psychologists were therefore working from the inside, using Psychology's master tools to try and shift the discipline away from homophobic abusive practice.

Others were tackling the issues from an outside perspective. The pathologization of homosexuality and the treatment of queer people by Psychology and Psychiatry was a key area of discussion for many queer activist groups (see Hubbard, 2020; Jennings, 2008; Spandler & Carr, 2021). This included the Gay Liberation Front (1970–1972) who even had a sub-group called the Counter-Psychiatry group. This group first met in London at the house of fellow member and sociologist Mary McIntosh (Hubbard, 2020; Jennings, 2008). Their specific objectives fed into the wider Gay Liberations Front demands from 1971, which included 'that psychiatrists stop treating homosexuality as though it were a problem or a sickness, and hereby giving gay people senseless guilt-complexes'. There is also evidence of other psychologists being involved in other activist groups in the UK (e.g. the Minorities Research Group, Hubbard, 2020) and psychologists supporting their queer clients despite pathologization (Hubbard, 2021).

Eventually, following further debate and discussion, the American Psychiatric Association committee held a vote in 1973 (see Bayer, 1981). With a vote of 13 to 0 (2 abstentions) 'homosexuality' was deleted from the DSM (yay!). *However*, Sexual Orientation Disturbance was added, including 'ego-dystonic homosexuality' (boo!). It is this precise reason why many consider this as the removal of homosexuality *per se*. Psychologists and psychiatrists were still able to 'treat' or attempt to 'cure' homosexuality if patients were unhappy with their sexualities. Ongoing *activism* inside and outside of Psychology led to removal of 'ego-dystonic homosexuality' from the DSM by 1987.

It is of course a relief that homosexuality was depathologized, though as this brief history shows, it was not straightforward (if you'll excuse the pun). Some people have argued that the *depathologization* of homosexuality itself didn't have an immediate impact on queer people on the ground (King, 2003) and certainly a lot of damage had already been done. So depathologization was in effect a removal of a bad thing in Psychology and Psychiatry, rather than an introduction of a good thing. But it was without doubt the actions of activists (inside and outside of Psychology) which made a significant difference. Equally, Psychology has had a very complicated, worrying and pathologizing history with trans people (Eisfeld, 2014; Riggs, Pearce, Pfeffer, Hines, White & Ruspini, 2019; Suess, Espineira & Walters, 2014).

For the most part, the nurses and mental health professionals, including psychologists, did not deliberately set out to cause great distress and pain in those they 'treated' (Dickinson, 2015). In fact, some of those who conducted aversion therapies, and other 'treatments', were themselves gay or lesbian. Usually, those practising often believed they were helping someone who was voluntarily there (which was often the case). However, this highlights the issue that homophobic social attitudes were legitimatized by Psychology, as a powerful institution. King and Bartlett (1999) in their review of homosexuality and Psychiatry argued that the history of aversion therapies and institutionalized homophobia has 'exposed the conservative social bias inherent in psychiatry and psychology, damaged the lives of gay men and lesbians and provided grounds for discrimination' (p. 111).

Psychology has of course changed since *depathologization*, though some similarities remain. Peter wrote about these changes in his book *A Recent History of Lesbian and Gay Psychology: From Homophobia to LGBT* (2017). Many histories locate the 1970s and de-pathologization as the 'end' of a bad history for lesbians and gay men. Instead, Hegarty (2017a) picks up what happened afterwards, including the HIV/AIDS epidemic, the formation of gay/lesbian groups in Psychology organizations, psychologists' support for lesbian and gay rights, such as marriage rights, in court, and later expansions of the field beyond 'lesbian and gay' to address fluid sexualities, bisexuality, trans and intersex people. This history therefore shows the impact social attitudes and beliefs can have on apparently scientific, objective and unbiased disciplines such as Psychology and vice versa.

Katherine has previously argued, alongside wonderful colleague and friend David Griffiths, that LGBTQI Psychology is (sadly) not a simple story of progress (Hubbard & Griffiths, 2019). Things do not get better and more enlightened all the time and unfortunately we do not get closer and closer to more equal rights, fairness and equality as each day passes. Progress is actually often more precarious and doesn't impact everyone in the same way. For example, despite *depathologization* and the actions of the Gay Liberation Front and other activist groups, Section 28 was introduced in 1988 which in effect banned schools from saying anything positive about queer sexualities (until 2000 in Scotland and 2003 in England and Wales). There was also a very slow response to HIV/AIDS both in and outside Psychology, largely because of homophobic stigma, and it cost thousands of (often very young) lives (Hegarty, 2017). When positive changes *do* occur, they can often take longer than anticipated for their effects to be felt and this sometimes only impacts a select group of people (with more marginalized people remaining side-lined). Indeed, for some, definitions of 'progress' actually include disavowing the rights of others so it's worth being very attentive to what people think constitutes progress. It is also important to avoid viewing 'progress' through a WEIRD lens (western, educated, industrialized, rich and democratic) and recognize the complexities of LGBTQ emancipation outside of these contexts. Horne (2020) argued we need a transnational LGBTQ Psychology which expands beyond WEIRD ways of thinking for this reason.

But that is not to say bad things are inevitable. The important thing to remember about social change, and what this history above exemplifies, is to not take it for granted. Powerful institutions take away as well as give, in fact sometimes it's easier and recently there have been examples of marginalized groups having their rights rolled back. This is being felt at the time of writing in the UK and the USA especially in regard to trans and gender non-conforming people's rights (e.g. so-called 'drag bans' in various US states and relentless media scrutiny towards trans people in the UK). Hegarty (2017a) described a period of history when the US Supreme Court often sided with LGBT rights. We are not living in that era any more. It is the actions of people that make *social change* and force powerful bodies to shift. It's up to us in the present to appreciate the actions of those in the past, to be grateful for the social changes that they fought for, and to keep fighting for ongoing equality in the future.

Box 4.2: Equal marriage

Psychologists Sue Wilkinson and Celia Kitzinger have never been ones to shy away from feminist action and have been responsible for a number of changes within and outside of Feminist Psychology. As mentioned in Chapter 2, Sue Wilkinson was involved in the setting up of POWES, and they were also both instrumental in establishing the Lesbian and Gay Section of the BPS (now called the Psychology of Sexualities Section). But perhaps the most well-known *social change* they've been involved with has been equal marriage.

In 2003 Sue and Celia got married in Canada (only a few weeks after it became legal for same sex couples). 'We got married in part because, in the international social and political context in which we find ourselves, we believe it was more politically important to marry than to refuse to do so' (Kitzinger & Wilkinson, 2004, p. 131). However, unlike marriages between men and women aboard, their marriage was not recognized by British Law upon their return. Two years later, when the Civil Partnership Act came in, their marriage was automatically allocated as a civil partnership. But they hadn't got a civil partnership, they were married.

So Sue and Celia went to the high court! They argued that civil partnerships were both practically and symbolically lesser than marriage and asked the court to recognize their marriage in the same way that it was in other countries. They said that their human rights were being breached, including a) their right to respect for privacy and family life; b) their right to marriage; and c) their right to live without discrimination.

This is fundamentally about equality. We want our marriage to be recognised as a marriage – just like any other marriage made in Canada. It is insulting and discriminatory to be offered a civil partnership instead. Civil partnerships are an important step forward for same-sex couples, but they are not enough. We want full equality in marriage.

In 2006 it was announced that they had sadly lost their case. Without same sex marriage in the UK, their marriage just wouldn't be recognized in the same way. Celia and Sue talk about their decisions and provide a feminist critique of marriage in their 2004 article 'The Re-branding of Marriage: Why We Got Married Instead of Registering a Civil Partnership' in *Feminism & Psychology*. You can also hear Sue and Celia talk about their experiences of this in their Psychology's Feminist Voices *oral history* (available on YouTube and the PFV site). However, their case had made the headlines and made big waves in the fight for marriage equality for many queer people. In 2014, when the Marriage (Same Sex Couples) Act came in, their marriage was finally recognized, over a decade after actually getting married.

TOOL 3: Queer theory

Queer theory is another *interdisciplinary* idea that we'd like to introduce to you as a tool to investigate the history of Psychology. It was developed from the early 1990s onward and is associated with various topics (including desires, behaviours, identifies, histories, spaces, etc.) and spans across several disciplines (Sociology, History, Political Science, Philosophy, etc.) Key people involved in the development of *queer theory* are Judith Butler, Eve Kosofsky Sedgwick and Adrienne Rich. Queer theorists tend to come from critical and *social constructionist* positions, and have often been inspired by the work of Michel Foucault as a key theorist in this area.

Berlant and Warner (1995) argued that *queer theory* isn't so much a 'thing' but a queer commentary, and so doesn't function as a theory *per se*. They said that even within the first five years of queer theory being something people spoke about, there was already a sense that people want to know what it was and what it could do. In their paper 'What does Queer Theory tell us about X?' they argued that queer theory arose from the queer activism, specifically around HIV/AIDS, and that it emerged in this **context** because it 'provoked intellectuals to see themselves as bringing a queerer world into being' (p. 344). Crucially, they said queer theory has the 'power to wrench frames' (p. 348).

At its core queer theory disrupts and decentres norms around sex, gender and sexuality. In particular, it decentralizes heterosexuality as a key frame of reference. It challenges heteronormativity, that is, the assumption and default position of heterosexuality. Rich (1980) described a form of compulsory heterosexuality – that is, that heterosexuality is often presumed and presented as being natural or intrinsic. Consider this example: it's very common to hear about or see signs for a 'man cave'. This discourse or imagery makes particular assumptions such as: a) that the domestic space is that controlled and maintained by women; b) that they are in relationships with men; and c) that men require their own space outside of or adjacent to this. This is telling not only about norms of relationships, but also of gender roles, and of domestic expectations. So queer theory takes wide and various objects, ideas, concepts etc. under consideration and shifts, or wrenches, the perspective. If men need a 'cave' and, as Virginia Woolf argued, women need 'a room of one's own', what do non-binary people need? What kind of space do agender people require?

Queer theorists have often disrupted ideas of stability in particular and show the complexities of sex, gender and sexuality. Foucault in *The History of Sexuality* (1976), argued that sexuality needed to be understood as products of historical and cultural **context**. It's not a fixed, permanent and stable thing, but something which was constructed as such in nineteenth-century Psychiatry, is implicated into histories of power and institutions and changes over time and place. While Foucault centred on Europe, post-colonial theorists looked at power mechanisms that make up sexuality and race in interaction with each other that originated in encounters between Europeans and the people they colonized (Stoler, 1995). Judith Butler continued such wrenching work and applied similar thinking to gender. In *Gender Trouble* (1990), they argued that gender is not a biological reality of bodies, but instead is the repetition of gendered acts – that is, it's performativity. These ideas therefore *wrench* away from standard expectations and frames of reference giving and centralizing a queer perspective.

The term 'queer' was used deliberately by theorists as a form of reclaiming the term from its use as a slur. It is a deliberately inclusive term which defies definition and encompasses broad conceptualizations about marginalized forms of sex, gender and sexuality. *Queer theory* is not a dead intellectual discussion, but is grounded in current political conversations (Berlant and Warner, 1995). It's live and the topics it refers to are often embroiled and relevant to the lives of those who are using it. It is a political and active area which is undergirded by, and in engagement with, *activism* – it's not a purely academic area. Because of its flexibility and lack of clear definition, Butler (1993b) suggests that 'queer' as a term should not be 'owned' but instead always be ready for redeployment to the most urgent current political purposes. Such flexibility has been criticized by some, but proponents of queer theory argue that it means queer theory can then be adjustable to the needs and experiences of people who are marginalized based on their sex/gender/ sexuality as those needs change.

Queer theory can be a bit confusing sometimes because of the lack of definitions and its political and disruptive nature. Initially Psychology paid little attention to queer theory (but see Bem, 1995, Hegarty, 1997, and Minton, 1997 for early exceptions to the rule). Since there has been greater attention (e.g., Downing & Gillett, 2011). Despite its complexity there's a really excellent book by Meg-John Barker and Jules Scheele called *Queer: A Graphic History* which outlines it all really well. (It's a very accessible text with clear illustrations throughout to really explain all the different aspects of it – we strongly recommend it and you can even see pictures of Peter and some of those that he mentions in his acknowledgements inside!)

How might we *use* queer theory as a tool to study the history of Psychology?

1 **Consider what is being taken for granted** and what the standard frames of reference are. Think about the things that seem to 'go without saying'. What would it be like to name those things? (Are there any assumptions around gender or sexuality?)

2 **Question any underlying assumptions** going on. These are often around binaries when we think of sex, gender and sexuality (they get framed as female/male, women/men and gay/straight) but these binaries don't hold up to any form of scientific or social scrutiny. So what and who is being left out?

3 Queer theory is political and centralizes the lives of those who are marginalized by sex, gender and sexuality. **Imagine what the history of Psychology looks** like from these perspectives. (What are the implications for marginalized queer people, e.g. trans people of colour, queer intersex people or queer disabled people?)

4 **Once you've identified the norms underlying a historical narrative, imagine how such norms might be disrupted.** What other options are there? How might you begin to expect the unexpected? There are alternative ways of looking at things in the history of Psychology. (What does it look like if we take trans, disabled or working-class queerness as the norm?)

5 **Think queerly!** All of this disruption and perspective changing can be considered a verb as well as a noun. The doing of queer theory is active and remains political. So think about what your perspective and context is in this (and what you are aiming to do).

SUMMARY

We started this chapter by questioning whether Psychology is a force for good and this led into a deep dive into feminist understandings of power. We then thought about **activism** and Psychology and presented queer theory as a tool to interrogate the history of Psychology. In doing this, we looked at aversion therapy and the de/pathologization of homosexuality as key examples throughout the chapter to illustrate our main points. This crucially showed some of the downright awful things Psychology has done and how activists inside and outside of Psychology fought for social change.

One of the main ties between Psychology and **social change** is their lack of inevitability. Psychology isn't inevitably or inherently good and social change is not inevitable or automatically for the better. As you may have guessed it from the chapter, it's all about power and the various forms that takes. Powerful institutions and organizations don't tend to be at the forefront of positive social change because their current circumstances are exactly ripe for them to hold power. They are not therefore going to provide the tools to help change those circumstances. This is what Lorde was explaining. Psychologists can utilize the power of Psychology and the outcomes of this can be for good. Likewise, social change can be good, but it requires a great deal of work often from activists for this to occur. They're just not inevitable, we have to keep resisting rollbacks and working towards further positive social change. We think its therefore important to not just rely on the methods from Psychology, but to borrow from other areas too, which is why **interdisciplinary** ideas like queer theory are so useful. If the master's house won't give us the tools we need, we need to a) diversify our tools, and b) ensure as many people as possible have them too.

QUESTIONS TO CONSIDER

1 What sorts of 'power-to' and 'power-over' forms of power can you identify in your own life? What things make you feel empowered and what forms of structural power have forms of control over you?
2 What are the areas of the world that you think still need substantial social change? What are you passionate about and what can you do to contribute towards this change?
3 How easy do you find it to think queerly? To what extent do you think your own gender and sexual identities assist in this?
4 Can you come up with an example of a underlying norm in the history of Psychology? How might you look at it from a different (queer) angle?

Key resources

Berlant, L., & Warner, M. (1995). Guest column: What does queer theory teach us about X?. *Proceedings of the Modern Language Association, 110*(3), 343–349.

Barker, M.J., & Scheele, J. (2016). *Queer: A graphic history.* Icon Books: London.

Carr, S., & Spandler, H. (2019). Hidden from history? A brief modern history of the psychiatric 'treatment' of lesbian and bisexual women in England. *The Lancet, 6*, 289–290. https://doi.org/10.1016/S2215-0366(19)30059-8

Dickinson, T. (2015). *Curing queers: Mental nurses and their patients, 1935–1974.* Manchester, UK: Manchester University Press.

Davison, K. (in press). *Aversion therapy: Sex, psychiatry and the Cold War.* Cambridge: Cambridge University Press.

Hegarty, P. (2017). *A recent history of lesbian and gay psychology: From homophobia to LGBT.* Routledge: New York.

Hubbard, K.A., & Griffiths, D.A. (2019). Sexual offence, diagnosis and activism: A history of LGBTIQ psychology. *American Psychologist, 74*(8), 940–953. https://doi.org/10.1037/amp0000544

King, M. (2003). Dropping the diagnosis of homosexuality: Did it change the lot of gays and lesbians in Britain? *Australian and New Zealand Journal of Psychiatry, 37*(6), 684–688. https://doi.org/10.1111/j.1440-1614.2003.01275.x

King, M., & Bartlett, A. (1999). British psychiatry and homosexuality. *The British Journal of Psychiatry, 175*(2), 106–113. DOI: 10.1192/bjp.175.2.106

King, M., Smith, G., & Bartlett, A. (2004). Treatments of homosexuality in Britain since the 1950s - an oral history: the experience of professionals. *The British Medical Journal, 328*(7437), 1–3. DOI: 10.1136/bmj.37984.442419.EE

Lorde, A. (2018). *The master's tools will never dismantle the master's house.* Penguin UK.

Minton, H. L. (2002). *Departing from deviance: A history of homosexual rights and emancipatory science in America.* London: University of Chicago Press.

Riggs, D. W., Pearce, R., Pfeffer, C. A., Hines, S., White, F., & Ruspini, E. (2019). Transnormativity in the psy disciplines: Constructing pathology in the Diagnostic and Statistical Manual of Mental Disorders and Standards of Care. *American Psychologist, 74*(8), 912. DOI: 10.1037/amp0000545

Smith, G., Bartlett, A., & King, M. (2004). Treatments of homosexuality in Britain since the 1950s—an oral history: The experience of patients. *British Medical Journal, 328*(7437), 427–429. DOI: 10.1136/bmj.37984.442419.EE

5 | Gender on the Brain

Learning objectives

Study of this chapter will enable you to:

- Expand your understandings of constructionism from Psychology and History to Biology
- Learn more about how key feminist thinkers described sex and gender as social constructions
- Consider how gender differences are often presented as biological and based in the brain and give you some suggestions to question whether that is really the case
- Explore what Psychology has said about LGBTQI people's brains
- Gain Feminist Biology as a critical tool for doing CHIP, providing you with a whole new lens to consider biological approaches to sex and gender

Introduction

In this chapter, we get to what is often thought of as the hard stuff: bodies, brains and biological mechanisms. You could be forgiven for thinking that somehow gender is possible to find in the brain somewhere. Perhaps, once technology hits a particular point we might be able to point to part of it and say, 'Behold, I have found where the brain keeps gender identity!' As we'll discover in this chapter, these ideas are common, often well-intentioned but can often have dangerous implications.

This chapter is all about dismantling the notion that biology and *biological determinism* deliver a simple story free of questions about politics, power, values, and interpretation. Biological determinist perspectives in Psychology have supported scientific racism, ableism, sexism and homophobia in the far and recent past. As Weisstein (1968/1971) noted half a century ago, biological accounts in Psychology can make gender unfair arrangements seem natural (aka legitimate) by attributing gender differences caused by social structures to biological causes. In other words, gender inequality can become seen as automatic, natural and therefore unchangeable by appealing to the *nature* of sexed bodies. A feature of biological *discourses* is that they seem to go without explanation; biological matters are seen as if they were true, have always been true, and will always be true (see Smyth, 2001).

In this chapter we aim to equip you so you can critically engage with sexist claims that use biology as evidence. Biology seems somehow pre-historical, pre-cultural, or pre-political, something 'harder' than a *reflexive* kind of **human science** (Hacking, 1995). But claims about biology and its impact on behaviour are always constructed within particular *socio-historical contexts*: data and findings always require interpretation. The science is not 'found' in the wild, but constructed via technologies, ideologies, and the questions we pose. From this basis we untangle some of the aforementioned key areas from which sexist ideas often emerge, and pay close attention to 'sex differences'. Finally, we explore the importance of considering the implications of so-called biological 'explanations' via LGBTQI brains. What would happen if the goal to 'find' a gene or a brain location which 'caused' gender or sexuality was to be achieved?

Biology is constructed (and so is sex)

We are often given the strong impression that Biology is an infallible science whose 'facts' are fully trustworthy. Unlike reflexive sciences like Psychology, biology seems fully reliable and not liable to influence, right? In this section we are taking you on a quick tour of some of the central *CHIP* related points which put biology on somewhat more shaky ground. It's still people doing the biological science. Here, we outline how biology is historical, the complexity of biological *discourse* and concepts, and show how the often disembodied sense of biology gives this impression.

Indeed, biology seems to be taking over more and more aspects of twentieth-century psychological sciences on an almost daily basis. The 'mind' is out, the 'brain' is in. Neuroscience findings have also become ever-more popular in the media (O'Connor & Joffe, 2013), and laypeople seem more ready to form meaningful social identities from brain differences, a phenomenon called *biosociality* (consider the newish term 'neurotypical' for example). Biological determinist arguments might be circling around your own future career plans right now. In Psychology, career paths are still gendered. Men still seem more likely to be involved in academic research and women in areas of applied Psychology such as Clinical and Educational Psychology. What would you do if someone argued such patterns are *natural*? They might attempt to argue that science requires intelligence and that there are large sex differences in spatial intelligence, so that women can't compete. Indeed, Larry Summers, the president of Harvard University, made a very similar argument in 2005. Such comments inevitably provoke familiar *nature/nurture* debates (as Summers' comments did between cognitive scientists Elizabeth Spelke and Steve Pinker for example, Ruck, 2021). For this reason, we are going to look at recent feminist criticisms of the literature on sex differences in spatial abilities, often thought to be a cognitive ability that explains men's great involvement in science than women's.

The first thing to notice is that 'Biology' (the academic field) is not the same as 'biology' (what our diverse fleshy bodies are, how we experience being those bodies, or how we know the world through being (in) a body. This is similar to how we distinguished types of P/psychology in Chapter 1. Historian of science and cyborg goddess Donna Haraway (1991, p. 132) described the particular version of cold war biology in which feminism grew as dominated by a *gender identity paradigm* made of the 'constructions and meanings and technologies of sex and gender in normalizing, liberal interventionist-therapeutic, empiricist, and functionalist life sciences, principally in the United States, including psychology, psychoanalysis, medicine, biology, and sociology'. This was also the context of Weisstein's (1968/1971) critique, within which *second wave* feminists in Psychology and other disciplines asserted that what seemed to be biological sex was really only socialized *gender* all along (see Unger, 1979 on Psychology).

In Psychology, the rise of 'gender' as a concept resulted in *nature/nurture* debates and our long-standing *interactionism*, which imagines biological 'sex' and social/cultural gender to be separate domains that compete to explain variance or interact to produce the diverse human beings that we are. As ever it is worth looking outside Psychology for *interdisciplinary* feminist insights. Anthropologist Gayle Rubin (1975) coined the term 'sex/gender system', to describe the cultural mechanisms that make gendered people out of sexed bodies. These mechanisms included the ways in which females were domesticated to become women who would be inserted into kinship systems organized by men. Like lesbian theorists such as Adrienne Rich (1980) and Monique Wittig (1980), Rubin called attention to the possibility of interrelated revolutions in kinship, sexual desire and gender oppression that would radically unseat what was later called *heteropatriarchy*. Returning to these women's studies classics will show you the greater influence of *socialist feminism* then than now, and less attention to 'race'. Biology determinist accounts of gender have a history. So does the history of its feminist critics.

Second wave feminist Psychology drew critical attention to gender stereotypes in entirely new ways. Gender stereotypes are sometimes thought of as just beliefs about women's and men's psychological attributes, but have you ever wondered if *parts of the body* are seen through their lenses? Take for instance, cells. In your Biology classes you may learned that the egg waits patiently in a fallopian tube for the sperm cell. The sperm cells are racing against each other for the fittest to win and fertilize the egg. In a classic early study of Biology textbooks, anthropologist Emily Martin (1991) revealed how this aspect of physical 'sex' is made intelligible to Biology students through the lens of gender stereotypes about heterosexual romance. (There is even a memory experiment showing the effect of the gendered script on memory for the Biological details, Bangerter, 2000). Likewise Hankinson Nelson (2017) argues you'll often hear about specific hormones such as testosterone and oestrogen being classified as 'male' or 'female' without qualification, although both are present in women's and men's bodies. Indeed, the occasional Biological Psychology textbook will warn you *against* such simplistic assumptions that all biological entities labelled 'male' (such as XY chromosomes, testosterone, testes, penis, etc.) only exist in men, while those labelled 'female' (such as XX chromosomes, ovaries, a vagina, a clitoris, breast tissues, etc.) only exist in women (Pinel & Barnes, 2022).

In discussions about gender there is often the underlying idea that sex is biological and gender is social. But in reality, sex and gender can't be so easily distinguished. Kit Heyam (2022) explains:

> ...Similarly, why do we think of some sexual characteristics (like genitals and chromosomes) as 'fundamental' parts of sex, which make a difference to how we categorise a person's body, and others (like facial hair and fat distribution) as comparably insignificant? Why so we think of sex as a binary, dividing humans into two clear biological types, when in reality, it's a spectrum, on which comparatively few people tick all of the boxes required to slot neatly into one of those two categories? Why do so many societies still carry out violent, non-consensual and medically unnecessary surgery on intersex children (children whose bodies don't fit clearly into one of the categories we label 'male' and 'female')? The answer to all of those questions is gender – that social constructed idea which carries all of the social baggage we associate with 'male-ness' and 'female-ness'– informs, even *produces*, our ideas about sex.
>
> (p. 6 emphasis original)

Sex is therefore not a simple binary, but the *concept* of binary gender makes it seem like it is (or should be). Indeed, the more Biological advances we have, the more *queer* sexed bodies become (both in the sense of being diverse and of troubling our norms for 'proper' bodies). Why then does sex seen like a simple variable to many? Often one level of physical sex stands in for and signifies 'sex' in its totality. At birth, external genitals seem to 'sex' an infant, while other sex characteristics are usually not considered (e.g. gonads, hormones, chromosomes, genetics, many of which are not simply *binary* in humans). Pioneering social psychologist Suzanne Kessler (1998) first examined how doctors think when an infant is born with genitals that do not allow onlookers an easy binary sex classification. Here doctors re-assure parents that the child has one of two binary *genders* (that can't be seen on the body), and that the genitals can be 'corrected' to fit the right gender. Surgical interventions in such circumstances are common despite the fact they are rarely medically necessary, and are increasingly described as infringing children's human rights (see Hegarty, 2023 for a very quick update). Unsurprisingly, people who believe the core principles of the **gender identity paradigm** – that there are only two sexes or genders, and that biology grounds sex, are also more likely to think those surgeries are good and should not be prohibited by law (Hegarty, Donnelly et al., 2021). Indeed, in UK law, dominant constructions of how people have sex with one another impacted how the law defined what legal sex is and is not (Griffiths & Hubbard, 2022).

Judith Butler (1990, 1993a) made an important intervention in feminist studies that became foundational to both *queer theory* and *trans studies*. Central to this complicated book is the idea that *realness* is never real (no matter how real it feels or how much biological *discourse* is involved). Rather, gender is 'a kind of persistent impersonation that poses as the real' (Butler, 1990, p. viii). This approach allowed Butler to dodge the question of who is or is not a 'real woman' (or a real anything else), and to replace it with questions about when and how the realness of gender is successfully socially constructed, and how it feels when gender performance fails. Butler argues that just as we've worked out gender is constructed, so too is sex.

That's not to say biology isn't relevant to gender. As Barker and Scheele (2016, see also 2019) explain, gender is biopsychosocial. This combines biological, psychological and social aspects together, because they can't really be teased apart anyway. They're all interactive and interweaved in complex ways to produce how we understand our gendered selves. Other more biologically inclined feminists have likewise supported the breaking down of the sex/gender distinction that was so central to second wave feminism. Biologist Anne Fausto-Sterling (2012) challenged this idea of a clear distinction between biological understandings of sex and social understandings of gender by pointing out how there is so much diversity in all levels of biology. Likewise, Cordelia Fine (2010) argued against biological theories that claim that our gender roles aren't 'hard wired' into our brains. She argues that they become engrained in our brains by the repetition of doing them.

The repetition of norms, often at the implicit level of meaning, is key to Butler's explanation of how some things come to appear as biological sex that are 'real' and outside *social construction*. Butler (1993a) used the metaphor of 'citing' norms to explain this.

So it's the social world that, over time, can impact our brains rather than the other way around: our habits change our neural connections over time. And the more primed people are to what gender 'ought to be', the more stereotyped their attitudes and behaviour can become. Recently, Amanda Swarr (2023) has taken this point literally, and shown how the common idea among Western biologists that African women are particularly likely to have intersex variations rests on a chain of citations to a single master's thesis, conducted during the apartheid era, that did not have enough data to evidence the case one way or the other. Examples like Swarr's point out how the social world of academic research creates biological sex differences, that there is more than one way to think about bodily variation, and that the differences between them matter.

Looking closely at gender differences

In this section, we will take this approach to tackling some of the central ways that men have been theorized to be superior to women in Cognitive Psychology. As embodiment theorists argue, Western Philosophy and Biology have tended to associate women with the weaknesses of the body and men with the powers of reason (Rooney, 1991; Grosz, 1994). A good example of this conflation, which feminist psychologists Mary Brown Parlee (1973) challenged early on is the persist literature associating the menstrual cycle with irrationality. But here we take aim at sex differences in spatial ability, thought to explain why men do science more than women do.

In 1971, Roger Shepard and Jacqueline Metzler (1971) introduced the topic of mental rotation to Psychology in a pivotal experiment. Eight male participants looked at pairs of 2-D images which each represented 3-D block figures rotated by different angles.

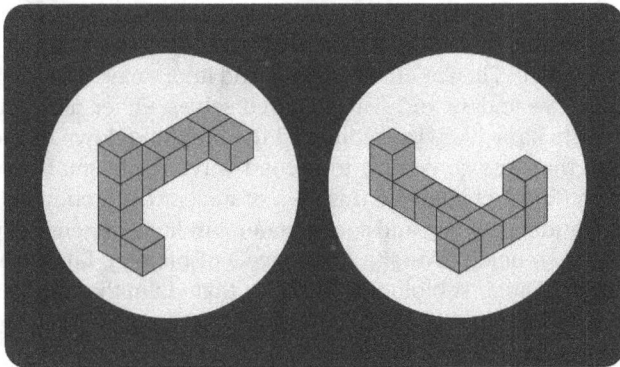

When asked to verify if the figures were the same, the participants' reaction times were strongly correlated with the size of the angle of rotation between the two figures. This result suggested that participants relied on a process of 'mental rotation' to answer the questions within the experiment. The experiment kicked off an ongoing debate about whether Cognitive Psychology needs to account for analogue mental imagery processes like mental rotation or whether other computational explanations are sufficient.

The next development in the story is Vandenberg and Kuse's (1978) Mental Rotation Test (hereafter MRT) of individual differences in mental rotation ability. When psychologists shift from the lab to the field of measuring individual differences, they often lose sight of the dependence of concepts on the methods used to operationalize them. The meaning of concepts can 'creep' as the methods used to study them change for social reasons (such as convenient mass testing). The MRT used abstract block stimuli as Shepard and Metzler (1971) had done. However, each MRT item showed a target block and four figures including 'true' rotations and two incorrect 'foils'. Test-takers had to detect the right answers and avoid the foils. But did this test measure 'mental rotation' as Shepard and Metzler had defined it, or had the concept crept?

The mental imagery debate took shape in Cognitive Psychology during the period of influence of second wave feminism. In the 1970s, *empirical feminists* pored through the empirical literature to determine which purported psychological sex differences were real and which were only *textbook myths*.

Those reviews conceded that men and boys did outperform women and girls in spatial ability tests (see also Hyde, 1981; Maccoby & Jacklin, 1974). However, does the *measure* matter? And if so, how? An early meta-analysis found that gender differences measured by Vandenberg and Kuse (1978) MRT were larger than differences in mental rotation assessed by other tests, which were larger than gender differences measured by other tests of spatial ability (e.g., Linn & Petersen, 1985, pp. 1487–1488).

Bartlett and Camba (2023) drew together a number of innovative pieces of research that inform this question. First, girls and boys agree that boys are more familiar with the abstract blocks used in mental rotation tasks than girls are (Ruthsatz et al., 2017). In fact, girls and boys were found to perform equally well on tests of mental rotation when items were introduced as assessing 'artistic abilities' rather than 'spatial imagery' (Neuburger et al., 2015). Men may also complete the MRT using strategies to detect the 'foils' without mentally rotating the figures at all. And when women are taught the same strategies, their performance on the MRT increases (Boone & Hegarty, 2017; Hegarty, 2018 – this isn't Peter's work but that of his sister Mary!). Men and boys not only bring more embodied familiarity with the stimuli and their construction as 'scientific' to the MRT, they also bring learned strategies of how to complete MRT items without having to mentally rotate anything.

As Bartlett and Camba (2023) note, the fact that the MRT shows a large gender difference is one of the reasons why it has become popular. They point to several lines of abandoned research to support their argument. When Peters et al. (1995) explored an extension of the test which required mental rotation in different axes, the test got harder and gender difference got smaller. As the researchers could not explain why the gender differences were decreasing, they abandoned this line of research! An unpublished meta-analysis of *unpublished* studies on the MRT found small gender differences and went largely uncited (Druva-Roush & Wu, 1989). Clinching the argument, test manuals for the Vandenberg and Kuse (1978) MRT argue that *because* it yields a gender difference, it must be valid test of spatial abilities!

Critically then, 'spatial ability' (in general) is not the same thing as 'mental rotation ability' (specifically) which is not the same thing as 'scores on the MRT' (in particular). This distinction is not purely 'academic'. Bartlett and Camba (2023) note that many psychologists argue that enhancing the educational pipeline of talented scientists might require assessing spatial abilities early in life and the Vandenberg and Kuse (1978) test has become the tool for this job; a 'gold standard' measure of spatial abilities. Its results create sex differences in terms of who does or does not get educational advantages, a 'looping effect' (Hacking, 1995) if ever we saw one.

Bartlett and Camba's (2023) analysis shows a number of conceptual moves you might make around psychological attributes used to justify treating groups differently. Consider (1) the stubborn particulars (Cherry, 1995) of how the concept was made up in a particular time and place; (2) 'concept creep' as the method and goals of research expanded; (3) group differences which became *intrinsic* to the concept's meaning (but seem to be the 'effects' it 'reveals');

and (4) how concepts create methodological norms about the right and wrong way to study them. *Empiricist*, *standpoint* and *postmodern feminist epistemologies* can all be useful in these contexts where scientific practices construct psychological concepts and gender differences can be an effect of gendered academic cultures and the larger dominant patriarchal culture.

Another area which is often highlighted as a biological difference between women and men is around 'biological clocks' and having children. The topic of 'instincts' takes us back to Darwinism. From the 1970s onwards Darwinism underpinned various reactions to second wave feminism in popular discourse and academic Psychology. Reversing the feminist political claim that a woman can determine what happens to her own body, 1970s' sociobiology emphasized how the 'whispering within' (Barash, 1979) of 'selfish genes' (Dawkins, 1976) determined gender differences in sexuality, reproduction and aggression (see Wilson, 1975 for the classic statement). Sociobiology didn't 'stick' with Psychology in the 1970s, but the Evolutionary Psychology of the 1990s emerged as an (apparently) new hot theory that served to popularize Psychology in new ways with the larger public, often by reifying gender stereotypes (Cassidy, 2006; McCaughey, 2012). For example, evolutionary theories of sex differences in 'mating preferences' were a staple of British lads mags which dominated the market for men's magazines throughout the 1990s and 2000s (see Gill, 2003). It's basic philosophy is that all human behaviours have a foundation in 'survival of the fittest' frameworks (Hankinson Nelson, 2017). Darwinism has long horrified people of conscience – from the nineteenth century to twenty-first-century feminists – because of its tendency to legitimize actions that can be attributed to natural 'adapted' causes, including horrific forms of human aggression. In recent decades, the argument that human men are evolved to commit rape has been a boundary object in debates between evolutionary and feminist psychologists (Ruck, 2021).

LGBTQI brains

When technologies advanced and neuroscience became more prominent, the study of sex differences in brain structure, and then sexuality differences, received a lot of attention. It was believed these studying LGBTQI people could answer *nature/nurture* questions about gender identity (of which sexual orientation was sometimes presumed to be a part, and sometimes treated as a separate thing). The people targeted by this research derived little benefit from it. Here, we explore some conceptual implications of the history of the search to find the key to sexuality in Biology.

Following the first decade of the HIV/AIDS pandemic in the 1980s, gay men and their rights to sexual expression became legitimate subjects of mainstream conversation. Hitherto, biological studies on homosexuality had tended to presume that gay men (and lesbians, who got less attention, by far) were abnormal creatures, whose biology was defined by an improper deficiency of this or an excess of the other hormone (Sedgwick, 1990). A very different narrative emerged in the early 1990s anchored by the work of neuroanatomist Simon LeVay (1991) and geneticist Dean Hamer (Hamer et al., 1993). The former claimed to have found a portion of the anterior hypothalamus that was different in size between gay and straight men and suggested it was a biological determinant of sexual orientation. The latter claimed to have isolated a gene on the X-chromosome that varied between gay and straight men, suggesting that male homosexuality was inherited from one's mother. Now it seemed, Biology could support the narrative that homosexuality (at least male homosexuality) was biologically fixed and determined. In the United States where collective anti-gay action was often organized by Christian groups who described homosexuality as a moral sin or a choice, where sex between men was subject to heightened scrutiny because of HIV, and courts upheld states' sodomy laws criminalizing sex between two men (or women), biological determinism began to seem like a very gay-friendly narrative.

Hamer and LeVay became openly gay public scientists who appealed to the liberal mainstream, showing how far acceptance had moved since the closeted appearance of 'Dr Anonymous' at the APA in 1973. Their research paradigms were copied in other domains – another part of the anterior hypothalamus distinguished *trans* women from *cisgender* men, suggesting a biological basis of gender identity (Zhou et al., 1995). (Yes, somebody did really claim that they found gender identity in the brain!) Lawyers explored the possibility of using their science in court to support claims for lesbian/gay rights (Halley, 1994). Social psychologists began to describe how biological *essentialist* arguments might be responsible for making heterosexual people less homophobic in their attitudes (see Hegarty, 2020).

This sounded really positive to a certain extent. But biological explanations for identities that remain subject to stigma can also lead to fantasies of biological 'solutions' particularly when the biological pathways to those identities are littered with signs that say 'deficiency' 'abnormal' and 'excessive'. This is not as far-fetched as you might think; LeVay (1996) seemed enthusiastic about a new form of 'eugenics by choice' allowing women to selectively abort a foetus if it proved to have biological markers of homosexuality. This sinister implication was picked up far more in the gay press than in the mainstream press in the USA (Conrad & Markens, 2001).

Peter has repeatedly argued that this was not a moment when 'Biology made people gay friendly' but when the public were becoming more gay-friendly and biologists used that to their own advantage. He came out in the USA at this time, while doing his PhD and noticed the irony between enthusiasm for the biological determinist narratives in a research-intensive heteronormative university context versus the apathy about it in the queer community where he was living. He and others who conducted Social Psychology studies showed that this biological research on its own did very little to turn homophobic people gay-friendly (Hegarty, 2020). The research was also a fad. If biological *essentialism* about male sexuality was the hot topic in LGBTQ Biology in the 1990s, it was replaced by a focus on the fluidity, or flexibility, of women's sexual orientation in the 2000s, coinciding with Biological Psychology research on the question of whether bisexual people existed or not (Hegarty, 2018).

One area where dubious claims about the biological basis of sexual orientation has long been made is in regard to people with intersex variations. This interest has a long history. In 1955, when psychologist John Money first defined the psychological concept of gender identity/role, he included eroticism within the range of gender role behaviours that were thought to signify an underlying gender role. He came up with that definition in the context of the clinical protocols for the management of children born with intersex variations that Suzanne Kessler (1990) studied three decades later. Money's framework, which reiterated the assumption that gender identity was binary, even when 'sex' gave it only weak support, influenced academic and popular Psychology profoundly. This influence was amplified particularly after the publication of Money and Ehrhardt's (1972) *Man and woman, Boy and girl* which summarized (sometimes untruthfully) the effects of clinical interventions, assigning gender to people born with intersex characteristic (see Morland, 2015 for an excellent analysis of Money's psychological concepts).

It is no exaggeration to say that intersex and trans folk were largely researched in Psychology from the late 1960s onward to satisfy scientific curiosity about **nature/nurture** questions about gender identity, sexuality and other aspects of human psychology. But trans and intersex folks had virtually no hand in shaping that research or derived any benefit from it. It spoke for rather than to them, largely presuming that they never could (or should) speak for themselves (see Alcoff, 1991). Little research took a non-pathological approach to children who expressed gender identities other than those assigned at birth, and such affirmative research was rarely cited (Ansara & Hegarty, 2012). An upswing in research on trans and non -binary populations, increasingly by trans and non-binary psychologists in the early twenty-first century presented a key moment where LGB Psychology became LGBT Psychology. The American Psychological Association (APA) 2009 Task Force report on gender identity and gender variance representing the culmination of work within APA that aimed to recognize the psychological aspects of trans folks' lives. Although it remained torn between psychiatric and social identity paradigms of understanding of trans people and did not address intersex, the report sedimented the fact that what had once been 'lesbian and gay psychology' was now quite firmly LGBT (Hegarty, 2017).

Around 2014, decades of trans **activism** began to pay off with what historian Susan Stryker described a 'tipping point' in the recognition of trans people (2017).This moment followed the DSM formally depathologizing trans identity by dropping the category of 'gender identity disorder' in favour of 'gender dysphoria' in 2013. The aim of this change was to shift attention away from pathologizing gender diversity *per se*, and to target instead distress that is the result of dysphoria (see Riggs et al., 2019 for a longer history of these psychiatric classifications related to gender, and the norms that they leave in place). However, research on trans populations has remained focused on identity issues, and less attention has been paid to social **contexts** or on positive aspects of mental health (Moradi et al., 2016).

Box 5.1: Fact-check your History of Psychology

Psychologists' output of trans-related research continues to accelerate but let's explore this in a bit more depth. Figure 1 shows the results of a search that Peter conducted on 15 February 2023 using APA's archive *PsycInfo*. It shows the proportion of peer reviewed articles written in English in each year from 1991–2021 that are tagged by *Psycinfo's* own tag 'transgender or transsexual or transexual or gender variant or gender non-conforming'. As you might expect, given the wide range of fascinating and important topics that psychologists could study, the percentage of studies so tagged in *Psycinfo* is small, and always below 1 per cent. Nonetheless, there has been a swift and recent rise in attention trans people and their psychologies, and the change is accelerating. In 1991, only 7 articles were so tagged, amounting to 0.02 per cent of the literature archived on *Psycinfo* in that year. By 2021, 1019 articles were so tagged, and the proportion had risen to 0.69 per cent.

It is possible to make claims that there is either (1) no research on a topic, or (2) lots of research on a topic. Often both are used to argue for more research! You might sometimes hear statements like: 'research has quadrupled in this area in the past decade'. When critically evaluating such claims it's important to draw a distinction between raw numbers of publications and proportions of publications in a field. Over historical time, scientific publications overall are growing and diversifying in Psychology and elsewhere. For example this search found a total of 35,149 *Psycinfo* articles for 1991, but 148,082 for 2021 – more than four times as much. So our claim that research on

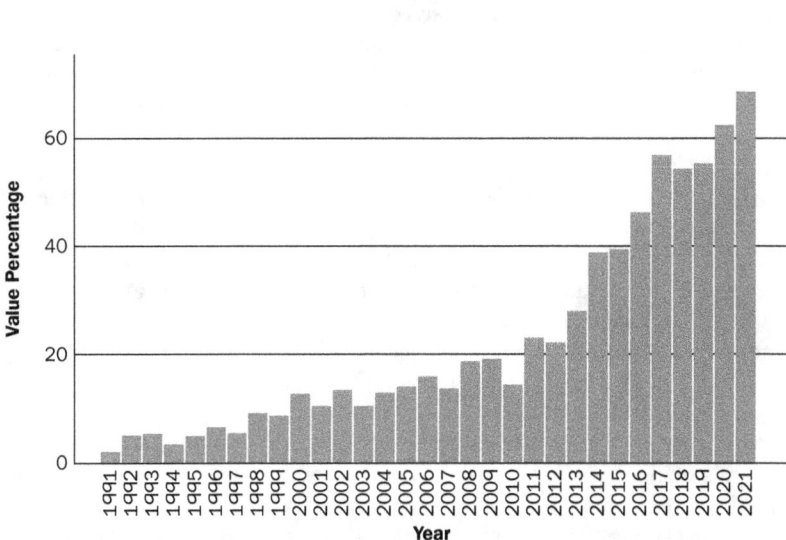

Figure 5.2: The percentage of trans-related literature found in 1 per cent of Psych journals from 1991–2021

transgender and non-binary folk is growing is based on the (harder) criterion or proportions rather than the (softer) criterion or raw counts of articles.

Through this example, we have just introduced you to the field of **scientometrics**, which is about the measurement and quantitative analysis of scientific and other academic literatures, science communication and science policy. Your Psychology degree prepares you to look at the research literature in quantitative ways like this more than other degree programmes do. It's a powerful tool to tease apart different narratives about historical change. A person could make spurious claims about historical growth in research interest in a topic if the raw numbers of research papers are going up but they neglect to look at proportions. Just like 'mental rotation' there might be feminist stakes in cleaving apart meanings of 'growth in the research literature'. To go further, look at **scientometric** research on bias against gender bias research (Cislak et al., 2018), the impact of editors' race on the publication of race-related research (Roberts et al., 2020), or **cisgenderism** (Ansara & Hegarty, 2012).

The growing recognition of trans and nonbinary people in Psychology nonetheless represents a historical conceptual shift. The assumptions that gender is unambiguously grounded in physical sex characteristics which are simply binary is now challenged. Here in the UK, this cultural shift is evident in society. The 2004 Gender Recognition Act in the UK allowed some trans people to change their legal gender revising earlier marriage law from the late 1960s that had determined that physical sex characteristics defined legal gender in the UK (Griffiths & Hubbard, 2022). In the first research on transphobia in Europe, Peter and Nicola Tee described the beliefs and attitudes that predicted students' endorsement or opposition of those new trans rights (Tee & Hegarty, 2006).

Sex no longer seems like the simple binary 'biological basis' of gender in the way that it once was, and the norms of talking about other people's genders are thankfully shifting. More recently, neuroscientist Daphna Joel has argued that there is simply no such thing as the 'male' brain and 'female' brain (2016). With colleagues, she has also argued against the idea of a gender binary utilizing psychological research as well neuroscience and neuroendocrinology (Hyde et al., 2019). The question of what trans-inclusive neuroscience might be is currently being vigorously debated.

Greater recognition of the reality and possibility of non-binary gender identification is evident on campuses and elsewhere. Just as an early generation of feminists successfully shifted the field's authors way from using 'he' and 'man' to refer to everyone (Gannon et al., 1992), the current APA publication manual encourages authors to clarify if participants are **trans** or **cisgender** rather than assuming that everyone has a cisgender identity (American Psychological

Association, 2020; see Ansara & Hegarty, 2013 on these intersecting histories). The APA also provide guidelines on terms including two-spirit and gender non-conforming, and explain how it's best practice to use the terms people use to describe their own genders. This development is obviously resonant with feminist *empiricism* (reform the science), *standpoint feminism* (use the subordinate group's reality) and feminist *postmodernism* (take seriously the idea that language constructs reality).

Despite such positive shifts however, trans people's rights have been increasingly targeted in UK media and elsewhere, being described as a threat to social order. We are living and writing this book in 2023 in a national context where contemporary authors write of 'a rift between trans inclusive and gender critical feminists in the UK' (Shaw, 2023, p. 1) and mainstream media refer to a 'transgender debate' which often refers to the question of whether trans people should or should not be allowed to be themselves and enjoy civil rights (see also Chapter 1). Around the world, populist leaders are increasingly targeting LGBT groups, particularly trans people, to single out a 'scapegoat' to be hated in political *discourse*. In the United States alone there were hundreds of new anti-LGBT laws in 2023.

It does sound nice and neutral, to be having a 'debate,' doesn't it? It sounds narrow-minded and authoritarian to say any debate shouldn't be happening in academia. But cisgender readers of this book might want to remember that insisting that we must have a 'debate' about some people's lives can also be an authoritarian move. (Consider debates such as 'the Irish question' in nineteenth-century Britain, 'the Jewish question' in nineteenth-century Germany or, or E.G. Boring's framing of 'the woman question' in mid-twentieth century Psychology.) If you are required to be the topic of other people's debates, and your rights are on the line, you won't be feeling much freedom. As Shon Faye has articulated (2022), trans liberation doesn't just benefit trans people – it offers a more free and joyous world for everyone.

TOOL 4: Feminist Biology

Feminist Biology, and/or *feminist Neuroscience*, is focused on removing gender inequality from research practice including *androcentrism*, and aims to highlight the role of social factors in the production of biological/neuroscientific knowledge (see Bluhm, Maibom & Jacobson, 2012; Schmitz & Höppner, 2014). In staking a claim on the ways to do Biology and Neuroscience from a feminist perspective, we are arguing that it is possible to not throw the baby out with bathwater when it comes to criticizing biological approaches to understanding and exploring gender.

Rather unsurprisingly, criticisms within Biology around its gendered practice and assumptions came to the fore in the 1980s as *second wave* feminism abounded. Ruth Bleier wrote *Science and Gender: A Critique of Biology and Its Theories on Women* ([1984] 1997) which tackled Biological ideas of women's inferiority and how this could be 'explained' via biology. Four years later, Ruth Hubbard (no relation to our Katherine as far as we're aware!) wrote a paper in feminist journal *Hypatia*, 'Science, facts and feminism' (Hubbard, 1988). The abstract for which is:

Feminists acknowledge that making science is a social process and that scientific laws and the "facts" of science reflect the interests of the university-educated, economically privileged, predominantly white men who have produced them. We also recognize that knowledge about nature is created by an interplay between objectivity and subjectivity, but we often do not credit sufficiently the ways women's traditional activities in home, garden, and sickroom have contributed to understanding nature.

Soon after, in 1990 she also wrote *The Politics of Women's Biology* and explicitly discussed how the anti-war sentiments and the women's rights movements influenced her thinking from the 1960s. She remained politically active and vocal against sociobiological accounts of gender and also cautioned against the popular goal to identity genes to explain all facets of human behaviour. Overall, she argued that politics seem to vanish in the sciences yet women's biology is profoundly political (Hubbard, 2001).

Here, we want to go into a bit more detail about one key feminist biologist who applied her thinking to a key study in Psychology. In *Primate Visions: Gender, Race, and Nature in the World of Modern Science* (1989) Donna Haraway (who we first introduced in Chapter 2) wrote about the history of animal research in the twentieth-century USA, including that of psychologist Harry Harlow (1905–1981).

Harlow is best remembered for research showing the importance of touch (an operational definition of 'maternal love' or even 'love'). In a very famous line of laboratory experiments, he startled baby rhesus monkeys with diverse stimuli, and allowed them to run to one of two dummy 'mothers' (wire frames with weird fake monkey faces). The baby monkeys consistently ran to the 'mother' covered in cloth with no food rather than the one that offered food but wasn't snuggly. Harlow argued (as you may have read in your textbook) that the experiment exemplified the natural basis of love among rhesus monkeys, and by analogy, in humans as well. Harlow achieved control over the meaning of 'love' through experimental storytelling, by directly comparing the relationship between lab-locked baby monkeys and wire frames, and the nature of human love, violence and despair.

An irony of Harlow's work – which is typical of the primatologists in Haraway's history – is that while he exerted an almost sadistic control over his primate subjects, he also regarded them with affection. As Harlow's biographer Deborah Blum (2002) narrates it, Harlow was also ironically a neglectful husband who married three times (including marrying the psychologist Clara Mears twice). He chose to spend his time studying 'love' in the laboratory, rather than experiencing it at home.

Harlow's later work took quite sinister turns that may merit a content warning. His experimental apparatus expanded to include a device which he jokingly referred to as the 'rape rack' on which female monkeys were forcibly impregnated and a 'well of despair' in which monkeys were isolated from birth, to model the onset of depression. Haraway (1989) interprets the sadism of Harlow's apparatus not as an exception to patriarchal science, but as a typical feature of male primatologists' *partial perspectives* in this era of the *gender identity paradigm*. By controlling the monkeys, making them signify human mothers and placing his 'discovery' at the centre of the narrative, he renders himself the all-powerful hero in a way that is typical of male scientists. Harlow's work was seen as humanist, for demonstrating the importance of motherly love. But his later even more cruel research became an early target of the animal rights movement.

Rather than 'cancelling' it because it projects capitalist, colonial, racist, sexist or sadistic values, Haraway stayed with Harlow's narrative to learn from it. You could describe her reading as a reparative one that assumes that, whatever its flaws, there is some merit in every position, particularly one with which you disagree. Haraway emphasized Harlow's light-hearted, often jokey style of research writing, noticing the meaningful relationship between what Harlow said, and how he said it. For Haraway, this jokey style is an advantage. Unlike the textbook construction of Biology as a singular truth that does not need to be tied to evidence, Harlow's story-telling does not convince us that it is the only reading of events – it is open to critique and to counter-narrative. Haraway concludes that joking is a 'reading strategy' that takes the scientists seriously as one set of actors in the story, but not the only one. Indeed humour is and 'the only available way to stay in the story' (Haraway, 1989, pp. 242–3).

There are many ways that feminists have grappled with biology and/or neuroscience, and several have taken a *CHIP* perspective. Nora Ruck has done this around the construction of scientific boundaries in Evolutionary Psychology (2016) and around the concept of there being a 'beauty' gene (2013). Natasha

Bharj called attention to the naturalization of the orientalist concept of the harem in western primate studies and Evolutionary Psychology (Bharj & Hegarty, 2015). Likewise, Victoria Pitts-Taylor (2015) brought a feminist eye to the contemporary science of the mirror neuron. She urges social scientists to engage neuroscience, but to do so in a way that is watchful for assumptions about embodiment and socialization that are baked into narratives about how the mirror neuron system recognizes others. We've also already briefly explored the work of Anne Fausto-Sterling and Cordelia Fine in this chapter, and in Chapter 2 we also explored how physicist Evelynn Hammonds used concept of the Black (w)holes to explain with the ways that Black women's sexuality is represented as a 'void' or empty space that is simultaneously exposed and invisible (1994).

How might we *use* Feminist Biology as a tool to study the history of Psychology?

1 **Take a moment to reflect on what you have been told or assumed about biology and gender.** What are the things you've taken for granted? (What surprised you in this chapter?)

2 **Remember and maintain what you've already learned about textbook myths** (Chapter 3) **and Feminist Science Studies** (Chapter 2). These are highly related and can help in dismantling the ideologies which underpin science and its presentation.

3 **Ask 'what does this actually show'?** It's easy to get swept up in the cool technology and findings of bio/neuro studies. But what is actually shown in the data and what are the authors inferring from that? (E.g. MRIs don't prove brain areas are *doing* the task the person is doing at the time, they show blood flow not 'neurons firing'.) (Keep an eye out for the dead salmon coming in the next chapter.)

4 **Question and consider if there are any underlying ideologies, metaphors or applications to human behaviour.** Be critical of these and question how and when animal studies or particular psychological tests are argued to show us something about humans. (These are often around legitimizing a normative way of being, such as heterosexuality, and are assumed in the analogy making across species, and we forget the super varied ways some species live.)

5 **Consider using scientometrics.** As a method this can really help reveal the patterns of scientific thinking about a topic, letting you be a *feminist empiricist* while also making critical historical claims about academic cultures. (How and when are particular topics more or less popular? How do social events shift scientific focus?)

6 **Read. Read. Read.** Engage with the array of great Feminist Biological and Neuroscientific work that is out there. (Find your Feminist Biological heroes!)

SUMMARY

Overall, this chapter has taken aim at Biological understandings of gender in Psychology. In doing so, we are not intending to say that biology has nothing to do with gender. Instead, we are cautioning against what can be simple, neat and dangerously deterministic narratives that are often the loudest stories coming out of the biological sciences. We encourage you to view 'Biology' and 'biology' as distinct, just as 'Psychology' and 'psychology' are. That is the way to keep in mind how science takes place embedded within social, socioeconomic and political context, that science finds its subjects in a history created by colonialism and capitalism, and that scientific authors make meaning by telling stories imbued with ideology.

Our goal here was to explain how sex is not some sort of biological precursor to gender, but rather how understandings of gender have greatly shaped and informed how scientists in Biology, Medicine and Psychology have made sense of sex (and continue to do so). We explored the concept of spatial skills as a key area where sex differences have been claimed to be found and exposed some of the nuances within that. And finally, we've explored how LGBTQI brains have been researched, how this has changed over time, and the current *context* of such thinking. In all we argued that Biology is like Psychology in that ideologies around gender are implicated in research in sometimes subtle but impactful ways. The counter point here, and the Tool supplied, is therefore to use the insight that Biology provides in positive ways from a feminist standpoint and remain cautious and critical of assumptions around the value-free or objective nature of Biology.

QUESTIONS TO CONSIDER

1 What are the main essentialist or Biological deterministic claims you hear most in regards to gender?
2 Can you think of any conflicts between biological approaches and feminist thinking? To what extent do you think they are fully compatible?
3 What do you think are the benefits of understanding gender as biopsychosocial?
4 In what ways do you think nature/nurture debates and realist/constructionist perspectives are present in thinking about the biological basis of gender?
5 In your opinion what are the implications of thinking about gender from a solely biological perspective and a solely social perspective?

Key resources

Barker, M.J. & Scheele, J. (2019). *Gender: A graphic guide*. London: Icon Books.

Fausto-Sterling, A. (2012). *Sex/gender: Biology in a social world*. London: Routledge.

Faye, S. (2022). *The trans-gender issue: An argument for justice*. London: Verso Books.

Fine, C. (2010). *Delusions of gender. How our minds, society, and neurosexism create difference*. New York: WW Norton & Company.

Hankinson Nelson, L. (2017) *Biology and feminism: A philosophical introduction*. Cambridge: Cambridge University Press.

Haraway, D. (1989). *Primate visions: Gender, race, and nature in the world of modern science*. New York: Psychology Press.

Hegarty, P. (2017). *A recent history of lesbian and gay psychology: From homophobia to LGBT*. New York: Routledge.

Hubbard, R. (2001). Science and science criticism. In Lederman, M. & Bartsch, I. (Eds.) *The Gender and Science Reader* (pp. 49–51). London: Routledge.

Hyde, J. S., Bigler, R. S., Joel, D., Tate, C. C., & van Anders, S. M. (2019). The future of sex and gender in psychology: Five challenges to the gender binary. *American Psychologist, 74*(2), 171–193. https://doi.org/10.1037/amp0000307

Joel, D. (2016). VIII. Captured in terminology: Sex, sex categories, and sex differences. *Feminism & Psychology, 26*(3), 335–345. https://doi.org/10.1177/0959353516645367

Psychology's Feminist Voices Video Series Gender Matters. https://feministvoices.com/projects/gender-based-analysis (Video 2 discusses sex vs gender distinctions)

Ruck, N. (2021). Public sciences, public enemies. Boundary work and cultural hegemony in public controversies between evolutionists and feminists. *Social and Personality Psychology Compass, 15*(3), e12582. https://doi.org/10.1111/spc3.12582

6 CHIP in the present

Learning objectives

Study of this chapter will enable you to:

- Bring what you've learned so far about history to the present
- Consider central issues for contemporary Psychology – including replication and Open Science – and meet some of the feminists working in the field right now
- Recognize how when we do research it can often bring up all sorts of emotions – and how that can be a good thing
- Reflect on your own journeys of coming to CHIP and read about our experiences
- Gain Your Lived Experience as a critical tool for doing CHIP, helping you recognize the value of your own embodied perspective and what you bring to your studies that is unique

---

Introduction

It might initially look a little odd to be considering history in the present. Surely it's all about the past? While History (the discipline) tends to take the past as its subject matter, history is always being made in the here and now. By the time this sentence is done, writing it will be in the past. By the time you read this, it will have been written quite a while ago. If you're finding this book in a dinky old second hand shop in 2076, it was over half a century ago. Some historians do pay particular attention to more recent histories and it's generally agreed that it's really challenging to do history when we're still sort of living in it. Another challenge of more recent histories is that the over-production of digital documents in the age of computers, the internet and social media has changed the rules of history. The past does not really 'decay' like it once did and we have much more text available about very recent history that it is possible to analyse (Hoskins, 2013). Usually, time and space away from something often allow for greater perspective, but that's not to say that considerations and reflections *at the time* aren't important. This sense of what things looks like right now and our reflections in the present on how things feel, are the main focus of this chapter.

In this chapter we're considering the state of Psychology in the present and how emotions, identities and perspectives come into play. In Chapter 1, the very first map key/legend we gave was that 'History is Made Up'. Here, we explained the interpretive nature of history (and how that *subjectivity* is not necessarily a bad thing). We outlined how history depends on what is *able* to be said and by *whom* (which is linked to the power that they hold) and that it's written in stories, and based on the perspective and interest of the historian. Historians, psychologists and biologists are led, after all, by the questions we find interesting, personally pertinent, and feasible to study in particular contexts. We all have beliefs, attitudes and investments in what we research – we all have a perspective or a 'lens' through which we are looking at the world and constraints on how we do our research within our socio-historical contexts.

In the first section we're going to consider a current issue in Psychology that is worth taking into consideration: the replication crisis. Second, we think about what it's like to be a feminist in Psychology at the moment. These sections are really complimented by Box 6.1 which is a little mini interview with Dr Sarah Marks who is a historian-of-psychological-science-superstar. Box 6.2 provides a key resource and case study about feminist historical practice in the present: Psychology's Feminist Voices. After this, we delve into the emotional aspects of historical work more and consider how doing history makes us feel, and vice versa, how feelings can also lead us to doing history. This leads to the next section in which we both provide an account of how we first came to do *CHIP* research projects.

This all leads to the final tool in the book: your own lived experience. By reflecting on our own experiences, identities and perspectives we hope to show how your own lived experience can also inform the kinds of CHIP questions you want to ask. This results in you being fully ready to embark on the final chapter, which will explain in more detail a) how to compile your own tool kit, and b) how we would advise you to do your own CHIP projects!

A present crisis

In 2011 a Dutch social psychologist (previously professor), Diederik Staupel, was suspended for manipulating and fabricating his data. To date, over 50 of his publications have been retracted, creating considerable damage to the reputation of Social Psychology and the lives of many people (especially students and junior colleagues) who had worked with him. It was also around this time that a number of other publications demonstrated a serious unease around the reliability of data in Psychology. For example, one article showed that questionable research practices, used knowingly by Bem (2011) in his experiments, could routinely be used by psychologists in favour of any impossible hypothesis (Simmons, Nelson & Simonsohn, 2011). Simmons et al. (2011) argued that while Psychology has collectively agreed that 5 per cent is the acceptable level of a false positive in statistical analysis (which is where our $<.0.05$ level of statistical significance comes from), researchers still had a wide degree of freedom in data interpretation allowing the *production* of statistically significant findings – choosing which groups to compare, what variables to transform, when to stop collecting data, etc. But this confusion of hypothesis-testing and exploration meant that researchers were likely to come across more false negatives. They explained:

> This exploratory behavior is not the by-product of malicious intent, but rather the result of two factors: (a) ambiguity in how best to make these decisions and (b) the researcher's desire to find a statistically significant result.

The following year, even more fraud cases became evident. Uri Simonsohn was named the 'data detective' (Yong, 2012). Similarly, a survey of over 2000 psychologists showed psychologists routinely engaged in questionable research practices (John, Loewenstein & Prelec, 2012). In all, Psychology came under increasing scrutiny and concerns developed swiftly as to how reliable data really was.

Even neurological methods, ones that we might often think of as more 'reliable' and more 'objective' were not immune. One great example of this showed how the questionable research practice of testing a large number of comparisons in search of statistically significant effects could even materialize fMRI evidence of brain activity in a dead salmon (Bennett, Baird, Miller and Wolford, 2010).

Indeed, many of neuroscientists' published correlations about brain activity were suspiciously high, suggesting a publication bias in favour of positive results (and fishing in the data to find them). Psychology researchers and journals appeared to have invested in junk science, whose illusory value had been exposed along with the publish-or-perish culture that had given rise to perverse incentives to continually publish statistically significant results rather than honest and complete accounts of research data. Indeed, the replicability of Simon LeVay's neuroscience research on the 'gay brain' was itself by this time a case in point (see Byne et al., 2001).

In Social Psychology, many celebrated counter-intuitive 'effects' were found to be less-replicable than advertised, casting doubt on the scientific standing of the researchers who had built their reputations around them. Amy Cuddy had achieved considerable fame for a TED talk describing her research on the 'power pose,' a stance which was described as increasing your testosterone, and making you feel powerful and take risks. This was not found to be possible to fully replicate (e.g. see Garrison Tang & Schmeichel, 2016). As such high-profile examples indicated, and as Pettit (2024) astutely notes, psychologists were realizing the shortcomings of investing in methods that allow you to progress swiftly without having to think too much about it or pause to reflect on what was occurring (or not occurring) in data.

The replicability of psychological science was thrown into further doubt when the new Open Science Collaboration (2015) published a test of the replicability of 100 'effects' reported in Psychology's top peer-reviewed journals. Whilst 97 per cent of the original publications reported significant results, only 36 per cent of replications had significant results, and the statistical effect sizes in the replication studies were about half of what they had been in the original published works. The *open science* movement became the dominant response to this 'replication' 'replicability' or 'reproducibility' crisis. Open science practices include: (1) the public pre-registration of hypotheses in advance of data collection; (2) greater attention to power calculations in advance of data collection balancing risks of type 1 and type 2 errors; (3) making research data accessible for other researchers to investigate, as on the Open Science Framework, for example; and (4) a move towards open-access publication both in commercial publishers and online preprints.

As your feminist, conceptual and historical companion, we urge you to think about what skin you might have in this game. Let's first use our historical orientation to take a step back from the high drama of the present moment. While the language of 'crisis' suggests that 'the replication crisis' is unique and unprecedented, you can see it as just one of many revolutionary 'crises' which have demarcated shifts between schools of thought throughout the history of Psychology and other sciences (Driver-Linn, 2003; Kuhn, 1962).

In fact, Thomas Kuhn in *The Structure of Scientific Revolutions* argued that sciences develop in a number of key stages. First a science is 'pre-paradigmatic' meaning it is very new and so its practitioners aren't organized or in agreement. When developments lead to some sense of unity and there is an agreed upon language and tenets, they are 'paradigmatic'. From this point, significant progress can occur. But at some point there will be a 'crisis', where an anomaly is identified which cannot be explained by the current broad understandings of the science. Emerging from this might be a new point of view, that is at odds with the old one. This eventually leads to a *'paradigm shift'* or a 'revolution'. But critically, this shift isn't necessarily about getting closer to *truth* – it's a new way of understanding. Driver-Linn (2003) explains how Kuhn's ideas are often rather appealing to psychologists because as a discipline there is a general lack of scientific identity and agreed upon dogma. We also of course can recognize that if a scientific discipline is experiencing some form of crisis, then perhaps it's reassuring to think that maybe it's heading towards a revolution.

Furthermore, the problem of replication has been with Psychology – and science – from the beginning (and will always be here). As sociologist Harry Collins (1992) makes clear, if one scientist fails to replicate another's findings, should we conclude that one of the scientists did the research badly, or that they were describing qualitatively different phenomena? There are no good immediate logical answers to this problem of what Collins (1992) calls the 'experimenter's regress', but it has been around since the very earliest modern science (Shapin, 1996).

We also urge you to consider how the moral lines between 'good' and 'bad' science are shifting in the present – and how this shift is evident in new concepts, which seem to matter, that didn't exist in quite the same way before. On the face of it, the *open science* movement argues for the research virtues of 'replicability', 'transparency' or 'openness' and against the sins of 'questionable research practices', such as making up your hypotheses to fit the data you have observed (or HARKing, see Kerr, 1998). Psychologists have new concepts that they didn't use 20 years ago such as the 'replicability' of a study, or 'researcher degrees of freedom' which allow then to *express* those social norms (and describe others as falling short of them). What has changed in recent history is not the existence of these critiques; the ideas are not new. What has changed is that these new norms now affect the publication of psychological research via researchers' and journal editors' behaviour, shaping what is and what is not deemed publishable research now. And researchers are now keen to show that they are 'good' scientists with respect to the new dominant norms it this context. Papers can even get special badges for adhering to the norms of the *open science* movement by these newly invented criteria.

Feminist Psychology and the *open science* movement have a lot in common. While both critique organizational incentives and individual research practices that lead to 'bad science' feminism tends to point the finger at patriarchy while the open science movement points it at the norms of the dominant research culture (Gervais et al., 2021). In the 1970s and 1980s, meta-analysis allowed an earlier generation of feminist empiricists to draw together findings to nuance claims about gender differences that had trundled along as *textbook myths* (e.g., Hyde, 1981). Open science may similarly expose the extent to which purported sex differences in neuroscience are the consequence of the questionable research practice of multiple statistical testing (Persson & Pownall, 2021).

But some of the most high profile targets of the open science movement have been women, such as Amy Cuddy. Moreover, many of its most outspoken champions are men. Indeed, Whitaker and Guest (2020) coined the term 'Bropen Science' out of concern for the ways that asserting the new norms of open science – and the targeting of individuals – reproduces a sexist culture of bullying women psychologists. They point out that the open science movement is less diverse than Psychology as a whole, and critique the 'bros' of open science for explaining the new norms without listening to others' *lived experience* of science or the reasons for nuancing some arguments. For example, Open Science Collaboration replication reports present incomplete information about participant characteristics making it very difficult to gauge if failures to replicate may have been due to participant characteristics or not (Sabik et al., 2021).

What does this recent transformation mean for a feminist companion to *CHIP*? First, we note that many problems named during the replication crisis were already acute in the psychology of women and gender some decades earlier. Feminist psychologists have long critiqued the focus on gender differences in the Psychology of gender because they were concerned with the problem of 'false positive' sex difference results, and of how the selective favouring of reports of statistically significant difference weighs against findings of sex similarities polarizing gender stereotypes (McHugh et al., 1986; Hare-Mustin & Marecek, 1990; Hyde, 2005).

Second, the *replication crisis* shows that feminist psychologists were right all along to emphasize that individual psychologies were nested within social, historical and cultural frameworks (e.g. Stewart & McDermott, 2004; Matsick et al., 2021). Such arguments were always in tension with a value system in Psychology's academic culture which presumed that psychological science was important to the extent that it could be replicated and generalized far and wide. However, feminists often do their research (including their experiments) not to uncover the timeless nature of human psychology but to prompt social change, in quest of impact validity (Massey, Barreras & Levy, 2013). As Gervais, Baildon and Lorenz (2021, p. 437) put it in the context of the #MeToo movement: 'We hope that many previously published findings fail to replicate as women have become more collectively empowered to voice their own experiences of gendered violence.' Failure to replicate can be a sign of social progress that feminist psychological research has achieved its goal, not a 'failure' of theory.

Third, there is a clear logical relationship between the critique of experimental culture which has not tested the replicability of findings across meaningful social group boundaries and the self-promoting practices of experimental psychologists operating under the norms of the 'publish-or-perish' culture. If a psychologist can materialize an effect in their lab, then there is a safe route to publication by continuing to explore this effect with closely related experiments, to the neglect of the diversity of samples. Consequences of this have been a neglect of diversity, such that Black participants became *less* common in American Social Psychology as social cognition became the dominant paradigm (Graham, 1992). American psychologists often conceptualize that racial and ethnic minorities 'have' culture that explains their psychology (Causadias Vitriol & Atkin, 2018), and studies on ethnic minorities have been published particularly rarely when authors and editors are exclusively white (Roberts et al., 2020). In mainstream Psychology, asserting group differences and similarities has always been about investigating whether theory generalizes or 'fails to replicate'. In practice, Psychology has been an engine for attributing gender difference to women more than men, and race differences to ethnic minorities more than majorities (that is, 'marked' rather than 'unmarked' groups, Haraway, 1988). Psychology has not only been an academic culture dominated by white men, it has long functioned to make those groups available for psychological interventions.

Co-occurring with the rise of open science there have been severe cut-backs in universities following the financial crisis of the late 2000s. In the UK and elsewhere this has – if anything – created greater competition between universities meted out through the scientific labour of their academics, giving early career researchers more precarious career prospects than before. As Persson and Pownall (2021) point out, women, feminists and Black, indigenous, and people of colour in Psychology may especially be particular risk when *open science* becomes a form of bullying in the context of this precarity because of *neuroracism* and issues of binaried understandings, as well as a lack of *intersectional* thinking. *Open science* should not become 'open season' on psychologists at the forefront of decolonizing the field among those drawn to the discipline's internal crises. Instead, Feminist Psychology may find expression by keeping the field's methods, theories and values open to the public with whom we can face a number of economic, political and environmental crises (Siegel, Calogero, Eaton & Roberts, 2021). Diversity in open science requires not only empiricism, it seems to also require an understanding of why epistemologies from a *standpoint feminist* perspective matter. In light of these resonances with the history of Feminist Psychology, we now explore what it's like to be a feminist in Psychology at the moment.

Box 6.1: An interview with Sarah Marks

Dr Sarah Marks is a historian who researches the history of science, medicine and technology and she pays particular attention to the **Psy-disciplines** (i.e. Psychology, Psychotherapy and Psychiatry). She's really interested in the history of mental health broadly and also works on histories of modern Africa and Europe. She is currently the Director of the Birkbeck Centre for Interdisciplinary Research on Mental Health and the Editor for the journal *History of the Human Sciences*.

Question 1: What sorts of research do you conduct and why do you think you're interested in that topic?

A lot of my work has been on the history of psychotherapies (Marks, 2017; Marks, 2018), trying to promote this as an area of historical study in its own right, especially going beyond psychoanalysis to understand other therapeutic approaches, e.g. from the CBT tradition, art therapies or non-western traditions. Many people access forms of psychotherapy: it's a powerful force in society and ever more so globally. It's important to understand where the ideas have come from, how they have been justified, and what they mean in practice. I'm also particularly interested in how psychotherapeutic approaches are adapted for different cultural contexts. I started out working on Eastern Europe, and now I work with colleagues in Africa – particularly Ghana and Zimbabwe – to understand the take up of therapies in local settings.

There is a strong critique of Global Mental Health which sees these often as western therapeutic ideas being imposed from outside. There are of course risks and complications of scaling up therapies, not least because they can have the effect of individualizing problems that are actually rooted in socio-economic, political or environmental factors. But the work we are doing shows that it's not just a simple case of practitioners from the 'West' or the 'Global North' exporting ideas in a neocolonial manner. African psychologists and psychiatrists make use of different modes of therapies in ways that make sense to the local context, and have been doing for decades. I don't think the history of psychotherapy outside of Europe and America is very well understood, so it's important to work with in-country partners to uncover these stories, and to prioritize the experiences and agency of the African practitioners who have been working in mental health.

Question 2: In what ways is your feminist identity relevant to the research you conduct?

As a feminist historian there is always an impetus to foreground the voices of women in the histories we are writing, and psychology and psychotherapy is still very often written as a History of Great Men. Freud, Jung, Rogers, Beck, etc. In some of my forthcoming work, on contexts such as the former Czecho-slovakia and Ghana, I'm telling the stories of female clinicians who really innovated in therapy, and sometimes also campaigned to change policy in mental health. For example, Eva Syřišťová, a Czech psychotherapist who developed new creative therapies for the treatment of psychosis, drawing from phenomenological philosophy, whose work has largely been forgotten. And in Ghana, the work of Clinical Psychologist Araba Sefa-Dedeh, who adapted cognitive and behavioural approaches for a multi-lingual Ghanaian context from the 1970s onwards, where clients come to therapy with a wide range of belief systems informed by spiritual commitments. Both women were also involved in training multiple generations of clinicians and had a huge impact within their countries. While it's important for historians not to get too caught up in uncritical, celebratory narratives, there is an aspect of historical work which is also about remembrance, and we still need more gender balance in our histories.

In addition to that I think it's important to acknowledge the role of feminist historians in the development of *oral history* as a method, which is really crucial for the history of psychology, and for reorientating history as a profession towards understanding individual experiences from a variety of diverse backgrounds.

Question 3: What do you think are the most pertinent or key issues at the moment when thinking about the history of Psychology?

We are at an important moment for the *decolonization* of history in general, and the history of the psychological disciplines is being internationalized in particular, both in terms of what we write about, and also in terms of author-ship. And it's about time too, but there's still much more work to be done here, and some of that is about us taking responsibility for being more inclusive and having conversations and collaborations across national and continental boundaries.

I think the other really pressing imperative is to genuinely include the *lived experience* of service-users, clients or patients in the therapeutic encounter, and people who have been on the receiving end of psychological technologies such as testing. There is a lot of great work in this area, particularly around the use of patient records, memoirs and letters as archival and printed sources. I'm keen to see more *oral histories* of lived experience, and I think we should do more to think about how oral history as an approach could also learn from qualitative research on health experience in the social sciences. I'm working with colleagues in Interpretative Phenomenological Analysis (IPA) at the moment to think through some of the methodological challenges of understanding the lived experiences of psychotherapeutic treatments in the past.

Question 4: What advice would you give feminist historians of the future?

I think the main thing I've learned in recent years is not to be afraid to experiment and challenge yourself to try new methods, or work on new areas. I think history as a field can be quite conservative as a discipline – we are often encouraged to work on one region or time period, with the same methods for our whole careers, and this can lead to knowledge silos and a lack of comparative thinking or methodological innovation. There is always risk involved with *interdisciplinary* working, experimenting with new approaches, or working on topics that are new to you. But collaborative work – e.g. with anthropologists or other social scientists, and with people who have expertise on different areas or are from different geographical locations themselves – can really challenge our assumptions, and forces us to find new ways to think about our research questions.

Being a feminist in Psychology now

We'd certainly like to hope that being a feminist in Psychology now is markedly different to those in the past, like the women we identified in Chapter 2. Inspired by the 30th Anniversary of the Psychology and Equalities of Women Section (POWES) of the BPS, Katherine and colleagues Lois Donnelly and Rose Capdevila embarked on a project to uncover the experiences of feminist psychologists in Britain in their everyday working lives.

This began has a short survey to people who considered themselves to be feminist psychologists in and around the POWES community (see Capdevila, Hubbard & Donnelly, 2019). The story completion task survey revealed that on the whole everyone was very positive about POWES and highlighted the importance of a feminist community (even if they weren't allowed to call themselves that explicitly). In respondents' reflections about POWES, they constructed the feminist community to be a) a movement, b) a supportive community and environment, c) intellectually stimulating, d) an arena for opportunity, and e) a site of recuperation. In particular we noted how participants described POWES (especially the conference) as like 'coming home'. Participants also highlighted key challenges and hopes for the future. They indicated a certain level of apprehension at first engaging with POWES, a nervousness around the conference, and frustration at visibility and accessibility issues (namely, around financial accessibility and with the BPS).

In 1994, Shields described feminist organizing in Psychology as 'dazzling' but stated it had had 'a surprisingly muted impact on scientific psychology as a whole' (p. 93). But our research and the work of others showed that such feminist work had had a big impact on feminist individuals themselves. Austin, Rutherford and Pyke's (2006) study focused on Canadian feminist psychology and argued the Canadian equivalent group of POWES, the Section on Women and Psychology (established 1976, SWAP – originally the Interest Group on Women in Psychology) of the Canadian Psychological Association, was critical in promoting change around gender equality. Radtke (2011) has more recently argued, in the Canadian context, that continued engagement with such organizations and conferences remained important to maintain this agenda. Capdevila et al (2019) argued overall that POWES, like many feminist organizations, exists in 'loyal opposition' to mainstream Psychology, where the mainstream is criticized with the hope of re-shaping rather than abandoning it (Marecek, 1995).

Based on this survey Lois, Katherine and Rose decided to delve a bit deeper and interview people about their experiences of being feminist psychologists and their experiences of POWES (see Donnelly, Hubbard & Capdevila, 2022). Three research questions addressing: the boundary between activism and academia; the provision of support; and differing approaches to knowledge production were investigated. Together, they found that it was incredibly important to participants to stake claim on POWES as a feminist organization which helped them navigate the sometimes difficult boundary between feminist activism and academic Psychology, and activism and academia more broadly. The value of a feminist community was vital, especially one that was deemed inclusive and welcoming. More difficult boundaries abounded, including those around work/academia and fun/home.

This was often challenging for feminist psychologists for two reasons. The first reason is that we noted how while the nurturing, supportive community was invaluable, there was an invisible quality to the emotional labour behind the making of such an environment. While it was valued, the agents of this work were often unrecognized (this was also evident in the survey, see Capdevila et al., 2019). Rickett and Morris' (2021) research similarly demonstrated that working-class female academics often find themselves 'mopping up the tears in the academy' and that emotional labour is not often recognized; as do Thompson, Turley, Frances, Donnelly and Lazard (2023) who highlighted once again that the emotional labour of feminist work is often invisible.

The second was that the dichotomy between work/academia and home/fun was complicated by ideas of what rigorous Psychology is. There was sometimes a sense that while feminist Psychology was valued, it was perhaps not 'proper' Psychology or rigorous enough to qualify as good science, precisely because it often related to a nice or kind supportive community. This is reminiscent of the findings of Eagly and Riger (2014) and Rees (2011) about how feminist epistemologies can be seen as less prestigious and so this appeared to echo though some of the interviews showing how pervasive and difficult it is to do this work sometimes even in actively feminist communities.

The prevailing message of this collective work has been that having a feminist 'home' in Psychology is not only crucial for the survival of Feminist Psychology as a sub-discipline but for feminists in Psychology as well (Donnelly et al. 2022). We noted, like others have, that there is evidence of joy and genuine love for feminist community in Psychology. Several of the participants said they loved POWES and one stated they 'wouldn't be the person I am now without it'. Similarly, Segal (2017, p.xiv) said 'those participating in resistance to or a process of collective deliberations on the harms of the present, sometimes trying to build alternatives, often do find in these strategies sources of fulfilment, resilience, even moments of shared joy' (2017, p. xiv). Such joy is especially valued in a context of *neoliberalist* academia (Gill, 2009).

Recent work by Thompson et al. (2023) presents the current challenges and opportunities for critical feminist psychologists. They found in their round table discussion that doing feminism in Psychology remained 'sweaty' work (borrowing from 'sweaty concepts' coined by Ahmed, 2014). In all they showed how feminist work on the ground is still a story of resistance and pushing at doors that are just cracked open, but that by finding other feminists, and having open discussion, collective strength can be found.

The research especially highlighted the need to make intersectional and inclusive forms of feminism more explicit within communities and there is perhaps a need to still resist adversarial approaches in order to ensure feminist communities in Psychology remain kind. So overall, there is still feminist work to be done but doing it and finding your fellow feminists can be exceptionally lovely.

Box 6.2: Psychology's feminist voices

Psychology's Feminist Voices is perhaps the most exciting ongoing project around feminist histories of Psychology. It's a multimedia digital archive of the past and presence of women and feminism in Psychology. Check out the website plus their various social media outputs too:

https://feministvoices.com/

Psychology's Feminist Voices (or PFV) is the brain-child of the one, the only... Prof. Alexandra Rutherford!

Alex is what is known as a feminist historian extraordinaire! She is a professor in the Historical, Theoretical, and Critical Studies of Psychology program at York University (Toronto, Canada) and has edited some of the biggest journals in the field of Psychology. She's gained several major awards for her work including the Carolyn Wood Sherif Award (2023) from the Society for the Psychology of Women; the Career Achievement Award (2022) from the Society for the History of Psychology; the Florence Denmark Distinguished Mentoring Award (2016) from the Association for Women in Psychology and the 2011 Award of Distinction (2011) from the Section on Women and Psychology of the Canadian Psychological Association. Alex founded PFV in 2004 with the intention to collect, preserve and share the narratives of diverse feminist psychologists from all over the world. By 2010 it had its first website and it's just grown and grown. Now with a dozen collaborators and international teams and a team base of nearly 30 individuals, PFV has become a cornerstone of feminist histories for Psychology.

On the website you can find not only profiles of feminists in Psychology's past, but also a really wide selection of *oral history* interviews with feminists in the present. It is truly a wealth of wonderful feminist knowledge and archival information. In addition to these there are also projects and exhibits on the website. These include:

- 'The Changing Face of Feminist Psychology' (their very own documentary)
- 'Women of Color in Psychology' (a timeline)
- 'Feminist Psychologists Talk About...' (a series of short teaching videos)
- 'I am psyched!' (virtual exhibit of women of colour in the history of Psychology)
- 'Queer(ing) Psychology' (an online interactive conversation exhibit)

- 'Takin' It to the Streets' (activism and protest exhibit)
- 'Gender Matters' (series of videos about gender focused analysis)
- 'Lasting legacies and feminist futures' (exhibit of feminist Psychology in the UK)
- 'Collecting Asylum Postcards' (exhibit of 20th century postcards of asylums)
- 'Standpoints' (a blog of all things relevant to feminist history in Psychology)

While the base of PFV is in Toronto, Canada, there are people from three continents associated with the project. There is a big effort to think about the history of Feminist Psychology from an international perspective. In all, they aim to use critical historical, feminist, constructionist and intersectional approaches to analyse Psychology's engagement with gender issues.

PFV represents what is happening right now in feminist histories of Psychology. It's a growing and continually developing resource. It really represents feminist historical practice in the present as it's not just about collecting things from the past, but seeking out the stories of those in the present. It's actively archiving in order to preserve and save feminist history for the future.

The website is well worth engaging with – it's a fantastic resource, especially if you're thinking about doing your own **CHIP** project (more on that in Chapter 7).

The emotions involved when doing history

So hopefully being a feminist in Psychology now feels a little different to how we might imagine those in the past felt. In keeping with this idea of feeling, here we explore how feelings don't just come up when doing Psychology, they also come up when doing History. Emotions and history are a bit more integrated than you first might expect, especially when it comes to conceptual and historical issues in Psychology. In many ways emotions are psychological objects: psychologists study them. Fundamentally, psychologists (and those of us who study Psychology) are interested in how people *feel*. This can then be more complicated when we come to understand emotions as not just psychological objects, but historical ones too. Million (2009) poignantly argues that in the context of indigenous histories in Canada, academia has suppressed voices of First Nations people precisely because they are *felt* as well as thought about.

There is in fact a whole field of the history of emotion. These can take a more *essentialist* perspective (emotions have a core unchangeable essence, they are the same for everyone and have or less stayed the same over history and across cultures) or a more *constructionist* perspective (how we describe, understand and experience emotions is context-specific and has changed over time and across cultures).

Barclay (2021a) articulates two important things in the field: (1) how we convey emotions can be understood as performative and this can also be gendered, and (2) historical objects are emotionally weighty. First, drawing upon the work of Judith Butler's concept of performativity, Barclay explains how repeated gestures become engrained to gender the expression of emotion. Stephanie Shields (2007) has also done some fantastic work in this area and argued that in the nineteenth century, British and American Psychology very much framed women and men as having different emotional experiences and capacities. Men were understood to be able to 'harness the power of emotions' to be more reasonable, whereas women's emotions were viewed as a consequence of their bodies (and thus were less reliable/rational, limited and often child-like). Feminine emotions were seen as complimentary to men's and Shields argues such constructions of emotions serviced to maintain power divisions. See Chapter 2 for further details about this.

The second key point is that objects can also carry a certain emotional weight. In many ways objects, technologies and other 'things' can work as extensions of the self and this can mean they are also attributed this emotional weight. Barclay uses the example of wedding certificates (2020) and of the charts and graphs used to illustrate the death rates of Covid-19 (2021b). She begins the 2021 article by stating:

> Over the weeks before I sat down to write this, news and social media have been dominated by statistics and graphs that track the spread of COVID-19 and the numbers of deaths in each country. Tracking pandemics through counts has occurred for hundreds of years as people have tried to feel in control of circumstances that were uncertain. Such data play a curious emotional role
>
> (p. 112)

This is in many ways a highly relatable experience for many of us. The 2020 onwards pandemic was a global tragedy which impacted everyone in often highly emotional ways. Those emotions were often attached to particular behaviours (like obsessing over the news) that caused or reduced particular emotions (like anxiety). But what is particularly insightful here is how this personal experience of engaging with the news and social media impacted Barclay's own reflections about the emotional role of *data*.

The crucial point here is that doing history itself can be an emotional experience and crucially this is not a bad thing. Historians are often driven by particular things they find personally pertinent and fascinating and this is all about understanding the conceptual and personal aspects of history. As such, how could good storytelling be anything other than emotional? Indeed, Lepore (2001) also questioned whether those conducting biography or microhistory (that is, those with a more specific, niche or individual level interest) can *love* too much. She argued that biographers in particular 'are notorious for falling in and out of love with the people they write about' (p. 133). There therefore seem to be particular emotional reactions to doing history and this can especially be around the people the researcher is writing about. In the next section we both outline how we first got into doing **CHIP** projects and the emotions that drove us to some extent. For example, Peter talks about turning feelings into research questions and Katherine talks about the feelings of being in an *archive*. We will leave it to you to decide if we love what we do too much.

Katherine has also written about this and her experiences of researching queer women and the feelings of queer kinship that she found in doing so (under review). As we've explained, who you are impacts the types of questions you ask. In the Introduction to her book *Queer Ink*, Katherine expressed how for her, the history she wrote was in many ways her history too as she was writing about queer women in Psychology. In doing so, she became a part of that history as well:

> There are various difficulties in doing such history (or 'herstory' as this book focuses on the workings of women) and its always worth thinking about who is telling the story and why. So why am I telling this history? I am telling this history because it is *my* history. As a queer woman studying psychological science what has come before me, for other queer women in the field is a part of my, and perhaps your, trajectory. In writing about it I now become, rather reflectively, a part of that history too. This embedded nature of doing history is rather important...
>
> (Hubbard, 2020, p. 4)

Others have argued that emotions are especially vital for queer history (and we could extend this to wider histories of marginalized groups). Cvetkovich (2003) for example argued that understanding queer archives as those of emotion and trauma often helps to actually understand them. Similarly, other scholars have also argued that for queer historians, doing historical work is an affective and personal 'touch across time' which draws upon a queer historical impulse (Dinshaw, 1999). This impulse is perhaps especially important for those who are writing histories of communities they themselves are a part of:

> The longing for community across time is a crucial feature of queer historical experience, one produced by the historical isolation of individual queers as well as by the damaged quality of the historical archive
>
> (Dinshaw, 1999, p. 37)

Drawing upon such work, Love (2009) paid closer attention to twentieth-century texts and argued in *Feeling Backwards* that when thinking about the emotionality of the queer *archive*, 'personal encounters and the feelings they elicit stand in for theories of history and of the social' (p. 12). Katherine argues (Hubbard, under review) that in the development of such deeply connected personal historical work, a type of queer kinship is formed between the researcher and the subject. There is, therefore, great value in having *inter-subjectivity* with one's historical subject – it is highly valuable to one's ability to 'read between the straight lines' of the archive (Koaureas, 2012). And this is of course applicable (though with somewhat less pun) for any groups whose history has been erased.

Perhaps Lepore (2001) is right, that we historians can love too much! But as we have argued throughout this book, *reflexivity* and transparency about our own identities and roles within the construction of history can begin to address this. We can place the historian into the narrative. For example, Jenn Shapland in *My Autobiography of Carson McCullers* (2020) beautifully untangles the complex relationships of conducting historical work and uniquely presents her own mental health, wellbeing, sexuality, sense of discovery and exploration into the very fabric of the (auto)biography of McCullers. Likewise, in *Before We Were Trans: A New History of Gender*, Kit Heyam excels in articulating a beautiful balance of deeply important historical work alongside personal reflection, awareness and honesty in regards to their own identities. We cover this to a greater extent in the Tool of this chapter when we discuss how drawing on your own *lived experience* can really assist in being more reflexive and transparent in the research process.

How we got into doing CHIP

Peter: Turning a feeling into a research question or how I became a psychologist-historian

Sometimes when you read a textbook history you may have a funny sort of feeling-of-knowing. It might feel like 'that's not right' and – if you are not feeling confident, it might feel like 'I'm not getting this right'. But rather than make sense of this feeling as a *problem* (about the text, or yourself), it can be the beginnings of surprise, curiosity, irony and historical storytelling. How does a feeling of wrongness turn into a research question? In response to this situation, I have learned to ask myself, 'Why does this thing I am reading feel strange?', 'What do I believe that seems to jar with what it evidences?'. I try to reflect explicitly on what-I-thought-I-knew, and how I think I know it (my common sense *epistemology*). I usually find that I can't explain the grounding of my assumptions as well as I thought when I look at them up close. Because this puts something I thought I knew in trouble, this can be anxiety-provoking.

Remember to breathe, and notice that your anxiety knows that you have invented a research question about the history of your own and others knowledge. Where does each of these two clashing versions of the past come from? How did you come to believe what-you-thought-you-knew? (You might be surprised about what you don't know about how you came to believe the things you believe!) Maybe your reflections will lead you to realize that what-you-thought-you-knew came from more than one source. Did you hear about the same thing from different authorities who gave different *partial* accounts of the story? Do you now have specific questions about how motivations, emphasis, morals and contexts shaped the factual details in those stories? Then you are on your way to a story about knowing from different *standpoints*, the history of those standpoints in groups, communities or cultures, develop, and even the *paradigm shifts* by which such understandings came about and how they change. You can look back and see how many of the stories in this book (about the Kitty Genovese murder, the depathologization of homosexuality, or the mental rotation test) were produced by this kind of thinking. If so, you are now not just a psychologist, but are becoming a psychologist–historian (Vaughn-Blunt et al., 2009). You are not going to satisfy anyone, least of all yourself, by concluding 'more research is needed' and switching off.

Here's how I (Peter) came to write my first article in a History journal (giving me licence to call myself a 'Psychologist-Historian' at terrifically fashionable parties). Studying judgement and decision-making as a budding cognitive psychologist in the early 1990s in the USA, I learned about the *illusory correlation*, a cognitive explanation of stereotyping. I also learned that one of the first studies demonstrating this phenomenon concerned psychiatrists 'illusory correlation' that male homosexuality could be diagnosed by certain common responses to the Rorschach inkblot test (Chapman & Chapman, 1969). I had also read a newspaper article several years earlier about psychologist Evelyn Hooker's influential research on the Rorschach responses of gay and straight men described in the story about the depathologization of homosexuality above (see Hooker, 1957, 1993). I had come out a few years earlier and this very much shaped my *standpoint* on/in Psychology at the time. It was when I was researching the gay brain stuff described earlier that I began digging into gay history to get a different angle on Psychology. By reading gay/lesbian history, I learned that it was in the Second World War that homosexuality became a reason for excluding gay men from the American military and psychologists and psychiatrists first invested in the hypothesis that the Rorschach could be a means of detecting gay men (or more precisely straight men, pretending to be gay to avoid military service, Bérubé, 1990). In reading American social history, I was also aware that many of my fellow American graduate students had a common sense version of the nation's history that I hadn't learned growing up in Ireland. Confronted with bits and bobs that I now knew from different vantage points (a student of Cognitive Psychology, a reader of newspapers, a gay man looking for histories in a foreign country), I took on the challenge of resolving their ironies into a historical narrative in which they were all part of the same thing.

I *constructed* this hypothesis – that the Rorschach could detect your sexuality – as the central topic of my story. (That's right, I *made up* the object of my study. I didn't 'find' it waiting for me in a dusty archive one day.) Investing my time in understanding this hypothesis set me the challenge of explaining the rise and fall in psychologists' confidence in this hypothesis between roughly 1941 (when the USA entered the Second World War) and 1973 (when homosexuality was depathologized). To research it, I read years of research by the Rorschach research community (particularly the publications of their key journal *Rorschach Research Exchange*, which became *The Journal of Projective Techniques* and then the current *Journal of Personality Assessment*). My first reading was pretty manic; you would not have known my excitement as the contours of this story took shape in my head as I sat with increasing piles of old journals around me in the Stanford University medical library one Friday night. I ultimately told a story about how the Rorschach rotated its gaze away from problematizing gay men's sexualities, to problematizing psychiatrists' claims to be objective. That story was bound up with shifts in the rise and fall in the confidence of psychoanalysis, testing, and Cognitive Psychology (see Hegarty, 2003). Maybe there is something to the ability to imagine mental rotation after all.

At the time, writing this history seemed like an adventure of discovery, story-telling and a step in my intellectual development. Looking back, it is easier to put this work into its own historical context, and to see that I was not so innovative really. At the time I wrote this, the 'new history' of Psychology had opened up interest in social history, but there was little work on sexuality (Minton, 1997, being an exception). However, in the emerging field of lesbian and gay studies (e.g., Halperin, Abelove & Barale, 1993), scholars were very fascinated by Foucault's thesis that sexuality was not a natural psychological category but one that could be historicized. (These are the beliefs that we measured years later in Katherine's dissertation study, Hubbard & Hegarty, 2014.)

Nor was I alone in charting a rise in faith in the Rorschach from the Second World War through to a decline in the 1970s. It's no surprise that other critical histories of Rorschach testing that came out about the same time focused on faith in the Rorschach to detect other 'others' of 1950s America apart from gay men, including displaced native Americans (Lemov, 2011) and convicted Nazi war criminals (Brunner, 2001). So when Katherine began her work on the UK Rorschach testers, my history was part of the 'history of criticism' of the Rorschach with which she engaged. Imagine my joy when I used my social psychological skills to persuade her to do that PhD. (Cue evil cackling laughter and thunderstorms here.)

So in closing, listen to that feeling, and don't be afraid of the anxiety of unknowing. Your anxiety knows that there is an open question there and that's a good start. (It's the *only* good start.) You will never know where curiosity can lead you unless you let it get the better of you once in a while.

Katherine: The feelings of the archive

As explained in Chapter 1, I got involved in conceptual and historical issues in Psychology precisely because of Peter. It's incredible what an enthusiastic lecturer can do. I did Peter's History of Psychology final year module and even though I was more focused in gender and sexuality studies throughout my Master's, I quickly combined these interests in my PhD.

One of the reasons I was so keen to write this book is because it's precisely the book I wanted at that time. Taking on a historical project when you've got a different disciplinary background can be tough. How do you even *do* history, especially when your methods training so far has probably stretched qualitatively only as far as interviews and focus groups?

For me, my first real historical project was writing a history of the Rorschach ink blot test in Britain. This involved going to *archives* (the British Library mainly) and exploring the journals associated with projective testing. I became a little fixated on what Peter called 'an annal' (cue some internal giggling). Which is basically writing a record, or a chronical of events, publications and important figures. My annal was extensive. In fact, I had multiple annals (okay, so it turns out I still find this pretty funny). But seriously, my annals were so big they stretched across Peter's office floor. Through my extensive annal work (ha, I can't stop), I began to be able to really chart in depth and detail the activities of people and the test itself.

I asked questions like: who is using this test? Where are they located? What is the test being used to do? What questions are being posed that are thought to be answered by the test? What theoretical background are people using the test from? What critiques are apparent about the test? When do they emerge? Who is being subjected to testing? How does the UK scene compare to other countries? Critically, I also learned the importance of asking: what is not evident that I might have expected?

I learned that this history had a surprising (for Psychology at the time) number of women involved. The Rorschach was often used in educational or developmental settings (linked unsurprisingly to the higher numbers of women in these areas, see Chapter 2). I also spotted that a number of the women involved seemed somewhat queer... this all eventually led to my first book *Queer Ink: A Blotted History Towards Liberation*.

In all, I fell in love with doing history and the people that I got to meet by doing it (both alive and dead). There is a real sense of discovery and curiosity when conducting archival research that I didn't get in the same way doing other methods. Of course, a lot of work goes into securing, collecting, archiving and recording materials in archives, and we must fully appreciate and recognize all the valuable work **archivists** do daily to ensure historical work can be done in collections of all sizes. So a historian never really 'discovers' something 'lost' in an archive. But nonetheless, there is still a real sense of being a detective when doing historical work. I still find the tingly excitement of what you're going to find in the archive a total thrill.

In the next chapter we outline a bit more about how to do you own history project so you can maybe get a sense of what this feeling is like for yourself too.

TOOL 5: Your Lived Experience

The final tool for the book is your own *lived experience*! As we've explained through various points in the book, who you are effects the kinds of questions you ask, the topics you're interested in and the perspective you take. In Psychology when students are taught about research methods they are usually first taught about quantitative approaches. Here, it is very common to hear that things like 'reliability' and 'objectivity' are important. But it's important to remember that these are also constructs and were made up in the cold war context by clinical psychologists and testers (see Morawski, 1994 and the original sources on this, Cronbach & Meehl, 1955). You might evaluate certain studies and be critical of them; this often includes questions around whether they have a generalizable sample or whether there has been any *bias*. Of course we can be highly questioning of the real extent to which any research method at all can truly be objective. By extension however, when qualitative methods are then taught, usually later and to a lesser extent, some of these criteria which are more appropriate for quantitative methods can become sort of automatically applied to qualitative approaches (Lazard & McAvoy, 2020). The fear of bias entrenches! This means that it can be difficult to accept that our lived experiences informing our research practice can actually be a really good thing.

When *lived experience* is conceptualized as 'bias' and work is written off immediately because of it, then the true value of what experience can add vanishes and the inherent *subjectivity* in all research is made invisible. We talked about this as well in the Chapter 2 Tool: Feminist Science Studies. Feminist Science Studies and the work of feminists such as Donna Haraway, Patricia Hill Collins and Sandra Harding have been critical in this area. The wider argument of this is that your lived experience can give you a particular *epistemological advantage*. Haraway (1988) described our lived experiences as providing *situated knowledges*. Our situations, our positions, our identities and how we are placed in the world inform all of the ways we can understand the world. They can be a source of irony, creativity, narrative and *social change* (as they have been for others in the past, and as we have explained above in regards to ourselves).

Applying this thinking to research often comes from having a more *interpretivist* stance, which likewise understands knowledge to be constructed and relational. This stance contrasts with more *positivist* stances, common in Psychology, which understands facts to be 'real' or 'true' out in the world lying around just waiting to be looked at via *empiricism*. By working in a more interpretivist way the researchers likes, dislikes, identities, their backgrounds, their expectations, etc. can all be taken into account and be objects of *reflexivity* (Bryman, 2016). Meaning:

> The researcher is an active, not passive, agent in acquiring knowledge of the processes, histories, events, language and biographies of the research context. Because of the importance of the nature of the relation between the researcher and research participants, the researcher's background – including class, gender, ethnicity, sexuality, age, ideas, commitments and national identity – needs to be made explicit.
>
> (Bukamal, 2022, p. 327)

In making these things explicit the researcher begins the process *positionality* and *reflexivity*. These two things are somewhat interrelated but can be considered separately.

Positionality is the accounting for the particular position the researcher holds. This is often in the form of a short biographical account which shows where the research is in relation to other relevant key features, demographics, characteristics etc. (see Bukamal, 2022). For example, in Chapter 1: Introduction, we explained a little bit about ourselves so you could get a sense of where we are coming from for this book – this is our positionality. It also has an additional important contribution and that is locating where the researcher is compared to any participants, data or materials. Indeed, the call for positionality statements in published work has increased.

A researcher might be considered an *insider*, an *outsider* or a combination of the two (Bryman, 2016). Toft (2012), for example, explains the value of explaining outsider positions alongside insider sentiments in interviews with bisexual Christians. The extent of 'insiderness/outsiderness' might also change throughout time, or shift, or be more complicated that this simple dichotomy (see McAvoy, 2009 as quoted in Lazard & McAvoy, 2020, for example). A researcher can be both insider and outsider to varying degrees and there are advantages and disadvantages to both. Being an insider often leads to quick rapport and understanding between researcher and participant (or data or material). But it also can come with the issue that sometimes it's difficult to see someone analytically when it's too close to you. Also, sometimes participants are less inclined to explain something in depth if they think you already understand it personally (see Bryman, 2016; Clark, Foster, Sloan & Bryman, 2021). You also, of course, have no obligation to necessarily share personal details in the process of your own research. *Ethics* includes protection of researchers as well as participants, so if it doesn't feel okay or appropriate to share then you don't have to.

Reflexivity is all about looking at your *positionality* and considering how it has shaped and informed the research. But not only that, it's about looking at the wider picture. Lazard and McAvoy (2020) argue that the point of reflexivity is to make visible specific personal, social, theoretical and/or political influences that shape the research so that claims made and conclusions drawn can be understood and evaluated in *context*. They also say that '[b]ecause of this, reflexivity is central to establishing rigour in qualitative and mixed method work' (p. 16). There has been a reluctance to examine experimental and laboratory-based research with the same critical reflexive consideration, even though it's possible to do that (Morawski, 2005). In the spirit of increasingly open science, the requirement for positionality statements about researchers' identities is becoming more common across Psychology (but not without critique). Because we humans embody the thing we are studying in Psychology, our knowledge is reflexive (Morawski and Agronick, 1991). Thinking about reflexivity has been especially advanced among feminist psychologists (Morawksi, 1994). Wilkinson (1988) identified various forms of reflexivity for feminist work within Psychology. These include the 'personal' and 'functional' reflexivity relating to the identity of the researcher as described above, as well as 'disciplinary' reflexivity which considers how the field of enquiry also has an influence.

In all, as feminist science studies scholars have articulated, our own viewpoints and experiences in the world can lead to valuable perspectives. This can often be especially true for those who have experience of some form of marginalization. That's not to say that marginalization automatically leads to ground-breaking theory, but that it has the potential to shed light in a new way. The lives and experiences of Black feminists, for example, are what led to incredibly vital Black feminist theory (see Hill Collins, 1990). It is through subjugated knowledge that problematic norms in science can be exposed. It is of course important remember the *intersectionality* regarding this, especially when thinking about identity and experience (see Crenshaw, 1989). We do not embody just a singular type of person, but are each unique and experience particular things based on how the various parts of ourselves intersect. *Structural oppression* also impacts some marginalized groups more than others and of course this is also highly context-dependant. So while valuing our *lived experience* and how it makes us come to particular questions, it is also important to be explicit in our positions and *reflexive* in the process.

We also need to be reflexive about our own *privilege*. There are ways in which each of us may benefit from, or at least not suffer from, systems in our social worlds. Ahmed (2017) describes privilege as a

> buffer zone; it is how much you have to fall back on when you lose something. Privilege does not mean we are invulnerable: things happen; shit happens. Privilege can however reduce the costs of vulnerability; you are more likely to be looked after.
>
> (p. 238)

Specific things here might include being: white, able-bodied or rich. These things mean that as you do not have to face structural racism, navigate a world not automatically designed for your bodily needs, or struggle with poverty and the mental and physical consequences of that. It's not to say things can't be really, really hard but you may be buffered in some ways and recognizing that can be important when being reflexive and positioning oneself.

How might we *use* our lived experience as a tool to study the history of Psychology?

1 **Work out who you are** (okay, this is a big one and we're not convinced anyone really gets to the bottom of it). But really think about what identities, experiences, beliefs, attitudes, politics, privileges and perspectives you hold. What is important to you?

2 **Follow your interests and instincts**. Allow yourself to explore various areas of interest and wonder what makes you drawn to certain things.

3 **Begin to adopt and embrace your epistemological standpoint.** As you're reading this we are guessing that being a feminist is probably a key aspect of this already. Great! Welcome to the club! (What other things might you draw in here? Is there anything more specific or additional you'd stake a claim to?)

4 **Question how your choices and assumptions have directed and shaped your research.** (This doesn't just have to be about your own internal features, but also external circumstances too. Was an archive nearby to you? Was something available online? Was there any other situation which meant your ideal project was im/possible?)

5 **Write about your positionality.** Be explicit in where you stand and explain where you're coming from. This doesn't have to be apologetic though, just explanatory. (Remember – it's not bias.)

6 **Reflect.** (This is the big one) You will have already done some reflexivity by this point, but it's worth remembering that it's a process, and reflexivity doesn't have a total end point. Respond accordingly to these reflections.

SUMMARY

This chapter began with a consideration of the main issues in the present for Psychology, namely the replication 'crisis'. This alongside the high rate of fraud which was uncovered shifted the conceptual and ethical standing of Psychology as a trustworthy 'science'. Continuing with our thinking about what Psychology looks like *now*, we also explored what feminists in Psychology are describing about their experiences. This makes an interesting contrast to Chapter 2. Before, we thought about how women gained access to Psychology and how their work was un/recognized. Now, we've considered how women find Psychology and perhaps depressingly, how sometimes their work continues to be invisible or challenging. Nonetheless, our considerations of feminist communities has showed one key thing: feminists need feminism and feminism needs feminists! In the words of Sara Ahmed:

'No wonder feminism causes fear; together, we are dangerous.'

(p. 2017, p.18)

The later parts of this chapter aimed to get into closer detail and consider how we as individuals might experience CHIP. We talked about the emotions involved, gave you a sense of how we both came to do such projects and introduced the final tool, Your Lived Experience. Here, we have tried to emphasize the importance and value of your own perspective and what that can contribute. As well as show you how to discuss this appropriately via *positionality* and *reflexivity*.

QUESTIONS TO CONSIDER

1 Upon reflection, what made you first identify as a feminist? Do you think of yourself as a specific type of feminist? Has that ever changed?

2 What other perspectives do you have and how do these inform the 'lens' through which you look at Psychology and the wider world?

3 What do you think are the current present issues for both Psychology and for feminism?

4 Can you name some of the emotions you've felt while studying Psychology? Perhaps sometimes there's been frustration. Have there also been times when you've felt like you found others just like you?

Key resources

Barclay, K. (2021). State of the field: the history of emotions. *History, 106*(371), 456–466. https://doi.org/10.1111/1468-229X.13171

Donnelly, L. C., Hubbard, K., & Capdevila, R. (2022). POWES is pronounced "feminist": Negotiating academic and activist boundaries in the talk of UK feminist psychologists. *Feminism & Psychology, 32*(4), 520–539. https://doi.org/10.1177/0959353522110006

Driver-Linn, E. (2003). Where is psychology going? Structural fault lines revealed by psychologists' use of Kuhn. *American Psychologist, 58*(4), 269. https://doi.org/10.1037/0003-066X.58.4.269

Heyam, K. (2022). *Before we were trans: A new history of gender.* Hachette UK.

Lazard, L., & McAvoy, J. (2020). Doing reflexivity in psychological research – What's the point? What's the practice? *Qualitative Research in Psychology, 17*(2), 159–177. https://doi.org/10.1080/14780887.2017.1400144

Lepore, J. (2001). Historians who love too much: Reflections on microhistory and biography. *The Journal of American History, 88*(1), 129–144. https://doi.org/10.2307/2674921

Love, H. (2009). *Feeling backward: Loss and the politics of queer history.* Harvard University Press.

Persson, S., & Pownall, M. (2021). Can open science be a tool to dismantle claims of hardwired brain sex differences? Opportunities and challenges for feminist researchers. *Psychology of Women Quarterly, 45*(4), 493–504. https://doi.org/10.1177/036168432110376

Siegel, J. A., Calogero, R. M., Eaton, A. A., & Roberts, T. A. (2021). Identifying gaps and building bridges between feminist psychology and open science. *Psychology of Women Quarterly, 45*(4), 407–411. DOI: 10.1177/03616843211044494

7　Feminist futures

Learning objectives

Study of this chapter will enable you to:

- Create your own personalized toolkit of things that will help you on your CHIP journey
- Design your own CHIP project having learned a wide range of various techniques you could use; including how to develop research questions, find and access archives and the other practicalities
- Learn how to actually do CHIP analysis
- Feel emboldened to embark on your own CHIP adventure

Introduction

Throughout this companion we've aimed to act as your navigators through the map of *CHIP* that we've drawn and used regularly. Our hand-drawn treasure map is metaphorically laid out across the last six chapters in a way that we hope you've found useful and enjoyable. Now we're at the end of the journey we want to pass over to you. We're at the edge of the map now and it's up to you to decide where to go next. To go into the uncharted territory and begin CHIP work in under explored and new areas that you are most passionate about.

In doing so we hope you are mindful and careful of how your tread might affect the environment you're in and to pay very close attention to evidence that people have been there before you. This is where *interdisciplinarity* comes in. Don't feel as if you can't use other disciplines' maps in areas that are relevant to your exploration. Be respectful of the land and decolonize your epistemology; just because something is new to you doesn't mean it's new to others. This is where good citation comes in; reference and refer to those who are helping you on your way.

This chapter is more about the future of *CHIP*. In order to have a *feminist* future, CHIP needs people just like you to be its agents! Here we will specifically outline how you might take what you've learned forward and do your own feminist research using the tools we've suggested in this companion. First, we combine the tools given throughout the book and encourage you to create your own feminist survival toolkit. Then, we explain how to practically *do* a CHIP project, for example, for a dissertation, thesis or larger project. Finally, we hand over to you as the future of feminist Psychology!

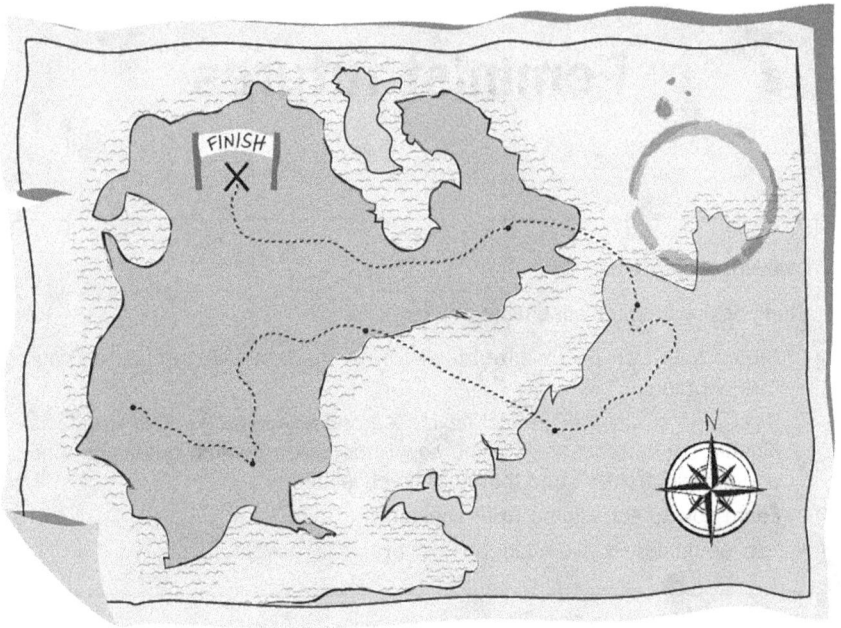

Your toolkit

As we explained in the Introduction, our thinking about tools emerged from the writing of Sara Ahmed from *Living a Feminist Life* (2017). Ahmed identified feminist tools as being critical for her own feminist survival kit. It's also worth reflecting on tools given what Audre Lorde said about the 'master's tools' (as we explored in Chapter 4). Similarly, Berlant and Warner (1995) described queer theory having the ability to 'wrench' frames which makes us think of wrenches/ spanners, the exact tool we've chosen to depict our Tools. In this book we've considered somewhat more conceptual and theoretical tools as being a part of the toolkit and have especially selected the tools we think are useful for doing the job of feminist *CHIP*. These are, of course, all metaphorical and we provide them to be used and applied to various areas by you, in the ways that you find suitable. The five tools we've outlined are:

Tool 1 (Chapter 2) – Feminist Science Studies

Our first tool aimed to begin to question some of the basic assumptions that underpin Psychology. By seeing Psychology as a science and applying Feminist Science Studies we revealed how it's a *social **reflexive*** science; we're studying the things that we are. Because of this, the science people produce reflects the beliefs of the people who make it.

Tool 2 (Chapter 3) – Critical Reading and Ethics

The communication of science is one way that it is social and in the second tool we outlined a method of how you might approach looking at such communications. By thinking critically about history and developing close reading skills, we explained how you may start to conceptualize the ethics and politics of Psychological research in greater depth. This is often all about thinking about context and intentions, and consciously taking the perspective of people (and animals and things) who are written about.

Tool 3 (Chapter 4) – Queer Theory

Here we somewhat expanded thinking critically by exploring queer theory. By attending to sexuality in more detail, we explored how a queer approach to *CHIP* might look. In particular, by wrenching the heteronorm evident in Psychology's history and how as a discipline it conceptualizes people. Psychology does a great deal of categorizing of people and so queering these lines and encouraging discovery into Psychology's past and present is important. This tool taught us more about the political nature of these enquires.

Tool 4 (Chapter 5) – Feminist Biology

This tool was all about questioning those ideas that Biology has all the answers and that it's super reliable and objective. By taking a feminist stance to Biology and Neuroscience we showed how it's possible to be understand how 'sex' and 'sex differences' are made up through gendered discourses and practices. They key thing here to remember is that all forms of science (including Psychology and Biology) are developed by people with ideologies in contexts, often through *discourses* which deny context and suggest infallible legitimacy.

Tool 5 (Chapter 6) – Your Lived Experience

Here we equipped you with the confidence that your own *lived experience* is valuable and informative. Specifically, we discussed how *positionality* and *reflexivity* allow you to account for our own perspectives but equally how *subjectivity* can be embraced. We really encourage you to think about your life and your own experiences in a new way. Not as something which makes you bias but as something which informs the lens through which you view the world. Everyone has their lens, it's just about being more transparent about it.

Each tool can be used as a form of critical questioning and a reluctance to accept the norm as its given to you. We hope that one, some or all of these 'spoke' to you in some way. Your tendency towards questioning, being critical and not accepting a (gendered, *patriarchal*) norm has already been established just by you picking up or downloading this book. Each feminist tool, Ahmed (2017) explains, is sharp, and as feminists, we need to keep sharpening our tools. But likewise, recognize when a blunt tool can work just as well.

Sometimes our sharp feminist voices are tools and we can say blunt things. But also sometimes, as recent Higher Education Union action demonstrates, it is important to down tools and strike.

It's now up to you to decide what tools you want to keep in your toolkit/ survival kit. Each toolkit is personal and individual, just like each individual *feminist killjoy*. As Ahmed (2017, p. 242) says:

Her killjoy survival kit, to fulfil the purpose for which it is intended, will itself become another useful thing. But hand that survival kit to another, and it might not be quite so useful. In fact: a killjoy survival kit might even be deemed as compromising the health and safety of other. In fact: a killjoy survival kit might be deemed useless by others.

The things in your toolkit, perhaps alongside the conceptual ones we've introduced to you (Feminist Science Studies, Critical Reading and Ethics, Queer Theory and Feminist Biology, as well as the recognition of the value of your own lived experience) can be varied and expansive. They are certainly not just academic.

Ahmed (2017) includes in her survival kit (alongside tools):

- Personal and important books and things (reminders and affirmative texts)
- Time (allowance to take time to make decisions or have a break)
- Life (things outside of us like pets)
- Permission notes (allowing yourself to decline, resign, be ill, etc.)
- Other killjoys (for community and to learn)
- Humour (to share the absurdity and lighten the load)
- Feelings (live in the stew of your feelings and see what they stir up)
- Bodies (listen to the feminist ears of your body and dance)

Thinking about this, what do you want to put in your survival toolkit? What helps you do feminism? For us, certainly some of these ring true. Our dogs (Peter's Fergus and Katherine's Pig) are crucial to the everyday feminist lives that we live. Our toolkits also contain, in no particular order: the knowledge that it's okay to change your mind (Katherine); prog rock (Peter); The Bookclub (Katherine); feminist friends and those who have become family (Katherine); Dublin (Peter); lavender essential oil (Katherine); trail running (Katherine); chess culture (Peter); home grown tomatoes (Katherine); and swimming pools (Peter).

These might not all look like feminist things *per se*. But they are in the toolkit because they help us survive as feminists and that's the whole point. Your toolkit needs to sustain, nurture and encourage you. It needs to give you the ability to know when to rest, when to down tools and when to make new tools. Some of the ideas you need for feminist *CHIP* come slow. They don't happen when you are working but when you are walking the dog, running or swimming your laps. Some of the ideas don't come from academia but other learning communities (book clubs, chess clubs). As Audre Lorde explained to us that the master's tools will never dismantle the master's house, Ahmed (2017) articulates that we need feminist tools to make feminist tools and perhaps we can become feminist bricks to build something new.

In some ways, as Ahmed (2017) explains, your feminist toolkit/survival kit could be understood as a collection of things for self-care. And much of what we've described would fit within that. But this also struggles with the danger that self-care can sometimes be framed in individualistic terms as good only to ensure further resilience to work and oppression. So let's avoid thinking in that way too much. We don't just want you to survive as feminists but to grow – to become unstoppable and thriving, enriched and nurtured.

We want this not just for you, but for feminism too. We, as feminists have a symbiotic relationship with feminism. We depend on one another.

> Feminism needs feminists to survive... And the reverse too is very true: feminists needs feminism to survive. (Ahmed, 2017, p. 236)

The same is of course true for **CHIP** – without feminists to do CHIP it could be a very sad sub-discipline in our opinion. So, in the hopes that you want to take this further, we're now going to give some guidance on how to actually do a CHIP project.

How to do an archival project

Learning and doing **CHIP** is of fundamental importance to understand Psychology (Elcock & Jones, 2015), but there are a lot fewer guidelines available to you than in other areas. Here we want to give you some pointers on how to do a CHIP project to encourage you as our feminist researcher of the future!

Research questions

The first thing that usually happens when you decide on a research project is you develop your *research question*. This is also useful when doing historical work but they are often far broader because unlike in other methods you don't necessarily know what material is going to be available to you. Peter talked a bit about developing research questions from feelings in Chapter 6 and so you can see how research questions in **CHIP** might look a little different. Here's how one topic might be looked at through three different methods and how the research questions differ accordingly:

- For quantitative survey methods the research question might be: Is there statistical differences across gender in the reporting of depressive symptoms?
- For qualitative interview methods the research question might be: To what extent does gender impact people's experiences of depression?
- For historical methods the research question might be: In what ways are depression and depressive symptoms constructed by men in *Asylum* magazine 1986–2006?

So for a **CHIP** project your research question might be very broad in scope and more likely to change as the project develops. Historical work is incredibly *inductive,* meaning you go from what you find rather than impose questions onto the data to answer (which is more deductive). You also have to consider the trustworthiness and authenticity of the materials (Clark, Foster, Bryman & Sloan, 2021). In *Bryman's Social Research Methods*, Clark et al. (2021) also highlight the importance of recognizing the limited extent to which documents can reflect 'reality' and we agree with that sentiment. If we think of history as constructed, which is a more *relativist* perspective, there isn't ever going to be the possibility to truly reflect reality objectively (as reality is relative to individuals experiencing it) and instead we can work with the *subjectivity* and the *intersubjectivity* of the materials we have to hand (check out Chapter 22, Documents as Sources of Data, of Clark et al. 2021,).

Your project will be determined by the materials that are available to you. What makes historical topics so interesting, in our opinion, is how varied the materials for *CHIP* projects are. Unlike how data sets in SPSS or interview transcripts might vary in content but look the same, historical materials can range dramatically. They could be letters from famous psychologists from one hundred years ago, or articles on typewritten pages from 50 years ago, or organization meeting minutes, or diary entries, or photographs, or *oral history* interviews with survivors of psychiatric abuse, or testing manuals, or... So first things first: work out roughly what you're interested in, what kinds of materials you'd like to look at, and then find out what is available to access. One of the main ways that historians get access to such materials is via archives.

Archives

An *archive* is a collection of historical documents that are securely stored to preserve them. Archives that are linked to institutions and organizations are usually accessible for researchers. After a process of registration, researchers are usually allowed to order and select materials to look at. There are some huge archives in the UK, for example we have the National Archives, The British Library and the Wellcome Library in London. There are also more medium-sized archives, for example at universities or large libraries, and smaller archives on a more local scale, such as a village archive or history website. There are also archives which are more community led and housed in more informal locations (sometimes in garages or someone's living room!).

As indicated in Chapter 1 and Chapter 6 (see also Chapter 4), what is kept for the historical record is related to power. Archives are an exemplar of this, as what is considered valuable has been preserved and materials from people, groups and organizations which are deemed less important have not been preserved so well, if at all. This is why community-led archives have emerged to collect materials important to small, often marginalized communities. Because of this, archives are scaffolded and often maintain structural issues around sexism, colonization, racism, and ableism and broadly, the stigmatization of *'othered'* groups meant their histories have not been recorded so reliably.

Alongside this, the *archive* just simply doesn't contain everything. Items are donated, selected, preserved and kept following certain inclusion criteria at every stage. Many collections are incomplete, many things we know did exist simply don't in the material world any more. Materials in the archive are therefore incomplete, often damaged and sometimes fragile. Yet, they so often feel like treasure to the historian/explorer! The key thing when doing research in an archive is to remember what is available is not the full picture. It is likely what you have is available because of underpinning power related to the materials. For example, it is more likely to have the letters from eminent white men psychologists; group meetings from national level groups; or the personal ephemera (small often not long-lasting items) from those from richer, upper-class families. There's also an absence of queer materials in archives as so much of it has been destroyed. There's likely another story but you might not have to materials to tell it, but being aware that the narrative that you can tell from the treasure you do have access to is *a* history, rather than *the* history is vital.

When you personally discover something in an *archive* you're likely to encounter feelings as well as the materials themselves. We talked about this more in Chapter 6 and Katherine described her emotional experience in the archive in particular. But another important thing to remember is that while you might be discovering it for the first time, it's not you who actually found it. There has been a huge amount of work that has gone into maintaining and cataloguing the materials and the archivists (those responsible for the archive) have similarly discovered it before you, as did those who donated it, as did those who created it in the first place. A lot of work has gone into creating the circumstance in which you're able to view the materials. So absolutely, go and explore in the archive! Archivists want nothing more than people who are interested to work with the materials they look after. But tread carefully when framing your 'discoveries' and acknowledge and respect the work of others who have allowed you to do it.

There are some fantastic people working in archiving to disrupt the structural issues within it and who are working very hard to ensure materials are accessible. Some of these people are explicitly and unapologetically feminist, which we love to see. Ashton (2017) writes a continued manifesto for feminist archiving identifying: selection, type, facilitation, storage and time, and access, as key points where feminist intervention can occur in the archiving process. This work stemmed from a collective conversation which aimed to disrupt traditional archive practice and modes of knowledge production. You can read about it by searching for 'The Feminists are Cackling in the Archive'. Here, they describe an evening buzzing with 'feminist-activist flavour'. How good does that sound?

Box 7.1 The British Psychological Society Archive

The main *archive* for Psychology in the UK is at the History of Psychology Centre which is part of the British Psychological Society (BPS). Following an epic strategic review, the archive and collections are currently in the process of being fully updated and relocated to the BPS offices in Leicester. But don't worry, it's still accessible.

https://www.bps.org.uk/history-psychology-centre

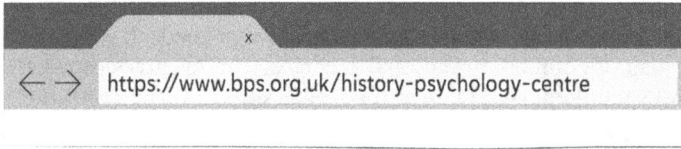

Their website holds a wealth of useful information, including most importantly, the catalogue for the materials they hold. You can also find a short history of the BPS written by Geoff Bunn, a history of Psychology in the UK by Claire Jackson, and a chronology of Psychology in Britain.

The Centre are especially keen at the moment to uncover 'hidden histories' – that is, those that have often gone overlooked. At present, they are very interested in paying close attention to the harms Psychology has done in the past and highlighting where in their archive materials are to make such 'hidden' histories more visible. Their written work in this part of the site has especially centred on the histories of Black psychologists and stories around racism, colonialization and Psychology. They have an appeal out at present for materials relating to minority groups and women so hopefully the feminist collections will be expanding to a greater extent!

For more information about this, or if you'd like to ask about specific materials, or arrange a visit, you can email the History of Psychology Centre at hopc@bps.org.uk.

There's a range of **archives** that might have materials that are of interest to you. Beyond the BPS archive, there are lots of materials elsewhere that will pertain to Psychology. For example, the Surrey History Centre (local to both of us), has the 'Mental Hospital Records' collection which includes all the records of patients and their treatments across the eight large-scale hospitals and asylums in Surrey from the 1800s. There is also lots of collections in the UK focused on feminist topics. To name just a few, you might be interested in:

• The Feminist Library (London)
• Feminist Archive North (Leeds)
• Feminist Archive South (Bristol)
• Women's Archive of Wales (Swansea)
• Glasgow's Women's Library (including the national Lesbian Archive, Glasgow)
• Sheffield Feminist Archive (Sheffield)

Check out the Feminist Libraries and Archive Network website for a more extensive list.

There are also archives which are about Psychology from specific perspectives. You could visit the Department of Experimental Psychology archive in Cambridge for example, or the Disability Archive in Leeds. If you're really keen there are also of course international archives. The Archives of the History of American Psychology is in Ohio at the University of Akron (with the National Museum of Psychology) and the University of Wisconsin has an online Virtual Psychology Museum (okay, you don't have to go far to get to that one).

There are also digital collections which make conducting **CHIP** research more accessible if travelling to archives is not a possibility for you right now (more on this in the next section). Digital collections are not necessarily just documents either, but can be multi-media. The example we've drawn upon several times in the book is the excellent Psychology Feminist Voices site. As a resource this acts as a full digital archive and this could easily be a source for materials for a feminist CHIP project. Other similar digital resources are also being developed, Glen Jankowski for example is also developing a Black and Ethnic Minority archive of psychologists doing anti-racist work (see bmepsychology.com). For another excellent resource in this area also see Carmichael-Murphy and Danquah's online document 'Hidden Histories, Black in Psychology'. There are also feminist resources and online archives available, for example: Greenham Women Everywhere; Rise Up! A Digital Archive of Feminist Activism; and the digital Women and Gender Studies collection at the University of Michigan.

Practicalities

Finding the *archive/s* that you'd like to go to is one thing. Then there are the practicalities of actually going to the archive and getting access. This brief section just outlines some of the key things to taken into consideration before you go deep into the archive and actually begin to analyse the materials you have.

- Library catalogues are essential when trying to find the archive/s you'd like to visit and the materials within them you're keen to see. Each catalogue usually has a search function where you can type key terms or names, and what is relevant should ideally pop up! You're likely to have to do some substantial searching and engage with some guess work. It's not possible to fully describe everything that's in each file and box. So you're going to have to be a bit investigative – if you're interested in letters you'll want to look at a person's correspondence but the description might not name who the letters are to and from. Or you might look at ephemera or family albums for more personal information.

- Often libraries and archives have 'research guides' to help support researchers. These can help indicate what a collection contains and where materials pertaining to particular topics can be found. The archivists who look after each archive are often the experts in what is there and what might also be useful to you. So pay attention to the materials they've provided and don't be afraid to ask for support if you need it.

- When searching in catalogues or looking through research guides you might notice variations of language. This is a critically important aspect of conceptual and historical work – the words we use to describe things are culturally and historically context specific. And so the terms within an archive change depending on what is being referred to when. Some of this language is now considered problematic and inappropriate – for example, we don't say 'feeble-minded' any more but this is a term that was used very commonly in Psychology. So when using key terms to search, you may have to expand your ideas of what words to use given the catalogue system will be picking up on terms used in the past.

- Once you've found something you'd like to see you can request it. Before you go to the archive you may have to register and give some details. There is usually a minimum request time too – sometimes from a couple of hours to a week or more (it depends on where the material you want to see is stored).

- When you're in the archive, or more specifically the room that you're allowed to access the materials (sometimes called a Rare Materials Room or Reading Room), there are sometimes particular rules. These really depend on how formal or informal the archive is that you're accessing. If you're in the British Library there are all sorts of rules to follow (e.g. only use the clear plastic bags provided, security checks your bags upon entry and exit), or if you're in a local library or community archive things are likely to be more relaxed. Nonetheless, it's worth recognizing some of the common features of these spaces. It is common for such rooms to be pencil-only spaces (so nobody can damage precious documents with ink). You have to use lockers for your things beforehand (because archival materials can and do get stolen). There are expectations of silence/quiet (to respect others' precious time to work in the archive without interruption). There can be specific rules about pho-tography (sometimes photocopies are allowed for a small fee if your own photos are not). Usually laptops are allowed so you can make notes, etc., but it can vary.

- You also may want to plan your visit if you are travelling some way and so you can confirm the materials are there in advance, work out exactly what times you'll aim to be there and factor in any costs of travel/food, etc. Doing intensive historical research in the archive can be very tiring so a lunch break is recommended and generally we advise you treat yourself to a lovely lunch or quick bite to eat before going back. Also set yourself a limit of how many hours you'll stay and rest afterwards.

- If you're interested in something very specific at an archive very far away, not all is lost! Sometimes if there aren't too many materials, archivists at the collection will agree to send you copies of what you'd like to see for a small fee. Archivists are really the key to historical research, so a friendly and polite email to ask for their help and expertise can lead to a lovely supportive exchange. It's all about asking for support in your investiga-tions if you need it and valuing all the work they do to make our research possible.

Likewise, of course there are digital archives that you can view with very little issue (or cost) and these are brilliant for making materials more openly accessible. Often archives have materials digitized and you can see them straight from the catalogue. Also, if there is something you're really keen on but aren't able to visit, it may be possible for the archivists to digitize multi-media material for you (again for a fee).

When you're actually in the archive and you're handling the materials you want to see, hear, touch and/or smell (!) it's generally a good idea to have a plan of action. So now you've got them, how are you going to analyse them? The next section takes you through various approaches to analysing documents and archival sources, plus gives some top tips for writing history.

How to conduct CHIP analysis

There are lots of ways to actually analyse conceptual and historical data and materials, so this section just gives a glimpse into some of the various options. Coming from a methods-heavy discipline like Psychology, it might be slightly alarming to learn that there's no singular 'right' way to do this (this section is somewhat deceptively sub-titled), but optimistically there's no really wrong way either! So long as your research question aligns with the materials and data you have, and both in turn align with the analytical approach, then you're all good.

We've already highlighted some of the approaches to analysis within this book already. For example, in Chapter 5 we introduced the field of ***scientometrics***. Using this method, researchers rather wonderfully use published outputs themselves as data to conceptualize about the field more broadly with critical historical reflection. This can be done quantitatively to assess patterns and test hypotheses or it can be done qualitatively (more on this soon). Chapter 6 also introduced the idea of creating annals – which are chronological timelines of events. Annals can be highly detailed context containing all sorts of relevant (and maybe later it turned out pretty irrelevant) information. This style of note taking can be really useful if you're planning on telling *a* history.

Other options depending on the type of materials you are using, include thematic analysis and discourse analysis. Both of these involve having textual material. The goal of a ***reflexive thematic analysis*** is exploring and interpreting patterned meanings, and the goal of ***discourse analysis*** is uncovering ***discourses*** (that is, units of meaning) and what they are doing. Thematic analysis is most often applied to interview data, though it can be used with a much wider range of materials, and you might find interview materials in archives and evidence of conversations. You can't get far in reflexive thematic analysis without coming across brilliant feminist psychologists Victoria Clarke and Ginny Braun! We would recommend their absolute classic paper 'Using Thematic Analysis in Psychology' (2006) and their book, *Thematic Analysis: A Practical Guide* (2021) (also see www.thematicanalysis.net). If you are more interested in what is going on discursively, then discourse analysis (or maybe even Foucauldian Discourse Analysis, which thinks even more about power structures) might be for you. Lamont (2015) specifically discussed the value of using discourse analysis in *CHIP* projects and highlighted it as an especially useful analytical approach for dissertations. Using discourse analysis allows for a qualitative approach to studying published work in Psychology. Lamont highlights the value of peeling back the layers of meaning in outputs from Psychology, like for example, textbooks. It reveals and contextualizes how psychological knowledge is produced, constructed and presented and ultimately, helps the researcher contextualize such knowledge and question where the line of science and non-science is.

To further a qualitative approach to more conceptual and historical materials, Clark et al. (2021) recommend *qualitative content analysis* and *semiotic analysis* as methods of analysis. Qualitative content analysis focuses on frequently recurring content much like its quantitative counterpart but embeds that within a richer and more detailed understanding of the contingent and fuzzy nature of contents. This might include explaining how frequent content is presented, what it looks like, how it's talked about, etc. to a greater extent. *Semiotic analysis* takes this one step further and is primarily useful for analysing visual images. It identifies what is literally being shown (the signs) and what that is meant to imply (the signified). It therefore combines both the denotations (what is there in the image) and the connotations (what that means/the implications/the impression it gives).

One final form of historical research is *oral history*. Oral history is a different type of interviewing whereby the person you're interested in isn't a participant but more of a respondent and they are usually not anonymous. This approach takes into account the expertise and *lived experience* of the person more, and they are understood as co-creating the interview. So there's usually something special about them that the interviewer is interested in, often a particular personal experience (which is why they are often named). For these reasons oral history has shared commonality with feminist ideas and has been used to feminists ends quite a lot (see Berger Gluck & Patai, 1991; Sarah Marks also commented on this in Chapter 6).

The interview takes a much more open format than usual structured or semi-structured interviews and may be more about their overall life (though it can retain a particular focus on a topic, or time-period or event). There is a wealth of *oral history* archives and so it's possible to analyse oral history testimony without doing the actual interview. The Psychology's Feminist Voices website is full of them! The British Library also has the Mental Health Testimony Archive plus others which contain video interviews with people explaining their experiences in this oral history style. Using sound archive materials can be a really fascinating way of exploring a topic and this means you can access really meaningful and important stories by using secondary sources of data (that is opposed to primary ones which you actively collected yourself).

When using secondary sources and doing *CHIP*-based work it's so important to uncover the contextual background to your materials. This is all about considering the authenticity and the background to what is being expressed in the materials and what is not able to be expressed. Considering the *context* allows you to consider *what is not there*, as well as what is. History is all about what is able to be said (or goes unsaid), by whom, and in what circumstances. Secondary sources (especially peer-reviewed academic ones) can help you discover more about how your materials were able to come into being and came to be valued enough to allow you to see them.

In addition to contextualization, there are some key things to take into consideration when writing up your *CHIP* project:

1   It is likely that there are some terms used in your materials which are no longer appropriate so be careful to use terms that are now considered offensive with due care and attention in your analysis and write up. You can make it explicit how and in what ways you use them. Demonstrate awareness of the dilemmas around language use. Make your *standpoint* on problematic language use from the past explicit. Perhaps only use outdated terms in direct quotes, or use 'x' to identify that it's a term and not something you're using directly (as we did with 'feeble-minded' earlier). Being careful and thoughtful with language demonstrates greater awareness of context of both the past and the present.

2   Generally, historians want to avoid *presentism* (that is the application of ideas from the present onto the past). This is seen as *anachronistic* (the inappropriate placement of something in the wrong time). So careful contextualization and explicit recognition of language changes, plus awareness of inappropriate or offensive language, is critical. But please remember, that doesn't mean as historians we can't be critical of the past (see Chapter 1). Sometimes being presentist is really useful when exploring a topic historically. Yes, something might not have been considered racist at the time, but we can certainly call out the past for this now! In fact, doing so in a way that untangles intentions, *contexts* and consequences can help us fight unfinished battles in the present too. Also, often historians are more worried about some things being applied to the past than others. In relation to gender and sexuality, terms referring to queer sexualities and nonconforming genders are applied very carefully onto figures of the past, far more so than heterosexual and cisgender identities. So while there are lots of reasons to not apply terms lightly, that's not to say it can't be done. Many of the women in Chapter 2 for example wouldn't have described themselves as feminists as the term wasn't understood in the same way then as it is now – but we feel pretty confident in claiming them as part of our feminist history of Psychology. Being aware of presentism and how you deal with it in your own projects is important. You don't want to write poor history, but equally all history is anachronistic in some way, so just be transparent and *reflexive* about this.

3   When telling a history (remember, not *the* history), there are particular ways that they tend to be told. White (1973) argued that the histories that historians tell are constructed by the types of questions they posed in the first

place. This means that no historical narrative can ever accurately reflect what actually happened and historians should accept that the past is confusing and uncontrollable. In order to therefore conceptualize and tell a history, decisions have to be made by the writer about where the story begins and ends, what is the arc of the story, and what the message is. White (1973) argued that historians could even learn a thing or two from fiction writers. In creating such historical narratives, White (1973) argues there are four *tropes*: romances, tragedies, satires and ironies, with writers themselves being anarchist, conservative, radical or liberal. So it's well worth reflecting on where your narratives fits within those. What sort of story are you telling?

4 Embrace *ethics*. Akhurst and Ewell (2015) identified *CHIP* as an especially useful area in which students learned and understood ethics on a deeper level. They found that via CHIP students valued ethics more, recognizing 'ethics is not a hurdle, it underpins all research' (p. 245) and it assisted future career planning. For a project, it is likely if you're using archival or published online resources that you'll not have to go through a full ethical review. However, that is not to say that there aren't still ethical considerations when doing CHIP projects. It is likely that you'll be identifying people by name and so careful consideration is required, including the power held by those people and the consequences of naming/not naming them. You should also remember issues of copyright if using any images (even if you took the photo yourself in the archive). Researcher wellbeing is also an important and often overlooked aspect of ethics. Take into account your own experience; it is possible you will encounter upsetting or distressing materials. Plan ahead as to how to cope and when to stop researching. Your wellbeing is important and should not be overlooked.

5 Relatedly, it is possible you may encounter or deliberately set out to look at the ways marginalized groups have been studied by Psychology. Psychology is powerful (as explored across the book and especially in Chapter 4) and as a discipline it has enacted great harms towards vulnerable people. There has been abuse and violence done in the name of Psychology and this has resulted in substantial trauma for some people. In writing about such topics it is therefore important not to replicate or continue such traumatic practice. Consider if images for example are appropriate or necessary for the write up. Perhaps you may want to consider using pseudonyms for people with substantially less power in particular situations. It is all about showing the utmost respect to people who have been oppressed by Psychology.

6 Consider your own citation practice. When writing up you'll be referencing all the relevant articles and books and sources used and this is great. But it's worth remembering who is more likely to get cited and who is not. Men are more likely to be cited than women in Psychology (and elsewhere, see Odic & Wojcik, 2020). This also has racial dimensions as well – for example, it's common to see references to *intersectionality* which don't identify Crenshaw (1989) as the person who first coined the term and developed it from

Critical Race Theory. For these sorts of reasons, Ahmed (2017) deliberately wrote a whole book without citing any white men. So just be careful of citing those who came before you, develop good literature search practices and consider the diversity of your references. And beware of secondary citations which may be creating myths (Swarr, 2023). Seek out the feminists and always check your sources; citation is political!

Over to you

The future of **CHIP** is exciting and we hope it is one with you in it. Recently, in the massive *Oxford Encyclopedia of the History of Modern Psychology* (Pickren, 2022), Wade Pickren explained that we are living in a time of change. Following the important Black Lives Matter movement and the Covid-19 pandemic, the urgency of **decolonization** has thankfully come to the forefront of modern Psychology, going far beyond WEIRD populations (see Chapter 4). He argued it is so vital to learn from disability studies. In 1998 the phrase 'nothing about us, without us' (Charlton, 1998) became critical as a message to researchers and Pickren (2022) argues it remains incredibly important to not be speaking to or about marginalized groups, but with them. Psychology still has a great deal to learn from the past to ensure present and future practices are genuinely and meaningfully helpful to those it studies. And CHIP is a key part of unlearning unhelpful practices and norms from the past as well as learning new ones.

In teaching **CHIP** we're been indebted to several brilliant feminist ideas which then inspired the way we have written this book. Two of the final ones we'd like to highlight are Shields' (2015) idea of transformational moments and Young, Rodkey and Rutherford's (2015) idea of sparking imaginations. Shields (2015) argues that when tracing the history of Feminist Psychology, it is possible to look at particular moments as transformational for the field or as times where an individual or group 'sparked' and advancement. Similarly, Young, Rodkey and Rutherford (2015) describe 'sparking imaginations' by using more innovative teaching approaches for CHIP. It's well worth asking yourself, what has sparked you? What has made you interested or passionate about feminist thinking, CHIP and Psychology? We encourage you to not let those sparks die out; fuel them. Writing this book has certainly been a spark-filled transformational moment for us.

Now in drawing this book to a close we want to hand over to you. You're the new **CHIP** adventurer and we want to embolden you to do what you think is most helpful for the future of Psychology. It might seem rather counterintuitive but we are firm believers that for the future of Psychology to be genuinely equal for all, we need to account for the past and be critical of the present. So we encourage you to draw your own map, collect your own tools and develop your own survival kit to carry on your own CHIP journey.

Conclusion

In living our own feminist lives, we draw once again back to Ahmed (2017) and have found her principles of living a feminist life incredibly validating. Especially Principle 5: 'I am not willing to get over histories that are not over' (p. 262). And that is what this book is about. If you're also not willing to get over histories that are not over, we're with you and we hope you have found this book has given you valuable tools to journey through rather than over unfinished histories.

Glossary

Activism – action taken by activists in an effort to positively reform, change or promote social, political or environmental change

Anachronism – the application of something to a time period that it doesn't belong in/didn't exist in (see also Presentism)

Androcentric/androcentrism – the tendency to centralize and prioritize men's perspectives and viewpoints

Archive – as a noun it is the located collection of historical records, and as a verb it is the act of the collecting and safe-keeping of those records, placing them in the collection

Archivist/s – is the person/persons who are responsible for the recording and safe-keeping of historical records; they maintain the archive

Biological determinism – the idea that characteristics, traits and behaviours are almost solely determined by biological factors known best by Biologists

Brown v. Board of Education Supreme Court – the landmark decision in 1954 by the US Supreme Court which argued segregated schooling was unconstitutional

CHIP – Conceptual and Historical Issues in Psychology

Cisgender – a term used to describe or identify someone whose gender identity aligns with the sex they were assigned at birth

Cisgenderism – ideology that values being cisgender more than being transgender, including assuming cisgender as norm. This is often related to denial, belittling or pathologizing beliefs about gender identities that do not align with assigned sex at birth

Colonial/colonialism – the practice of people from elsewhere gaining full or partial political and economic control over an area of country which exploits native or indigenous peoples and attempts to eradicate or undervalue their culture

Constructed – the idea that social concepts are created in meaningful ways in society usually via discourse and language (see also, Social Constructionism).

Constructionist – from the perspective of Social Constructionism

Context – the circumstances and wider cultural environment in which an event takes place (see Socio-Historical context)

Critical Reading – from literary criticism meaning the sustained and highly attentive practice of reading which takes nothing for granted and scrutinizes the text

Decolonial Feminism/Feminists – a form of feminism which aims to centralize issues of race and ethnicity alongside gender while recognizing the ongoing legacies and issues of colonialism with the goal to push towards a future without entrenched colonial understandings

Decolonization – the withdrawal of political and economic forces of settlers who have colonized an area or more conceptually, the removal of colonial ideas from other areas such as education

Depathologization – the removal of something as a pathologized and recognized mental disorder (usually under the Diagnostic Statistical Manual or the International Classification of Diseases)

Discourse – units of understanding within language or written text, usually about how something is said or what is being relied upon in communication rather than what is literally said

Discourse analysis – the analytical approach which aims to understand what discourses are being relied upon and what they are doing in a specific form of communication

Empirical Feminism/Feminists – the feminism approach which utilizes accepted empirical approaches (e.g. ways of measuring people in Psychology) and applies them to understand gender

Empiricism/empiricist – the theory of knowing the world as being reliant on our senses, so what we see, hear, measure, record and observe is how we best develop or create knowledge

Epistemic/epistemological advantage – a idea from feminism which says some people have particular advantages because of their lived experience and so have more reliable or valid knowledge on a topic

Epistemology – the approach and belief through which people approach studying the world; it is the philosophy of reality which informs how people go about gaining knowledge about something

Essentialist/essentialism – the idea that characteristics, traits or behaviours are intrinsic and often unchangeable; they make up what it means to be a particular kind of person or thing

Ethics – the moral principles and practices which govern our lives on varying levels; for Psychology it often refers to the procedures and guidelines in place to ensure the safety and protection of those involved in research

Eugenics – the immoral and erroneous idea (worryingly popular in the twentieth century) that the human race could be made better by controlling reproduction to ensure only people who were deemed suitable could procreate and eliminate social problems via heredity

Feminist Biology – an approach in the field of Biology which aims to dismantle problematic patriarchal ideas of gender, undo bias and use biological methods for feminist ends

Feminist epistemologies – there are different forms of feminist epistemologies but together this is the background philosophy and approach about how the world can be known and how knowledge can be gained which centralizes feminist goals and aims

Feminist killjoy – an identity and feminist characteristic formulated by Sara Ahmed which recognizes how feminists are often viewed as being serious and taking the fun out of things and which reclaims this as also a way to make room for new possibilities

Feminist Neuroscience – an approach in the field of Neuroscience which aims to dismantle problematic patriarchal ideas of gender, undo bias and use neuroscientific methods for feminist ends

Feminist Science Studies – an interdisciplinary theoretical sub-field of broader Science and Technology Studies which studies science itself from a feminist perspective

First wave – the description of feminist action in the early twentieth century especially focused on the right to vote and the work of both suffragists and suffragettes

Formal exclusion – explicit rules for excluding a group of people from higher education, for example, on the basis of characteristics such as gender and/ or race

Fourth wave – the description of feminist action from after around 2010 which especially uses the internet and social media as a format through which to enact feminism

Gender identity paradigm – the belief that sex always foregrounds gender in an essentialist fashion and that gender is a binary

God-Trick – the term coined by Donna Haraway to describe a tendency in scientific writing to write in a universal way to describe things as if there is a disembodied person who doesn't affect the environment they are in

Her-stories – histories from a feminist or woman-focused perspective

Heteronormativity – a general pattern that portrays heterosexuality as the primary 'normal' form of sexuality and centralizes it to the cost of other forms of sexuality

Heteropatriarchy – the combination of both heteronormativity and patriarchy; this recognizes how women and gender/sexually diverse people experience discrimination and oppression based on the same kinds of structures and beliefs

Historiography – the in-depth study and consideration of writing of history

Human Science – the study of human beings focusing on experience, behaviour and life processes

Imperialism – associated with colonialism, it is the practice of maintaining power over another nation

Inductive – an approach which involves working from data and information without imposing initial questions or ideas

Insider – sharing the same identity or identities with participants in research, so the study is also about the researcher's community to some extent

Interactionism – the combination of both nature and nurture in the development of key human and animal traits and characteristics

Interdisciplinary/interdisciplinarity – work that is in between or across more than one area of academic study (disciplines) to look at a particular topic or subject

Internalist – to look at something from the inside, that is to study something from the view of someone who is involved in the thing in some way

Interpretivist – the perspective that underpins Social Constructionism and is most related to qualitative research approaches, it is the understanding that the world is made meaningful by humans interpretation of it

Intersectional/intersectionality – the analytical framework developed by Kimberlé Crenshaw which considers how various social and political identities, primarily gender and race, interact and combine leading to multiple forms of oppression/discrimination and privilege

Intersubjectivity – the relational experiences or shared understanding between people who share a commonality, for example, sharing a relevant identity between participant and researcher

Liberal Feminism/Feminist – a form of relatively mainstream feminism which aims to ensure women have equal power and rights and are able to contribute politically as much as men

Lived experience – first hand or direct experience that someone has had in their life

Marxist Feminism – a form of feminism which explores how gender ideology impacts labour in a capitalist world following the doctrine of Karl Marx and Friedrich Engels (see also Socialist Feminism)

Mother-blaming theories – ideas which tend to put the responsibility of social problems on mothers and their parenting as the cause of such issues

Multidisciplinary/mulitdisciplinarity – work that uses multiple areas of academic study (disciplines) to look at a particular topic or subject

Nature/nurture – used to describe the debate in Psychology about the extent to which human behaviour can be explained by acquired socialization (nurture) or by inherited biology/ genetics (nature)

Neoliberalist/neoliberalism – a more conservative idea which promotes social institutions becoming privatized resulting in their existence being based on primarily economic and financial merit as opposed to social or moral good

Neuroracism – insidious as well as obvious forms of racism embedded within Neuroscience

Open science – efforts to make scientific findings and methods more accessible

Oral history – the study of history through people's spoken accounts (as opposed to using documents)

Othered – to treat a person or a group of people as distinctly different or abnormal in a negative way because of something about them; it is marginalizing

Outsider – not sharing the same identity or identities with participants in research, so the study is about a community to which the researcher doesn't belong

Paradigm shift – a fundamental change in the underlying assumptions or background belief in something

Partial perspectives – a term used to critique pretensions of objectivity by pointing out that all perspectives are located and come with interests

Pathologizing – the characterization of symptoms or differences being because of mental illness; treating someone as medically or pathologically abnormal

Patriarchy/patriarchal – a hierarchical ideological system which promotes and reproduces power as held by men and masculinity

Positionality – placing oneself explicitly within relevant social identities and locations to ensure perspective is clear

Positivist epistemologies – the idea that the world can be measured and understood via empiricism – that reality can be understood through developing knowledge through observation (opposite to Social Constructionist epistemologies)

Postcolonial Feminism – a form of feminism which aimed to shift feminist thinking away from primarily being concerned with western women and to consider those from formerly colonized places

Postmodern/postmoderism – a broad philosophical idea which takes a strong relativist perspective which aims to highlight the subjectivity and ideology involved in maintaining political and social power

Poststructuralist feminism – this form of feminism posits that power and knowledge are integrated to such an extent that science remains highly subjective, very similar to postmodern ideas

Presentism – the misapplication of something from the present being applied onto the past (see also **Anachronism**)

Privilege – a benefit, advantage or protection against experiencing something negative because of who you are, a multiple and complex buffer which protects from social disadvantage

Psy-disciplines – the combination of disciplines related to the psyche, including Psychology, Psychotherapy and Psychiatry

Qualitative content analysis – a form interpreting qualitative data inductively by concentrating on what is evident and the frequency that particular things occur within the data set

Queer theory – not really a theory but certainly queer, this approach sets to challenge the belief that cisgender and heterosexual are standardized ways of being (also known as cisheteronormativity) and is more political in its outlook than other efforts to study gender and sexuality

Radical Feminism/Feminists – a form of feminism mainly from the 1980s which called for a re-ordering of the social patriarchal system which conceptualizes men as being superior to women

Reflexive/Reflexivity – recognizes the circular and influential relationship between the person and knowledge, it is all about reflecting and considering any assumptions underlying

Reflexive thematic analysis – a way of interpretation qualitative data via the themes embedded within it, it reflexively reveals patterns of meaning

Relativism/relativist – the perspective which argues that nothing is absolute, but rather, knowledge and truth are grounded in particular contexts, they are relative to the circumstances

Replication Crisis – the problem that many scientific studies, including from Psychology, are difficult to reproduce and get the same findings

Science and Technology Studies – the interdisciplinary field which studies science itself, considering the contexts, communication and ideologies underpinning its production

Scientific racism – the highly problematic and discredited idea that there are intellectual, moral and physical differences between people from different racial and ethnic backgrounds; grounded in white supremacy, these ideas attempted to legitimize racism with science

Scientometrics – studying science and its outputs quantitatively

Second wave – the description of feminist action 1960s–1980s characterized by sexual revolutions and included liberal and radical forms of feminism emerging

Semiotic analysis – the interpretation of signs and what they signify within qualitative data sets, usually images, thinking about what the connotations are

Sexual harassment – a type of sexual violence in which sexual behaviour is conducted towards someone without consent and it makes them feel humiliated, scared, threatened, upset or offended

Situated knowledges – a term coined by Donna Haraway to indicate how forms of knowledge reflect the environment in which they are produced, meaning who we are impacts the type of knowledge we have

Social change – an alternation of the social order; a shift in how things are done or understood on a wide societal level

Social Constructionist/Constructionism – the idea that the world is rendered meaningful how humans interact with the world via norms and language, for example, knowledge is best developed through understanding how we construct such meaning (opposite to Positivist epistemologies, see also Constructed)

Socialist Feminism – a form of feminism which is similar to Marxist feminism in that it is concerned with class alongside gender in understanding and preventing social inequalities

Socio-historical context – the social circumstances and environment in which an event takes place alongside the precise historical time, often in regards to how these led to or impacted the event

Standpoint feminism/feminist – a form of feminism which emerged primarily from Feminist Science Studies, which argues that where people are from influences the type of science they produce and that by embracing such subjectivity, knowledges from those with less power can be valued more

Structural oppression – deep forms of discrimination which work on an institutional and societal level leading to the subordination of groups of people based on their characteristic (such as their gender and racial group)

Stubborn Particulars – a term coined by Frances Cherry to indicate historical details and specifics which complicate simple or neat narratives

Subjectivity – opposite to objectivity, it is the understanding that things are subject to influence and are understood in context, related to Relativism

Textbook myths – the stories perpetuated in textbooks which tend to over simplify and poorly portray stories in order to convey what is the expected or has been previously understood from them

Third wave – the description of feminist action from the 1990s especially focused on how gender is associated with other forms of marginalization; central to this time was growing Black feminist theorizing

Trans – an umbrella term used as an identity or to describe people whose gender identity does not align with the sex they were assigned at birth

Trans studies – the study and scholarship of trans-related topics

Tropes – a commonly used theme, often metaphoric, which tends to be over-used

White supremacy – the highly problematic belief that white people are superior and should be dominant over people from other racial and ethnic backgrounds

References

Agler, D. W., & Durmuş, D. (2013). Christine Ladd-Franklin: Pragmatist feminist. *Transactions of the Charles S. Peirce Society: A Quarterly Journal in American Philosophy, 49*(3), 299–321.

Ahmed, S. (2014). Sweaty concepts. https://feministkilljoys.com/2014/02/22/sweaty-concepts/

Ahmed, S. (2017). *Living a feminist life*. Durham, NC: Duke University Press.

Ahmed, S. (2023). *The feminist killjoy handbook*. London: Penguin.

Akhurst, J., & Elwell, C. (2015). 'Viewing ethics in a new light': Students' reactions to an under-emphasised yet important component of CHIP. *History and Philosophy of Psychology, 16*(1), 41–52.

Allen, A. (2016). Feminist perspectives on power. In Edward N. Zalta (ed.), *The Stanford encyclopedia of philosophy*. https://plato.stanford.edu/archives/fall2016/entries/feminist-power/

Alcoff, L. (1991). The problem of speaking for others. *Cultural Critique, (20)*, 5–32.

American Psychological Association. (2009). *Report of the American Psychological Association task force on gender identity and gender variance*. Washington, DC: American Psychological Association.

American Psychological Association. (2020). *Publication Manual of the American Psychological Association* (7th ed.). Washington, DC: American Psychological Association.

Ansara, Y.G., & Hegarty, P. (2012). Cisgenderism in psychology: Pathologizing and misgendering children from 1999 to 2008. *Psychology and Sexuality, 3*(2), 137–160.

Ansara, Y.G., & Hegarty, P. (2013). Masculine genetics as misgendering in English language contexts: Applying non-cisgenderist methods to feminist research. *International Journal of Multiple Research Approaches, 7*(2), 160–177.

Ashton, J. (2017). The feminists are cackling in the archive: A manifesto for feminist archiving (or disruption). *Feminist Review, 115*(115), 155–164.

Austin, S., Rutherford, A., & Pyke, S. (2006). In our own voice: The impact of feminism on Canadian psychology. *Feminism & Psychology, 16*(3), 243–257.

Bancroft, J. (1969). Aversion therapy of homosexuality: A pilot study of 10 cases. *The British Journal of Psychiatry, 115*(529), 1417–1431.

Bangerter, A. (2000). Transformation between scientific and social representations of conception: The method of serial reproduction. *British Journal of Social Psychology, 39*(4), 521–535.

Barash, D. (1979). *The whisperings within: Evolution and the origin of human nature*. London: Penguin.

Barclay, K. (2020). Doing the paperwork: The emotional world of wedding certificates. *Cultural and Social History, 17*(3), 315–332. DOI: 10.1080/14780038.2019.1589156

Barclay, K. (2021a). State of the field: The history of emotions. *History, 106*(371), 456–466.https://doi.org/10.1111/1468-229X.13171

Barclay, K. (2021b). Emotions in the history of emotions. *History of Psychology, 24*(2), 112–115. https://doi.org/10.1037/hop0000162

Barker, M. J., & Scheele, J. (2016). *Queer: A graphic history*. London: Icon Books.

Barker, M. J., & Scheele, J. (2019). *Gender: A graphic guide*. London: Icon Books.

Bartlett, K. A., & Camba, J. D. (2023). Gender differences in spatial ability: A critical review. *Educational Psychology Review, 35*(8). https://doi.org/10.1007/s10648-023-09728-2

Bartlett, A., Smith, G., & King, M. (2009). The response of mental health professionals to clients seeking help to change or redirect same-sex sexual orientation. *BMC Psychiatry, 9*, 11. https://doi.org/10.1186/1471-244X-9-11

Basow, S. A. (2010). Changes in psychology of women and psychology of gender textbooks (1975–2010). *Sex Roles, 62*, 151–152.

Bayer, R. (1981). *Homosexuality and American psychiatry: The politics of diagnosis*. Princeton, NJ: Princeton University Press.

Beck, H. P., Levinson, S., & Irons, G. (2009). Finding little Albert: A journey to John B. Watson's infant laboratory. *American Psychologist, 64*(7), 605–614.

Bem, S. L. (1995). Dismantling gender polarization and compulsory heterosexuality: Should we turn the volume down or up? *Journal of Sex Research, 32*(4), 329–334.

Bem, D. J. (2011). Feeling the future: Experimental evidence for anomalous retroactive influences on cognition and affect. *Journal of Personality and Social Psychology, 100*(3), 407–425. https://doi.org/10.1037/a0021524

Benjamin L. T. Jr, Henry, K. D., & Mcmahon, L. R. (2005). Inez Beverly Prosser and the education of African Americans. *Journal of the History of the Behavioral Sciences, 41*(1), 43–62.

Bennett, C. M., Baird, A. A., Miller, M. B., & Wolford, G. L. (2010). Neural correlates of interspecies perspective taking in the post-mortem Atlantic salmon: An argument for proper multiple comparisons correction. *Journal of Surreptitious and Unexpected Results, 1–5*. http://cda.psych.uiuc.edu/sgep_course_material/sgep_weekly_readings_posted/salmon_fmri.pdf

Berger Gluck, S., & Patai, D. (1991). *Women's words: The feminist practice of oral history*. New York: Routledge.

Berlant, L., & Warner, M. (1995). Guest column: What does queer theory teach us about X? *Proceedings of the Modern Language Association, 110*(3), 343–349.

Bernstein, M. D., & Russo, N. F. (1974). The history of psychology revisited: Or, up with our foremothers. *American Psychologist, 29*(2), 130–134. https://doi.org/10.1037/h0035837

Bérubé, A. (1990). *Coming out under fire: The history of gay men and women in World War II*. New York: The Free Press.

Bharj, N. & Adams, G. (2003). Dismantling the Master's House with the Mistress' Tools? The Intersection Between Feminism and Psychology as a Site for Decolonization. In R. Capdevila & E. L. Zurbriggen (Eds.), *The Palgrave Handbook of Psychology, Power & Gender* (pp. 173–189). Cham: Palgrave, Macmillan.

Bharj, N., & Hegarty, P. (2015). A postcolonial feminist critique of harem analogies in psychological science. *Journal of Social and Political Psychology, 3*, 257–75.

Bharj, N., & Hubbard, K. (2023). Power/History/Psychology: A Feminist Excavation of Power, History, and Psychology. In R. Capdevila & E. L. Zurbriggen (Eds.), *The Palgrave Handbook of Psychology, Power & Gender* (pp. 13–27). Cham: Palgrave, Macmillan.

Bhatia, S., Long, W., Pickren, W., & Rutherford, A. (2024). Engaging with decoloniality, decolonization, and histories of psychology otherwise. In H. Adames, L. Comas-Diaz, and N. Chavez (Eds.), *Decolonial psychology: Theory, research, training, and practice*. Washington, DC: APA.

Bleier, R. (1997). *Science and gender: A critique of biology and its theories on women*. New York: Teachers College Press.

Bluhm, R., Maibom, H. L., & Jacobson, A. J. (Eds.) (2012). *Neurofeminism: Issues at the intersection of feminist theory and cognitive science*. Cham: Springer.

Blum, D. (2002). *Love at Goon Park: Harry Harlow and the science of affection*. New York: Basic Books.

Bohan, L. S. (1990). Contextual history: A framework for re-placing women in the history of psychology. *Psychology of Women Quarterly, 14*(2), 213–227.

Boone, A. P., & Hegarty, M. (2017). Sex differences in mental rotation tasks: Not just in the mental rotation process! *Journal of Experimental Psychology: Learning, Memory, and Cognition, 43*(7), 1005–1019. https://doi.org/10.1037/xlm0000370

Boring, E.G. (1929). *A History of Experimental Psychology*. London: The Century Co.

Braun, V., & Clarke, V. (2006). Using thematic analysis in psychology. *Qualitative Research in Psychology, 3*(2), 77–101.

Brock, A. C., & Harvey, M. (2015). The status of the history of psychology course in British and Irish psychology departments. *European Yearbook of the History of Psychology, 1*, 13–36.

Brookes, M. (2004). *Extreme measures: The dark visions and bright ideas of Francis Galton*. New York: Bloomsbury.

Brownmiller, S. (1975). *Against our will: Men, women and rape*. New York: Simon & Schuster.

Brunner, J. (2001). 'Oh those crazy cards again': A history of the debate on the Nazi Rorschachs, 1946–2001. *Political Psychology, 22*(2), 233–261.

Bryman, A. (2016). *Social research methods*. Oxford: Oxford University Press.

Bukamal, H. (2022). Deconstructing insider–outsider researcher positionality. *British Journal of Special Education, 49*(3), 327–349. https://doi.org/10.1111/1467-8578.12426

Burman, E. (1990). *Feminists and psychological practice*. London: Sage.

Burman, E. (2011). Psychology, women, and political practice in Britain. In A. Rutherford, R. Capdevila, V. Undurti, & I. Palmary (Eds.), *Handbook of international feminisms: Perspectives on psychology, women, culture, and rights* (pp. 219–243). New York: Springer.

Butler, J. (1990). *Gender trouble: Feminism and the subversion of identity*. New York: Routledge.

Butler, J. (1993a). *Bodies that matter: On the discursive limits of sex*. New York: Routledge.

Butler, J. (1993b). Critically Queer. *GLQ: A journal of lesbian and gay studies, 1*, 17–32.

Byne, W., Tobet, S., Mattiace, L. A., Lasco, M. S., Kemether, E., Edgar, M. A., ... & Jones, L. B. (2001). The interstitial nuclei of the human anterior hypothalamus: an investigation of variation with sex, sexual orientation, and HIV status. *Hormones and Behavior, 40*(2), 86–92.

Capdevila, R., Hubbard, K., & Donnelly, L. (2019). Standing still whilst 'looking back and moving forwards': the personal accounts of POWS members in the here and now. *Psychology of Women & Equalities Section Review, 2*(1), 1–12.

Capdevila, R., & Lazard, L. (2015). 20 Psychology of Women: Questions of politics and practice. In I. Parker (Ed.), *Handbook of critical psychology*. Abingdon, Oxon: Routledge.

Carmichael-Murphy, P., & Danquah, A. (2022). *Hidden histories. Black in psychology*. https://documents.manchester.ac.uk/display.aspx?DocID=62182

Carr, S., & Spandler, H. (2019). Hidden from history? A brief modern history of the psychiatric 'treatment' of lesbian and bisexual women in England. *The Lancet, 6*, 289–290.

Carson, J. (2006). *The measure of merit*. Princeton, NJ: Princeton University Press.

Cassidy, A. (2006). Evolutionary psychology as public science and boundary work. *Public Understanding of Science, 15*(2), 175–205.

Causadias, J. M., Vitriol, J. A., & Atkin, A. L. (2018). Do we overemphasize the role of culture in the behavior of racial/ethnic minorities? Evidence of a cultural (mis)attribution bias in American psychology. *American Psychologist, 73*(3), 243–255. https://doi.org/10.1037/amp0000099

Chapman, L. J., & Chapman, J. P. (1969). Illusory correlation as an obstacle to the use of valid psychodiagnostic signs. *Journal of Abnormal Psychology, 74*(3), 271–280. https://doi.org/10.1037/h0027592

Charlton, J. I. (1998). *Nothing about us without us: Disability oppression and empowerment.* Berkley, CA: University of California Press.

Cherry, F. (1995). *Stubborn particulars of social psychology: Essays on the research process.* New York: Routledge.

Cislak, A., Formanowicz, M., & Saguy, T. (2018). Bias against research on gender bias. *Scientometrics, 115*, 189–200.

Clark, T., Foster, L., Bryman, A., & Sloan, L. (2021). *Bryman's social research methods* (6th ed.). Oxford: Oxford University Press.

Clarke, V., & Braun, V. (2021). *Thematic analysis: A practical guide.* London: Sage.

Clarke, V., & Hopkins, J. (2002). Victoria Clarke in conversation with June Hopkins. *Lesbian & Gay Psychology Review, 3*(2), 44–47.

Cole, E. R. (2009). Intersectionality and research in psychology. *American Psychologist, 64*(3), 170–180. https://doi.org/10.1037/a0014564

Collins, H. (1992). *Changing order: Replication and induction in scientific practice.* Chicago: University of Chicago Press.

Conrad, P., & Markens, S. (2001). Constructing the 'gay gene' in the news: Optimism and skepticism in the US and British press. *Health, 5*(3), 373–400.

Cook, K. (2014). *Kitty Genovese: The murder, the bystanders, the crime that changed America.* New York: Norton.

Cramblet Alvarez, L. D., Leach, J. L., Rodriguez, J. L., & Jones, K. N. (2020). Unsung psychology pioneers: A content analysis of who makes history (and who doesn't). *The American Journal of Psychology, 133*(2), 241–262.

Crenshaw, K. (1989). Demarginalizing the intersection of race and sex: A black feminist critique of antidiscrimination doctrine, feminist theory and antiracist policies. *University of Chicago Legal*, (1), 139–167.

Crenshaw, K. (1991). Mapping the margins: Intersectionality, identity politics, and violence against women of color. *Stanford Law Review, 43*(6), 1241–1299. https://doi.org/10.2307/1229039

Cronbach, L. J., & Meehl, P. E. (1955). Construct validity in psychological tests. *Psychological Bulletin, 52*(4), 281–302. https://doi.org/10.1037/h0040957

Cvetkovich, A. (2003). *Archive of feelings* (Vol. 2008). Durham, NC: Duke University Press.

Danziger, K. (1994). Does the history of psychology have a future? *Theory & Psychology, 4*(4), 467–484.

Darley, J. M., & Latané, B. (1968). Bystander intervention in emergencies: Diffusion of responsibility. *Journal of Personality and Social Psychology, 8*(4), 377–383.

Davison, K. (2021). Cold War Pavlov: Homosexual aversion therapy in the 1960s. *History of the Human Sciences, 34*(1), 89–119. https://doi.org/10.1177/0952695120911159

Davison, K. (in press). *Aversion therapy: Sex, psychiatry and the Cold War.* Cambridge: Cambridge University Press.

Dawkins, R. (1976). *The selfish gene.* Oxford: Oxford University Press.

Dickinson, T. (2015). *'Curing Queers': Mental nurses and their patients, 1935-1974.* Manchester: Manchester University Press.

Diehl, L.A. (1986). The paradox of G Stanley Hall: Foe of coeducation and educator of women. *American Psychologist, 41*, 868–878.

Dinshaw, C. (1999). *Getting medieval: Sexualities and communities, pre-and postmodern.* Durham, NC: Duke University Press.

Donnelly, L. C., Hubbard, K., & Capdevila, R. (2022). POWES is pronounced 'feminist': Negotiating academic and activist boundaries in the talk of UK feminist psychologists. *Feminism & Psychology, 32*(4), 520–539.

Downing, L. (2013). *The subject of murder: Gender, exceptionality and the modern killer.* University of Chicago Press.

Downing, L., & Gillett, R. (2011). Viewing critical psychology through the lens of queer. *Psychology & Sexuality, 2*(1), 4–15.

Driver-Linn, E. (2003). Where is psychology going? Structural fault lines revealed by psychologists' use of Kuhn. *American Psychologist, 58*(4), 269–278.

Druva-Roush, C. A., & Wu, Z. J. (1989). Gender differences in visual spatial skills: A meta-analysis of doctoral theses [paper presentation]. Annual Meeting of the American Psychological Association, New Orleans.

Eagly, A. H., Eaton, A., Rose, S. M., Riger, S., & McHugh, M. C. (2012). Feminism and psychology: Analysis of a half-century of research on women and gender. *American Psychologist, 67*(3), 211–230. doi.org/10.1037/a0027260

Eagly, A. H., & Riger, S. (2014). Feminism and psychology: Critiques of methods and epistemology. *American Psychologist, 69*(7), 685–702. https://doi.org/10.1037/a0037372

Eisfeld, J. (2014). International statistical classification of diseases and related health problems. *Transgender Studies Quarterly, 1*(1–2), 107–110.

Elcock, J., & Jones, D. (2015). Teaching conceptual issues through historical understanding. *History & Philosophy of Psychology, 16*(1), 4–12.

European Association of Social Psychology (EASP). (2019). Renaming the Tajfel award. www.easp.eu/news/itm/renaming_the_tajfel_award-947.html

Fancher, R., & Rutherford, A. (2016). *Pioneers of Psychology: A History* (5th ed.). New York: Norton.

Fausto-Sterling, A. (2012). *Sex/gender: Biology in a social world.* New York: Routledge.

Faye, S. (2022). *The transgender issue: Trans justice is justice for all.* Brooklyn, NY: Verso Books.

Fine, C. (2010). *Delusions of gender. How our minds, society, and neurosexism create difference.* New York: WW Norton & Company.

Foucault, M. (1954). *Maladie mentale et person-nalité [Mental illness and personality].* Paris: Presses Universitaires de France.

Foucault, M. (1976). *The history of sexuality (Vol. 1: An Introduction).* R. Hurley (Trans.). New York: Random House.

Fridlund, A. J., Beck, H. P., Goldie, W. D., & Irons, G. (2012). Little Albert: A neurologically impaired child. *History of Psychology, 15*(4), 302–327.

Friedan, B. (1963). *The feminine mystique.* New York: Norton.

Furumoto, L. (2003). Beyond great men and great ideas: History of psychology in sociocultural context. In P. Bronstein & K. Quina (Eds.), *Teaching gender and multicultural awareness: Resources for the psychology classroom* (pp. 113–124). American Psychological Association. https://doi.org/10.1037/10570-008

Furumoto, L., & Scarborough, E. (1986). Placing woman in history of psychology: The first American women psychologists. *American Psychologist, 41*(1), 35–42.

Gallo, M. (2015). *'No one helped': Kitty Genovese, New York City, and the myth of urban apathy.* Ithaca, NY: Cornell University Press.

Gallo, M. M. (2014). The parable of Kitty Genovese, The New York Times, and the erasure of lesbianism. *Journal of the History of Sexuality, 23*(2), 273–294.

Gannon, L., Luchetta, T., Rhodes, K., Pardie, L., & Segrist, D. (1992). Sex bias in psychological research: Progress or complacency? *American Psychologist*, *47*(3), 389–396.

Gansberg, M. (1964, March 27). 37 who saw murder but didn't call the police. *New York Times*, 1.

Garrison, K. E., Tang, D., & Schmeichel, B. J. (2016). Embodying power: A preregistered replication and extension of the power pose effect. *Social Psychological and Personality Science*, *7*(7), 623–630.

Gergen, K. J. (1973). Social psychology as history. *Journal of Personality and Social Psychology*, *26*(2), 309–320. https://doi.org/10.1037/h0034436

Gervais, S. J., Baildon, A. E., & Lorenz, T. K. (2021). On methods and marshmallows: A roadmap for science that is openly feminist and radically open. *Psychology of Women Quarterly*, *45*(4), 430–447.

Gieryn, T. F. (1983). Boundary-work and the demarcation of science from non-science: Strains and interests in professional ideologies of scientists. *American Sociological Review*, *48*(6), 781–795.

Gill, R. (2003). Power and the production of subjects: A genealogy of the new man and the new lad. *The Sociological Review*, *51*(1), 34–56.

Gill, R. (2009). Breaking the silence: The hidden injuries of neo-liberal academia. In R. Flood & R. Gill (Eds.), *Secrecy and silence in the research process: Feminist reflections* (pp. 228–244). London: Routledge.

Gould, S. J. (1981). *The mismeasure of man*. New York: Norton.

Graham, S. (1992). 'Most of the subjects were White and middle class': Trends in published research on African Americans in selected APA journals, 1970–1989. *American Psychologist*, *47*(5), 629–639. https://doi.org/10.1037/0003-066X.47.5.629

Griffiths, D. A., & Hubbard, K. A. (2022). Do you have to have sex to have sex? Defining sex in British law and medicine from the 1950s. *Sexualities*, 13634607221146504.

Griggs, R. A. (2015). The Kitty Genovese story in introductory psychology textbooks: Fifty years later. *Teaching of Psychology*, *42*(2), 149–152.

Griscom, J. L. (1992). Women and power: Definition, dualism, and difference. *Psychology of Women Quarterly*, *16*(4), 389–414.

Grob, G. N. (1991). Origins of DSM-I: A study in appearance and reality. *American Journal of Psychiatry*, *148*(4), 421–431.

Grosz, E. (1994). *Volatile bodies: Toward a corporeal feminism*. Bloomington, IN: Indiana University Press.

Guthrie, R. V. (2004). *Even the rat was white: A historical view of psychology* (2nd ed.). Boston, MA: Pearson Education.

Hacking, I. (1995). The looping effects of human kinds. In D. Sperber, D. Premack, & A. J. Premack (Eds.), *Causal cognition: A multidisciplinary debate* (pp. 351–394). Clarendon Press/Oxford University Press.

Hacking, I. (1999). *The social construction of what?* Cambridge, MA: Harvard University Press.

Haggbloom, S. J., Warnick, R., Warnick, J. E., Jones, V. K., Yarbrough, G. L., Russell, T. M., ... & Monte, E. (2002). The 100 most eminent psychologists of the 20th century. *Review of General Psychology*, *6*(2), 139–152.

Halley, J. E. (1994). Sexual orientation and the politics of biology: A critique of the argument from immutability. *Stanford Law Journal*, *36*, 301–366.

Halperin, D. M., Abelove, H., & Barale, M. A. (Eds.). (1993). *The lesbian and gay studies reader*. New York: Routledge.

Hamer, D. H., Hu, S., Magnuson, V. L., Hu, N., & Pattatucci, A. M. (1993). A linkage between DNA markers on the X chromosome and male sexual orientation. *Science*, *261*(5119), 321–327.

Hammonds, E. (1994). Black (w)holes and the geometry of Black female sexuality. *Differences, 6* (2–3), 126–145.

Hankinson Nelson, L. (2017) *Biology and feminism: A philosophical introduction.* Cambridge: Cambridge University Press.

Haraway, D. (1988). Situated knowledges: The science question in feminism and the privilege of partial perspective. *Feminist Studies, 14*(3), 575–599.

Haraway, D. (1989). *Primate visions: Gender, race, and nature in the world of modern science.* New York: Routledge.

Haraway, D. J. (1991). *Simians, cyborgs, and women: The reinvention of nature.* New York: Routledge.

Harding, S. G. (1986). *The science question in feminism.* Ithaca, New York: Cornell University Press.

Harding, S. G. (1994). Is science multicultural?: Challenges, resources, opportunities, uncertainties. *Configurations, 2*(2), 301–330.

Hare-Mustin, R. T., & Marecek, J. (Eds.) (1990). *Making a difference: Psychology and the construction of gender.* New Haven, CT: Yale University Press.

Harris, B. (2011). Letting go of Little Albert: Disciplinary memory, history, and the uses of myth. *Journal of the History of the Behavioral Sciences, 47*(1), 1–17.

Hearnshaw, L. S. (1964). *A short history of British psychology 1840-1940.* London: Methuen & Co.

Hegarty, M. (2018). Ability and sex differences in spatial thinking: What does the mental rotation test really measure? *Psychonomic Bulletin & Review, 25*(3), 1212–1219. https://doi.org/10.3758/ s13423-017-1347-z

Hegarty, P. (1997). Materializing the hypothalamus: A performative account of the 'gay brain.' *Feminism & Psychology, 7*(3), 355–372.

Hegarty, P. (2002). 'It's not a choice, it's the way we're built:' Symbolic beliefs about sexual orientation in the United States and in Britain. *Journal of Community and Applied Social Psychology, 12*(3), 153–166.

Hegarty, P. (2003). Homosexual signs and heterosexual silences: Rorschach studies of male homosexuality from 1921 to 1967. *Journal of the History of Sexuality, 12*(3), 400–423.

Hegarty, P. (2007). Getting dirty: Psychology's history of power. *History of Psychology, 10*(2), 75–91.

Hegarty, P. (2013). *Gentlemen's disagreement: Alfred Kinsey, Lewis Terman, and the sexual politics of smart men.* Chicago: University of Chicago Press.

Hegarty, P. (2017a). *A recent history of lesbian and gay psychology: From homophobia to LGBT.* London: Routledge.

Hegarty, P. (2017b). On the failure to notice that white people are white: Generating and testing hypotheses with the celebrity guessing game. *Journal of Experimental Psychology: General, 146*(1), 41–62.

Hegarty, P. (2020). Attitudes toward homosexuality and LGBT people: Causal attributions for sexual orientation. In D. Haider-Markel (Ed.), *Oxford Research Encyclopedia of LGBT Politics and Policy.* doi: 10.1093/acrefore/9780190228637.013.1173

Hegarty, P. (2023). The psychology of people with variable sex characteristics/ intersex. *Current Opinion in Psychology, 49,* 101539. doi.org/10.1016/j.copsyc. 2022.101539

Hegarty, P., & Bruckmüller, S. (2013). Asymmetric explanations of group differences: Experimental evidence of Foucault's disciplinary power in social psychology. *Social and Personality Psychology Compass, 7*(3), 176–186.

Hegarty, P., Donnelly, L., Dutton, P., Gillingham, S., Williams, K., & Vecchietti, V. (2021). Understanding of intersex: The meanings of umbrella terms and opinions about medical and social responses among laypeople in the USA and UK. *Psychology of Sexual Orientation and Gender Diversity, 8*(1), 25–37. https://doi.org/10.1037/sgd0000413

Hegarty, P., Hubbard, K., & Nyatanga, L. (Eds.). (2015). Innovative approaches to teaching Conceptual and Historical Issues in Psychology (CHIP). *History and Philosophy of Psychology, 16,* 1–68.

Hegarty, P., & Pratto, F. (2001). The effects of category norms and stereotypes on explanations of intergroup differences. *Journal of Personality and Social Psychology, 80*(5), 723–735.

Herman, E. (1995). *The romance of American psychology: Political culture in the age of experts.* Berkeley, CA: University of California Press.

Heyam, K. (2022). *Before we were trans: A new history of gender.* London: Hachette UK.

Hill Collins, P. (1990). *Black feminist thought: Knowledge, consciousness, and the politics of empowerment.* New York: Routledge.

Hinshelwood, R. (1999). Psychoanalysis and history. *Psychoanalysis and History, 1,* 87–102.

Hooker, E. (1957). The adjustment of the male overt homosexual. *Journal of Projective Techniques, 21*(1), 18–31.

Hooker, E. (1993). Reflections of a 40-year exploration: A scientific view on homosexuality. *American Psychologist, 48*(4), 450–453. https://doi.org/10.1037/0003-066X.48.4.450

hooks, b. (2013). *Dig Deep: Beyond Lean In.* https://thefeministwire.com/2013/10/17973/

Horne, S. G. (2020). The challenges and promises of transnational LGBTQ psychology: Somewhere over and under the rainbow. *American Psychologist, 75*(9), 1358.

Hornsey, M. J. (2008). Social identity theory and self-categorization theory: A historical review. *Social and Personality Psychology Compass, 2*(1), 204–222.

Hornstein, G. A. (1992). The return of the repressed: Psychology's problematic relations with psychoanalysis, 1909-1960. *American Psychologist, 47*(2), 254–263.

Hoskins, A. (2013). The end of decay time. *Memory Studies, 6*(4), 387–389.

Hubbard, K. (2017a). Treading on delicate ground: Comparing the lesbian and gay affirmative Rorschach research of June Hopkins and Evelyn Hooker. *Psychology of Women Section Review, 19*(1), 3–9.

Hubbard, K. (2017b). Queer Signs: The women of the British projective test movement. *Journal of the History of the Behavioural Sciences, 53*(2), 265–285.

Hubbard, K. (2018). The British projective test movement: Reflections on a queer feminist tale. *History and Philosophy of Psychology, 19*(1), 26–35.

Hubbard, K. (2020). *Queer ink: A blotted history towards liberation.* Abingdon, Oxon: Routledge.

Hubbard, K. A. (2021). Lesbian community and activism in Britain 1940s–1970s: An interview with Cynthia Reid. *Journal of homosexuality, 70*(4), 565–586. https://doi.org/10.1080/00918369.2021.1996098

Hubbard, K. (under review). Being captured by queer past: Margaret Lowenfeld, Margaret Mead.

Hubbard, K.A., & Griffiths, D.A. (2019). Sexual offenses, diagnosis, and activism: A British history of LGBTIQ psychology. *American Psychologist, 74*(8), 940–953.

Hubbard, K., & Hegarty, P. (2014). Why is the history of heterosexuality essential? Beliefs about the history of heterosexuality and homosexuality and their relationship to sexual prejudice. *Journal of Homosexuality, 61*(4), 471–490.

Hubbard, R. (1988). Science, facts, and feminism. *Hypatia, 3*(1), 5–17.

Hubbard, R. (1990). *The politics of women's biology*. New Brunswick, NJ: Rutgers University Press.

Hubbard, R. (2001). Science and science criticism. In M. Lederman & I. Bartsch (Eds.), *The gender and science reader* (pp 49–51). London: Routledge.

Hyde, J. S. (1981). How large are cognitive gender differences?: A meta-analysis using $\omega 2$ and d. *American Psychologist, 36*(8), 892–901. https://doi.org/10.4324/9780429035302-1

Hyde, J. S. (2005). The gender similarities hypothesis. *American Psychologist, 60*(6), 581–592. https://doi.org/10.1037/0003-066X.60.6.581

Hyde, J. S., Bigler, R. S., Joel, D., Tate, C. C., & van Anders, S. M. (2019). The future of sex and gender in psychology: Five challenges to the gender binary. *American Psychologist, 74*(2), 171–193. https://doi.org/10.1037/amp0000307

Intemann, K. (2010). 25 years of feminist empiricism and standpoint theory: Where are we now? *Hypatia, 25*(4), 778–796. doi.org/10.1111/j.1527-2001.2010.01138.x

Jennings, R. (2008). 'The most uninhibited party they'd ever been to': The Postwar encounter between psychiatry and the British Lesbian, 1945–1971. *Journal of British Studies, 47*(4), 883–904.

Joel, D. (2016). VIII. Captured in terminology: Sex, sex categories, and sex differences. *Feminism & Psychology, 26*(3), 335–345.

John, L. K., Loewenstein, G., & Prelec, D. (2012). Measuring the prevalence of questionable research practices with incentives for truth telling. *Psychological Science, 23*(5), 524–532.

Johnston, E., & Johnson, A. (2008). Searching for the second generation of American women psychologists. *History of Psychology, 11*, 40–69.

Joranger, L. (2016). Individual perception and cultural development: Foucault's 1954 approach to mental illness and its history. *History of Psychology, 19*(1), 40–51. https://doi.org/10.1037/hop0000014

Kerr, N. L. (1998). HARKing: Hypothesizing after the results are known. *Personality and Social Psychology Review, 2*(3), 196–217.

Kessler, S. J. (1990). The medical construction of gender: Case management of intersexed infants. *Signs: Journal of Women in Culture and Society, 16*(1), 3–26.

Kessler, S. J. (1998). *Lessons from the Intersexed*. New Brunswick, NJ: Rutgers University Press.

King, M. (2003). Dropping the diagnosis of homosexuality: Did it change the lot of gays and lesbians in Britain? *Australian and New Zealand Journal of Psychiatry, 37*(6), 684–688.

King, M., & Bartlett, A. (1999). British psychiatry and homosexuality. *The British Journal of Psychiatry, 175*(2), 106–113.

King, M., Smith, G., & Bartlett, A. (2004). Treatments of homosexuality in Britain since the 1950s - an oral history: The experience of professionals. *The British Medical Journal, 328*(7437), 1–3.

King, M. L., Jr (1968). The role of the behavioral scientist in the civil rights movement. *American Psychologist, 23*(3), 180–186. https://doi.org/10.1037/h0025715

Kitzinger, C. (1991). Feminism, psychology and the paradox of power. *Feminism & Psychology, 1*(1), 111–129. https://doi.org/10.1177/0959353591011016

Kitzinger, C., & Frith, H. (1999). Just say no? The use of conversation analysis in developing a feminist perspective on sexual refusal. *Discourse & Society, 10*(3), 293–316. https://doi.org/10.1177/0957926599010003002

Kitzinger, C., & Wilkinson, S. (2004). The re-branding of marriage: Why we got married instead of registering a civil partnership. *Feminism & Psychology, 14*(1), 127–150.

Kline, W. (2001). *Building a better race: Gender, sexuality, and eugenics from the turn of the century to the baby boom*. University of California Press.

Koaureas, G. (2012). Researching (homo)sexualitites: Working with Military and War archives. In C. N. Phellas (Ed.) *Researching Non-heterosexual Sexualities* (pp. 173–186). Ashgate: Surrey.

Kuhn, T. S. (1962). *The structure of scientific revolutions*. University of Chicago Press.

Kurtiş, T., Adams, G., & Estrada-Villalta, S. (2016). Decolonizing empowerment: Implications for sustainable well-being. *Analyses of Social Issues and Public Policy, 16*(1), 387–391.

Ladd-Taylor, M. (2001). Eugenics, sterilisation and modern marriage in the USA: The strange career of Paul Popenoe. *Gender & History, 13*(2), 298–327.

Lamont, P. (2015). Doing student projects in Conceptual and Historical Issues: The potential of discourse analysis. *History and Philosophy of Psychology, 16*(1), 53–60.

Latané, B., & Dabbs Jr, J. M. (1975). Sex, group size and helping in three cities. *Sociometry*, 180–194.

Latané, B., & Rodin, J. (1969). A lady in distress: Inhibiting effects of friends and strangers on bystander intervention. *Journal of Experimental Social Psychology, 5*(2), 189–202.

Lazard, L., & McAvoy, J. (2020). Doing reflexivity in psychological research – What's the point? What's the practice? *Qualitative Research in Psychology, 17*(2), 159–177.

Lemov, R. (2011). X-rays of inner worlds: The mid-twentieth-century American projective test movement. *Journal of the History of the Behavioral Sciences, 47*(3), 251–278.

Lepore, J. (2001). Historians who love too much: Reflections on microhistory and biography. *The Journal of American History, 88*(1), 129–144.

LeVay, S. (1991). A difference in hypothalamic structure between heterosexual and homosexual men. *Science, 253*(5023), 1034–1037.

LeVay, S. (1996). *Queer science: The use and abuse of research into homosexuality.* Cambridge, MA: MIT press.

Linn, M. C., & Petersen, A. C. (1985). Emergence and characterization of sex differences in spatial ability: A meta-analysis. *Child Development, 56*(6), 1479–1498.

Lorde, A. (2018). *The master's tools will never dismantle the master's house.* London: Penguin UK.

Love, H. (2009). *Feeling backward: Loss and the politics of queer history.* Cambridge, MA: Harvard University Press.

Lugones, M. (2010). Toward a Decolonial Feminism. *Hypatia, 25*(4), 742–759. http://www.jstor.org/stable/40928654

Luhrmann, T. M., Padmavati, R., Tharoor, H., & Osei, A. (2015). Differences in voice-hearing experiences of people with psychosis in the USA, India and Ghana: interview-based study. *The British Journal of Psychiatry, 206*(1), 41–44.

Maccoby, E. E., & Jacklin, C. N. (1974). *The psychology of sex differences*. Stanford, CA: Stanford University Press.

MacCulloch, M. J., & Feldman, M. P. (1967). Aversion therapy in management of 43 homosexuals. *British Medical Journal, 2*(5552), 594–597.

Macleod, C. I., Bhatia, S., & Liu, W. (2020). Feminisms and decolonising psychology: Possibilities and challenges. *Feminism & Psychology, 30*(3), 287–305.

Manning, R., Levine, M., & Collins, A. (2007). The Kitty Genovese murder and the social psychology of helping: The parable of the 38 witnesses. *American Psychologist, 62*(6), 555–562.

Marecek, J. (1993). Disappearances, silences, and anxious rhetoric: Gender in abnormal psychology textbooks. *Journal of Theoretical and Philosophical Psychology, 13*(2), 114–123.

Marecek, J. (1995). Psychology and feminism: Can this relationship be saved? In D. C. Stanton & A. J. Stewart (Eds.), *Feminisms in the academy* (pp. 101–132). Ann Arbor, MI: University of Michigan Press.

Marks, S. (2017). Psychotherapy in historical perspective. *History of the Human Sciences, 30*(2), 3–16. https://doi.org/10.1177/0952695117703243

Marks, S. (2018). Psychotherapy in Europe. *History of the Human Sciences, 31*(4), 3–12. https://doi.org/10.1177/0952695118808411

Martin, E. (1991). The egg and the sperm: How science has constructed a romance based on stereotypical male-female roles. *Signs: Journal of Women in Culture and Society, 16*(3), 485–501.

Massey, S. G., Barreras, R. E. & Levy, S. R. (Eds.). (2013). *Impact validity as a framework for advocacy-based research.* Wiley.

Matlin, M. W. (2010). Writing (and rewriting) about the psychology of women. *Sex Roles, 62,* 166–172.

Matsick, J. L., Kruk, M., Oswald, F., & Palmer, L. (2021). Bridging feminist psychology and open science: Feminist tools and shared values inform best practices for science reform. *Psychology of Women Quarterly, 45*(4), 412–429.

McCaughey, M. (2012). *The caveman mystique: Pop-Darwinism and the debates over sex, violence, and science.* New York: Routledge.

McHugh, M. C., Koeske, R. D., & Frieze, I. H. (1986). Issues to consider in conducting nonsexist psychological research: A guide for researchers. *American Psychologist, 41*(8), 879–890. https://doi.org/10.1037/0003-066X.41.8.879

Milar, K. S. (2000). The first generation of women psychologists and the psychology of women. *American Psychologist, 55*(6), 616–619.

Million, D. (2009). Felt theory: An Indigenous feminist approach to affect and history. *Wicazo Sa Review, 24*(2), 53–76.

Minton, H. L. (1997). Queer theory: Historical roots and implications for psychology. *Theory & Psychology, 7*(3), 337–353.

Minton, H. L. (2002). *Departing from deviance: A history of homosexual rights and emancipatory science in America.* Chicago: University of Chicago Press.

Mitchell, R. (2020). *Vénus Noire: Black women and colonial fantasies in nineteenth-century France* (Vol. 36). Athens, GA: University of Georgia Press.

Mohanty, C. T. (2003). 'Under western eyes' revisited: Feminist solidarity through anticapitalist struggles. *Signs: Journal of Women in Culture and Society, 28*(2), 499–535.

Money, J., & Ehrhardt, A. (1972). *Man & Woman: Boy & girl: Differentiation and dimorphism of gender identity from conception to maturity.* Baltimore, MD: Johns Hopkins.

Moradi, B., Tebbe, E. A., Brewster, M. E., Budge, S. L., Lenzen, A., Ege, E., ... & Flores, M. J. (2016). A content analysis of literature on trans people and issues. *The Counseling Psychologist, 44*(7), 960–995.

Morawski, J. G. (1992). There is more to our history of giving: The place of introductory textbooks in American psychology. *American Psychologist, 47*(2), 161–169.

Morawski, J. G. (1994). *Practicing feminisms, reconstructing psychology: Notes on a liminal science.* Ann Arbor, MI: University of Michigan Press.

Morawski, J. G. (2005). Reflexivity and the psychologist. *History of the Human Sciences, 18*(4), 77–105.

Morawski, J. G., & Agronick, G. (1991). A restive legacy: The history of feminist work in experimental and cognitive psychology. *Psychology of Women Quarterly, 15*(4), 567–579.

Morland, I. (2015). Gender, genitals and the meaning of being human. In L. Downing, I. Morland, & M. Sullivan (Eds.), *Fuckology: Critical essays on John Money's diagnostic concepts* (pp. 69–98). Chicago: University of Chicago Press.

Myers, D. G., & DeWall, C. N. (2018). *Psychology* (12th ed.). New York: Worth.

Neuburger, S., Ruthsatz, V., Jansen, P., & Quaiser-Pohl, C. (2015). Can girls think spatially? Influence of implicit gender stereotype activation and rotational axis on fourth graders' mental rotation performance. *Learning and Individual Differences, 37,* 169–175. https://doi.org/10.1016/j.lindif.2014.09. 003

O'Connor, C., & Joffe, H. (2013). How has neuroscience affected lay understandings of personhood? A review of the evidence. *Public Understanding of Science, 22*(3), 254–268.

Odic, D., & Wojcik, E. H. (2020). The publication gender gap in psychology. *American Psychologist, 75*(1), 92–103. https://doi.org/10.1037/amp0000480

Open Science Collaboration. (2015). Estimating the reproducibility of psychological science. *Science, 349* (6251), aac4716.

Parlee, M. B. (1973). The premenstrual syndrome. *Psychological Bulletin,* 80 (6), 454–465. https://doi.org/10.1037/h0035270

Parlee, M. B. (1975). Psychology. *Signs: Journal of Women in Culture and Society, 1*(1), 119–138. https://doi.org/10.1086/493210

Pearce, R., Erikainen, S., & Vincent, B. (2020). TERF wars: An introduction. *The Sociological Review, 68*(4), 677–698.

Persson, S., & Pownall, M. (2021). Can open science be a tool to dismantle claims of hardwired brain sex differences? Opportunities and challenges for feminist researchers. *Psychology of Women Quarterly, 45*(4), 493–504.

Peters, M., Laeng, B., Latham, K., Jackson, M., Zaiyouna, R., & Richardson, C. (1995). A redrawn Vandenberg and Kuse mental rotations test-different versions and factors that affect performance. *Brain and Cognition, 28(1),* 39–58.

Pettit, M. (2012). The queer life of a lab rat. *History of Psychology, 15*(3), 217–227. https://doi.org/10.1037/a0027269

Pettit, M. (2024). *Governed by affect: Hot cognition and the end of Cold War psychology.* Oxford University Press.

Pettit, M., & Davidson, I. (2014). Can the history of psychology have an impact? *Theory & Psychology, 24*(5), 709–716.

Pickren, W. (2022). Preface. In W. Pickren (Ed.), *The Oxford encyclopedia of the history of modern psychology* (pp. xiii–xx). Oxford University Press.

Pickren, W. E., & Tomes, H. (2002). The legacy of Kenneth B. Clark to the APA: The Board of Social and Ethical Responsibility for Psychology. *American Psychologist, 57*(1), 51–59. https://doi.org/10.1037/0003-066X.57.1.51

Pinel, J. P. J., & Barnes, S. J. (2022). *Biopsychology* (11th ed.). Harlow, Essex: Pearson.

Pitts-Taylor, V. (2015). A feminist carnal sociology? Embodiment in sociology, feminism, and naturalized philosophy. *Qualitative Sociology, 38*(1), 19–25. DOI: 10.1007/s11133-014-9298-4

Popper, K. R. (1959). *The logic of scientific discovery.* New York: Basic Books.

Porter, R. (1985). The patient's view: Doing medical history from below. *Theory and Society, 14,* 175–198.

Radtke, H. L. (2011). *Canadian Perspectives on Feminism and Psychology.* In A. Rutherford, R. Capdevila, V. Undurti, & I. Palmary (Eds.), *Handbook of international feminisms: Perspectives on psychology, women, culture and rights* (pp. 293–314). Cham: Springer.

Readsura Decolonial Editorial Collective Group. (2021). General psychology Otherwise: A decolonial articulation. *Review of General Psychology, 25*(4), 339–353. https://doi.org/10.1177/10892680211048177

Readsura Decolonial Editorial Collective Group. (2022a). Psychology as a site for decolonial analysis. *Journal of Social Issues, 78*(2), 255–277.

Readsura Decolonial Editorial Collective Group. (2022b). Decolonial approaches to the psychological study of social issues. *Journal of Social Issues, 78*(1), 7–26.

Rees, T. (2011). The gendered construction of scientific excellence. *Interdisciplinary Science Reviews, 36*(2), 133–145. https://doi.org/10.1179/030801811X13013181961437

Rich, A. (1980). Compulsory heterosexuality and lesbian existence. *Signs: Journal of Women in Culture and Society, 5*(4), 631–660. doi:10.1086/493756

Richards, G. (2010). *Putting psychology in its place: Critical historical perspectives.* Hove: Taylor & Francis.

Richards, G., & Stenner, P. (2022). *Putting psychology in its place: Critical historical perspectives.* Hove: Taylor & Francis.

Rickett, B., & Morris, A. (2021). 'Mopping up tears in the academy' – working-class academics, belonging, and the necessity for emotional labour in UK academia. *Discourse: Studies in the Cultural Politics of Education, 42*(1), 87–101.

Riger, S. (1992). Epistemological debates, feminist values: Science, social values, and the study of women. *American Psychologist, 47*(6), 730–740.

Riggs, D. W., Pearce, R., Pfeffer, C. A., Hines, S., White, F., & Ruspini, E. (2019). Transnormativity in the psy disciplines: Constructing pathology in the Diagnostic and Statistical Manual of Mental Disorders and Standards of Care. *American Psychologist, 74*(8), 912–924.

Roberts, D. (1997). *Killing the black body: Race, reproduction, and the meaning of liberty.* New York: Vintage.

Roberts, S. O., Bareket-Shavit, C., Dollins, F. A., Goldie, P. D., & Mortenson, E. (2020). Racial inequality in psychological research: Trends of the past and recommendations for the future. *Perspectives on Psychological Science, 15*(6), 1295–1309.

Romano-Lux, A. (2016). *Behave.* New York: Soho Press.

Rooney, P. (1991). Sex metaphor and conceptions of reason. *Hypatia, 6*(2), 77–103. doi. org/10.1111/j.1527-2001.1991.tb01394.x

Rosenthal, A.M. (1964). *Thirty-eight witnesses: The Kitty Genovese case.* McGraw-Hill.

Rossiter, M. W. (1982). *Women scientists in America: Struggles and strategies to 1940* (Vol. 1). Baltimore, MD: Johns Hopkins University Press.

Rubenhold, H. (2019). *The five: The untold lives of the women killed by Jack the Ripper.* New York: Houghton Mifflin.

Rubin, G. (1975). The traffic in women: Notes on the 'political economy' of sex. In R. R. Reiter (Ed.), *Toward an anthropology of women.* Monthly Review Press.

Ruck, N. (2013). Darwinian aesthetics? Criticizing the good-gene hypothesis of physical beauty. In A. Marvakis et al. (Eds.), *Doing psychology under new conditions* (pp. 31–40). International Society for Theoretical Psychology.

Ruck, N. (2021). Public sciences, public enemies. Boundary work and cultural hegemony in public controversies between evolutionists and feminists. *Social and Personality Psychology Compass, 15*(3), e12582.

Rutherford, A. (2015). Maintaining masculinity in mid-twentieth-century American psychology: Edwin Boring, scientific eminence, and the "woman problem". *Osiris,* 30(1), 250–271.

Rutherford, A. (2018). Feminism, psychology, and the gendering of neoliberal subjectivity: From critique to disruption. *Theory & Psychology, 28*(5), 619–644. https://doi. org/10.1177/0959354318979719

Rutherford, A. (2020). Encounters between feminism and psychology: Territories of critique and collusion. *Psychologie und Kritik: Formen der Psychologisierung nach 1945,* 289–307.

Rutherford, A., Capdevila, R., Undurti, V., & Palmary, I. (Eds.). (2011). *Handbook of international feminisms: Perspectives on psychology, women, culture, and rights.* Cham: Springer.

Rutherford, A., & Davidson, T. (2019). Intersectionality and the history of psychology. In *Oxford research encyclopedia of psychology*. https://doi.org/10.1093/acrefore/9780190236557.013.468

Rutherford, A., & Granek, L. (2010). Emergence and development of the psychology of women. In J.C. Chrisler & D.R. McCreary (Eds.), *Handbook of gender research in psychology* (Vol.1, pp.19–41).New York, NY: Springer Science Business Media.

Rutherford, A., Vaughn-Blount, K., & Ball, L. C. (2010). Responsible opposition, disruptive voices: Science, social change, and the history of feminist psychology. *Psychology of Women Quarterly, 34*(4), 460–473.

Rutherford, A., Vaughn-Johnson, K., & Elissa Rodkey, K. V. J. (2015). Does psychology have a gender? *The Psychologist. 28*(6), 508–510. https://www.bps.org.uk/psychologist/does-psychology-have-gender

Ruthsatz, V., Neuburger, S., Rahe, M., Jansen, P., & Quaiser-Pohl, C. (2017). The gender effect in 3D-Mental-rotation performance with familiar and gender-stereotyped objects–a study with elementary school children. *Journal of Cognitive Psychology, 29*(6), 717–730.

Sabik, N. J., Matsick, J. L., McCormick-Huhn, K., & Cole, E. R. (2021). Bringing an intersectional lens to 'open' science: An analysis of representation in the reproducibility project. *Psychology of Women Quarterly, 45*(4), 475–492.

Samson, C. (1995). Madness and psychiatry. In B. S. Turner & C. Samson, *Medical Power and Social Knowledge*. London: SAGE.

Sawyer, T. F. (2000). Francis Cecil Sumner: His views and influence on African American higher education. *History of Psychology, 3*(2), 122–141. https://doi.org/10.1037/1093-4510.3.2.122

Scarborough, E., & Furumoto, L. (1989). *Untold lives: The first generation of American women psychologists*. Columbia University Press.

Schmitz, S., & Höppner, G. (2014). Neurofeminism and feminist neurosciences: A critical review of contemporary brain research. *Frontiers in Human Neuroscience, 8*, 546. doi.org/10.3389/fnhum.2014.00546

Sedgwick, E. K. (1990). *Epistemology of the closet*. Berkeley, CA: University of California Press.

Segal, L. (2017). *Radical happiness: Moments of collective joy*. Brooklyn, NY: Verso Books.

Shapin, S. (1996). *The scientific revolution*. Chicago: University of Chicago Press.

Shapland, J. (2020). *My autobiography of Carson McCullers: A memoir*. Portland, OR: Tin House Books.

Shaw, D. (2023). A tale of two feminisms: Gender critical feminism, trans inclusive feminism and the case of Kathleen Stock. *Women's History Review, 32*(5), 768–780.

Shepard, R. N., & Metzler, J. (1971). Mental rotation of three-dimensional objects. *Science, 171*(3972), 701–703.

Shields, S. A. (2007). Passionate men, emotional women: Psychology constructs gender difference in the late 19th century. *History of Psychology, 10*(2), 92–110.

Shields, S. A. (2015). The legacy of transformational moments in feminist psychology. *Psychology of Women Quarterly, 39*(2), 143–150.

Shields, S. A., & Bhatia, S. (2009). Darwin on race, gender, and culture. *American Psychologist, 64*(2), 111.

Shilts, R. (1987). *And the band played on: Politics, people, and the AIDS epidemic*. New York: St. Martin's Press.

Siegel, J. A., Calogero, R. M., Eaton, A. A., & Roberts, T. A. (2021). Identifying gaps and building bridges between feminist psychology and open science. *Psychology of Women Quarterly, 45*(4), 407–411.

Simmons, J. P., Nelson, L. D., & Simonsohn, U. (2011). False-positive psychology: Undisclosed flexibility in data collection and analysis allows presenting anything as significant. *Psychological Science, 22*(11), 1359–1366.

Smith, R. (2007). Why history matters. *Revista de Historia de la Psicología, 28*(1), 125–146.

Smith, G., Bartlett, A., & King, M. (2004). Treatments of homosexuality in Britain since the 1950s—an oral history: The experience of patients. *British Medical Journal, 328*(7437), 427–429.

Smyth, M. M. (2001). Fact making in psychology: The voice of the introductory textbook. *Theory & Psychology, 11*(5), 609–636.

Somerville, S. (1994). Scientific racism and the emergence of the homosexual body. *Journal of the History of Sexuality, 5*(2), 243–266.

Spandler, H., & Carr, S. (2021). A history of lesbian politics and the psy professions. *Feminism & Psychology, 31*(1), 119–139. https://doi.org/10.1177/0959353520969297

Spivak, G. C. (1996). *The Spivak reader: Selected works of Gayatri Chakravorty Spivak.* Psychology Press.

Stewart, A. J., & McDermott, C. (2004). Gender in psychology. *Annual Review of Psychology, 55,* 519–544.

Stocking, G. W. (1965). On the limits of 'presentism' and 'historicism' in the historiography of the behavioral sciences. *Journal of the History of the Behavioral Sciences, 1,* 211–218.

Stoler, A. L. (1995). *Race and the education of desire: Foucault's history of sexuality and the colonial order of things.* Durham, NC: Duke University Press.

Stonewall, (2020). *2020 conversion therapy and gender identity survey.* www.stonewall.org.uk/resources/2020-conversion-therapy-and-gender-identity-survey

Stryker, S. (2017). *Transgender history: The roots of today's revolution.* London: Hachette UK.

Suess, A., Espineira, K., & Walters, P. C. (2014). Depathologization. *Transgender Studies Quarterly, 1*(1–2), 73–77.

Swarr, A. L. (2023). *Envisioning African Intersex.* Durham, NC: Duke University Press.

Tee, N., & Hegarty, P. (2006). Predicting opposition to the civil rights of trans persons in the United Kingdom. *Journal of Community and Applied Social Psychology, 16*(1), 70–80.

Thompson, L., Turley, E. L., Frances, T., Donnelly, L. C., & Lazard, L. (2023). (with participant authors Castellino, C., Christie, D., Hubbard, K., Jia, X., Keating, G., Lobban, R., Luo, T., Mishra, A., Moore, N., Smith, B.) Doing feminisms on the ground: Challenges and opportunities for critical feminist psychologies. *Psychology of Women and Equalities Section Review, 6*(1), 5–19.

Toft, A. (2012). Researching bisexuality and christianity: locating a hidden population and the use of reflexivity. In C. N. Phellas (Ed.), *Researching non-heterosexual sexualities.* Aldershot: Ashgate.

Tuck, E. (2009). Suspending damage: A letter to communities. *Harvard Educational Review, 79*(3), 409–428.

Tuck, E., & Yang, K. W. (2014). R-words: Refusing research. *Humanizing Research: Decolonizing Qualitative Inquiry with Youth and Communities, 223,* 248.

Tucker, W. H. (1994). Fact and fiction in the discovery of Sir Cyril Burt's flaws. *Journal of the History of the Behavioral Sciences, 30*(4), 335–347.

Unger, R. K. (1979). Toward a redefinition of sex and gender. *American Psychologist, 34*(11), 1085–1094. https://doi.org/10.1037/0003-066X.34.11.1085

Unger, R. K. (2010). Leave no text behind: Teaching the psychology of women during the emergence of second wave feminism. *Sex Roles, 62,* 153–158.

Valentine, E. R. (2008a). Alice Woods—Original Member of the (British) Psychological Society. *History and Philosophy of Psychology, 9*(2), 62–70.

Valentine, E. R. (2008b). To care or to understand? Women members of the British Psychological Society 1901–1918. *History and Philosophy of Psychology, 10*(1), 54–65.

Valentine, E. R. (2009). 'A brilliant and many-sided personality': Jessie Margaret Murray, founder of the Medico-Psychological Clinic. *Journal of the History of the Behavioral Sciences, 45*(2), 145–161. https://doi.org/10.1002/jhbs.20364

Valentine, E.R. (2010). Women in early 20th-century experimental psychology. *The Psychologist, 23*(12), 972–974.

Vandenberg, S. G., & Kuse, A. R. (1978). Mental rotations, a group test of three-dimensional spatial visualization. *Perceptual and Motor Skills, 47(2)*, 599–604. https://doi.org/10.2466/pms.1978.47.2.599

Vaughn-Blount, K., Rutherford, A., Baker, D., & Johnson, D. (2009). History's mysteries demystified: Becoming a psychologist–historian. *The American Journal of Psychology, 122*(1), 117–129.

Watson, J. B., & Rayner, R. (1920). Conditioned emotional reactions. *Journal of Experimental Psychology, 3*(1), 1–14. https://doi.org/10.1037/h0069608

Wattis, L. (2017). Revisiting the Yorkshire Ripper murders: Interrogating gender violence, sex work, and justice. *Feminist Criminology, 12*(1), 3–21. https://doi.org/10.1177/1557085115602960

Weisstein, N. (1968/1971). Psychology constructs the female. *Journal of Social Education, 35*, 362–373.

Whitaker, K., & Guest, O. (2020). # bropenscience is broken science: Kirstie Whitaker and Olivia Guest ask how open 'open science' really is. *The Psychologist, 33*, 34–37.

White, H. (1973). *Metahistory: The historical imagination in nineteenth-century Europe.* Baltimore, MD: Johns Hopkins University Press.

Wilkinson, S. (1988). The role of reflexivity in feminist psychology. *Women's Studies International Forum, 11*(5), 493–502.

Wilkinson, S. (1990). Women's organisations in psychology: Institutional constraints on disciplinary change. *Australian Psychologist, 25*(3), 256–269. https://doi.org/10.1080/00050069008260020

Wilkinson, S. (1999). Feminist psychology: Values and visions. *Psychology of Women Section Review, 1*(1), 20–30.

Wilkinson, S., & Burns, J. (1990). Women organizing within psychology: Two accounts. In E. Burman (Ed.), *Gender and psychology. Feminists and psychological practice* (pp. 140–162). London: Sage.

Williams, R. (2014). *Keywords: A vocabulary of culture and society.* Oxford: Oxford University Press.

Wilson, E. O. (1975). *Sociobiology: The new synthesis.* Cambridge, MA: Harvard University Press.

Winston, A. S. (2004). *Defining difference: Race and racism in the history of psychology* Washington, DC: American Psychological Association.

Wittig, M. (1980). The straight mind. *Feminist Issues, 1*(1): 103–111.

Yoder, J. D., & Kahn, A. S. (1992). Toward a feminist understanding of women and power. *Psychology of Women Quarterly, 16*(4), 381–388.

Yong, E. (2012). Bad copy. *Nature, 485*(7398), 298.

Young, R. M. (1966). Scholarship and the history of the behavioural sciences. *History of Science, 5*(1), 1–51.

Young, J. L., & Hegarty, P. (2019). Reasonable men: Sexual harassment and norms of conduct in social psychology. *Feminism & Psychology, 29*(4), 453–474.

Young, J. L., Rodkey, E. N., & Rutherford, A. (2015). Sparking the historical imagination: Strategies for teaching conceptual and historical issues in psychology. *History & Philosophy of Psychology, 16*(1), 61–68.

Zenderland, L. (1997). The Bell Curve and the shape of history. *Journal of the History of the Behavioral Sciences, 33*(2), 135–139. https://doi.org/10.1002/(SICI)1520-6696(199721)33:2<135::AID-JHBS4>3.0.CO;2-S

Zhou, J. N., Hofman, M. A., Gooren, L. J. G., & Swaab, D. F. (1995). A sex difference in the human brain and its relation to transsexuality. *Nature, 378*(6552), 68–70.

Index